American Cinema of the 1980s

SCREEN
DECADES

AMERICAN CULTURE / AMERICAN CINEMA

Each volume in the Screen Decades: American Culture/American Cinema series is an anthology of original essays exploring the impact of cultural issues on film and the impact of film on American society. Because every chapter presents a discussion of particularly significant motion pictures and the broad range of historical events in one year, readers will gain a systematic and progressive sense of the decade as it came to be depicted on movie screens across North America. We know that our series represents just one approach to the growth of the American cinema: to organize by decades establishes somewhat artificial borders and boundaries, and each author's thematic choices are but one way to understand the culture of a particular year. Despite such limitations, this structure contextualizes the sprawling progression of American cinema, especially as it relates to historical and cultural events. We hope that these books, aimed at scholars and general readers, students and teachers, will shed valuable new light on, will provide a better understanding of, American culture and film history during the twentieth century.

LESTER D. FRIEDMAN AND MURRAY POMERANCE
SERIES EDITORS

Ina Rae Hark, editor, *American Cinema of the 1930s: Themes and Variations*

Wheeler Winston Dixon, editor, *American Cinema of the 1940s: Themes and Variations*

Murray Pomerance, editor, *American Cinema of the 1950s: Themes and Variations*

Lester D. Friedman, editor, *American Cinema of the 1970s: Themes and Variations*

Stephen Prince, editor, *American Cinema of the 1980s: Themes and Variations*

American Cinema of the

1980s

Themes and Variations

EDITED BY

STEPHEN PRINCE

RUTGERS UNIVERSITY PRESS

NEW BRUNSWICK, NEW JERSEY

LIBRARY OF CONGRESS CATALOGING-IN-PUBLICATION DATA

American cinema of the 1980s : themes and variations / edited by Stephen Prince.
    p.   cm. — (Screen decades)
  Includes bibliographical references and index.
  ISBN–13: 978–0–8135–4033–7 (hardcover : alk. paper)
  ISBN–13: 978–0–8135–4034–4 (pbk. : alk. paper)
  1. Motion pictures—United States—History. 2. Motion pictures—United States—Plots,
themes, etc.   I. Prince, Stephen, 1955–
  PN1993.5.U6A8578   2007
  791.430973'09048—dc22

                                                                        2006021861

Visit our Web site: http://rutgerspress.rutgers.edu

Manufactured in the United States of America

For my parents

CONTENTS

ACKNOWLEDGMENTS

The editor wishes to thank the contributors to this volume. Their enthusiasm for the project and good will helped to bring this book forward in a timely fashion. Working with each of the contributors was a very pleasurable experience. Thanks also to Leslie Mitchner, Lester Friedman, and Murray Pomerance for their support and participation in the production of this volume.

T I M E L I N E

The 1980s

1980

29 APRIL — Director Alfred Hitchcock dies at age eighty.

4 NOVEMBER — Ronald Reagan defeats Jimmy Carter to become the fortieth president of the United States.

14 NOVEMBER — Martin Scorsese's *Raging Bull* premieres, subsequently cited by many critics as the best film of the decade.

19 NOVEMBER — United Artists releases *Heaven's Gate* to disastrous box office and critical reception.

8 DECEMBER — John Lennon is murdered by Mark David Chapman in New York.

1981

30 MARCH — President Reagan is wounded in an assassination attempt by a man influenced by the movie *Taxi Driver*.

9 JUNE — Oil executive Marvin Davis buys Twentieth Century Fox.

12 JUNE — Steven Spielberg's *Raiders of the Lost Ark* launches his popular series of films about adventurer Indiana Jones.

5 AUGUST — President Reagan fires the nation's striking air traffic controllers after they refuse his order to return to work.

20 OCTOBER — The Ninth Circuit Court of Appeals rules that home videotaping constitutes copyright violation.

1982

4 JUNE — *Star Trek: The Wrath of Khan*, with sixty seconds of computer graphics, and *Tron* (released 9 July), with forty minutes of computer graphics, signal the dawn of the age of digital special effects.

21 JUNE — The Coca-Cola Company buys Columbia Pictures.

23 JULY — During production of *Twilight Zone—The Movie*, actor Vic Morrow and two child actors are killed in a helicopter crash triggered by special effects explosions.

1 DECEMBER — Columbia Pictures, CBS television, and HBO announce plans to jointly form Tri-Star, a new major studio.

xii   TIMELINE — THE 1980s

1983

8 MARCH   In a speech before a conference of Evangelical Christians, President Reagan declares that the Soviet Union is "the focus of evil in the modern world."

23 MARCH   President Reagan proposes a missile defense shield that is quickly nicknamed "Star Wars."

15 APRIL   *Flashdance* is released, exemplifying high-concept filmmaking and lucrative marketing tie-ins with MTV.

23 MAY   Lucasfilm introduces the THX certification system for optimizing theater sound and projection. *Return of the Jedi* is exhibited as a demonstration of the process.

23 OCTOBER   In Beirut, 241 U.S. servicemen are killed by a Hezbollah truck bomb.

25 OCTOBER   The United States invades the small island nation of Grenada.

20 NOVEMBER   *The Day After,* a made-for-television movie about the aftermath of a nuclear holocaust, is viewed by 100 million Americans.

1984

17 JANUARY   The U.S. Supreme Court rules that home videotaping is a fair use activity.

9 MARCH   *Splash* becomes the first film released under Disney's new Touchstone label.

9 MAY   President Reagan calls the contras battling the Sandinista government in Nicaragua "freedom fighters."

1 JULY   Following criticism of the violence in the PG-rated *Indiana Jones and the Temple of Doom* and *Gremlins,* the Motion Picture Association of America (MPAA) adds a new ratings category, PG-13.

15 AUGUST   The MPAA requires that home videos of Hollywood films carrying the G, PG, PG-13, R, or X ratings must be the same version as the theatrical release so rated.

7 NOVEMBER   Ronald Reagan is reelected in a landslide.

1985

23 JANUARY   *Blood Simple* wins the first Grand Jury Prize (Dramatic) at the United States Film Festival, later known as Sundance, dedicated to independent films.

18 APRIL   Hal Roach Studios announces production of colorized home video editions of classic black-and-white films.

24 SEPTEMBER   Rupert Murdoch's News Corp. finalizes its purchase of Twentieth Century Fox.

2 OCTOBER   Popular romantic film star Rock Hudson, who earlier in the year became one of the first public figures to announce that he had AIDs, dies.

31 DECEMBER   The year's adult video releases climb to 1,600 titles, skyrocketing from 400 in 1983.

1986

28 JANUARY   The space shuttle *Challenger* explodes, killing all aboard.

10 FEBRUARY   Pixar is formed as a separate company from the computer graphics division of Lucasfilm.

26 MARCH   Turner Broadcasting Systems buys MGM/UA. In September, Turner sells MGM/UA but keeps its library of 3,650 films.

21 MAY   Studio marketing studies show a large decline in movie theater attendance as households with VCRs rent an average of four videos per month.

20 AUGUST   *She's Gotta Have It*, Spike Lee's debut feature, marks an emerging generation of African American filmmakers in Hollywood.

13 NOVEMBER   President Reagan denies that the United States attempted to trade arms for hostages with Iran.

19 DECEMBER   *Platoon*, considered by many to be Hollywood's most realistic depiction of the Vietnam War to date, is released.

1987

12 JUNE   At a speech in Berlin, President Reagan urges Soviet leader Mikhail Gorbachev to "tear down" the Berlin Wall.

19 OCTOBER   Stock market drops 23 percent, its largest single-day decline in history.

31 OCTOBER   The MPAA claims video piracy robs studios of $1 billion per year.

18 NOVEMBER   The committee investigating the Iran-Contra scandal concludes that President Reagan bears responsibility for the illegal arms-for-hostages operation.

1988

3 JULY   The U.S. Navy mistakenly shoots down an Iranian commercial airliner, killing all 290 people aboard.

12 AUGUST   Martin Scorsese's *The Last Temptation of Christ* angers conservative Christian groups over its depiction of Christ's last days.

27 SEPTEMBER	Congress passes the National Film Preservation Act, authorizing the Library of Congress to designate twenty-five films each year as national treasures, to be preserved and housed at the Library.
8 NOVEMBER	George H.W. Bush wins election to become the forty-first president of the United States.
31 DECEMBER	*E.T. the Extra-Terrestrial* sells 15 million copies on videocassette in its first year of release, earning $175 million (compared with $187 million at the box office in 1982).

1989

30 JUNE	Spike Lee's *Do the Right Thing* is released, stimulating wide-ranging national debates about race in America.
23 AUGUST	Time and Warner Communications announce merger terms, creating the world's biggest information and entertainment company.
9 AUGUST	*The Abyss,* with its computer-generated images (CGI), heralds the arrival of Hollywood's digital era.
8 NOVEMBER	Sony buys Columbia Pictures.
20 DECEMBER	President Bush orders the invasion of Panama to arrest President Manuel Noriega, a former CIA employee. The operation results in thousands of civilian deaths.

American Cinema of the 1980s

Robert De Niro as the boxer Jake LaMotta in Martin Scorsese's *Raging Bull* (United Artists). Many critics considered it to be one of the decade's best films, and yet Scorsese struggled to sustain his career during this period. Jerry Ohlinger's Movie Material Store.

INTRODUCTION

Movies and the 1980s

STEPHEN PRINCE

The 1980s significantly transformed the nation's political culture, as it did the Hollywood industry and its products. Today, the United States is an extremely conservative nation, and the turn toward right-wing policies began in the eighties with the administration of Ronald Reagan. Today, Hollywood filmmaking is beset by out-of-control production costs with no ceiling in sight, and these soaring costs, and the industry's turn toward the global film market for its blockbusters, have their origins in the 1980s.

The decade's most important developments, however, have given rise to a set of core myths in both domains, even as the realities of film and politics proved to be more complex, more nuanced, and more contradictory than the myths acknowledged. The myths about American film in the period are these: blockbusters took over the industry, leading to a general lowering and coarsening of the quality of filmmaking; the films of George Lucas and Steven Spielberg epitomized this blockbuster style and proved detrimentally influential on a generation of American filmmaking; and Hollywood film mirrored the politics of the Reagan period, shifting to the political right and helping to popularize the Cold War politics of the era.

Popular Perceptions

Each of these propositions is partially true, but like all myths each also distorts by oversimplifying complex and often contrary realities. Each proposes a monolithic view of Hollywood and American culture in the period when, in fact, a more diverse and heterogeneous set of films and influences was at work. Let's consider each of these propositions in turn as a way of building an introductory survey of the decade.

The critical tendency to equate eighties filmmaking with blockbusters is understandable because in that decade the industry did realize that motion pictures were capable of generating a tremendous amount of revenue, and the studios aimed to produce one or more blockbusters each year. As a result, when one looks back at the 1980s, the blockbusters seem to tower over other pictures because of the media attention and hoopla that surrounded them and the mass audience that turned out to see them. Although the industry's initial move toward blockbusters began in the mid-1970s, the eighties was the first full decade in which the top box office films consistently earned increasingly huge returns.

The Empire Strikes Back (1980), *E.T. the Extra-Terrestrial* (1982), *Return of the Jedi* (1983), *Ghost Busters* (1984), and *Batman* (1989) all broke the $100 million earnings threshold in the year of their release. At the time, that was a historic threshold, and many other films closed in on it, among them *Raiders of the Lost Ark* (1981), *Back to the Future* (1985), *Top Gun* (1986), *Beverly Hills Cop II* (1987), and *Who Framed Roger Rabbit* (1988). Media attention in the period increasingly focused on these popular pictures and on the question of which one was leading the box office in a given weekend.

The prevalence of sequels and series (today called franchises) was another symptom of the emphasis on blockbusters. James Bond continued as the most successful franchise in film history with four movies in the eighties, beginning with *For Your Eyes Only* (1981) and ending with *License to Kill* (1989), the character's popularity undiminished despite changes in leading men (Roger Moore in the decade's first three Bond offerings and the harder-edged, less jokey Timothy Dalton in the fourth). Sylvester Stallone's two most popular characters, Rocky and Rambo, romped through the eighties with *Rocky III* (1982), *Rocky IV* (1985), *Rocky V* (in production 1989, released 1990), *First Blood* (1982), *Rambo: First Blood Part II* (1985), and *Rambo III* (1988). Eddie Murphy reached his career height with *Beverly Hills Cop* (1984) and *Beverly Hills Cop II* (1987).

And it seemed as if the industry had been taken over by mathematicians. More and more movies had numbers in their titles: *Superman II* (1981), *Superman III* (1983), *Superman IV* (1987), *Star Trek II: The Wrath of Khan* (1982), *Star Trek III: The Search for Spock* (1984), *Star Trek IV: The Voyage Home* (1986), *Star Trek V: The Final Frontier* (1989), *The Karate Kid, Part II* (1986), *Police Academy 2* (1984), *Lethal Weapon 2* (1989), *Back to the Future, Part II* (1989). The imperative to sequelize a successful picture became so all-powerful in the period that the industry viewed the late appearance of *Ghostbusters II* (1989), five years after the success of the original film, as a major failure by the studio, Columbia Pictures, to capitalize on its momentum.

The widespread embrace of sequels in the eighties showcased the status of film as pure product merchandising. Sequels were like brand labels, and the studios sought to brand audience loyalty by developing characters and film properties that could be manufactured in perpetuity. As a result, the endings of many films in the period were not really endings, just the postponing of narrative until the next installments. Studios wanted sequels to offset the exploding costs of filmmaking. Runaway production costs plagued the industry, and the studios tried to recoup these with the guaranteed earnings of a sequel. In 1979, the average production cost of a film was $5 million. It rose to $9 million in 1980 and to $23 million by decade's end (MPAA "1996"). These numbers may sound meager when compared with current figures that often pass $100 million, but what we see today is the continuation of an inflationary process that began in the 1980s.

This explosion in the cost of filmmaking explains much about the importance of blockbusters for the industry. Blockbusters are planned as sure-fire winners. By bringing in an enormous amount of revenue, they help the studios stay afloat in a sea of rising costs. It is, however, a self-perpetuating cycle because blockbusters also cost a lot to produce. If the blockbuster was carefully tailored according to a "high concept," however, it had a very good chance of succeeding.

The emergence of high-concept filmmaking was a direct result of the industry's recognition of the earnings potential of a hit film. High concept offered a formula for manufacturing hits, and the producing team of Don Simpson and Jerry Bruckheimer embodied this approach. Their hits in the period—*Flashdance* (1983), *Top Gun, Beverly Hills Cop, Beverly Hills Cop II, Twins* (1988)—epitomized what Simpson and Bruckheimer described as a "clean" aesthetic. The stories were built on a catchy premise (the hulking Arnold Schwarzenegger and the diminutive Danny DeVito as twins, for example), were constructed without irony or ambiguity, were layered with slick imagery like icing on a cake, and were accompanied by pop rock scores that were cross-promoted with the movies. High-concept films were relentless in style, turning narrative into a series of music videos strung together along a thin narrative line. The Simpson-Bruckheimer formula proved extremely influential and continues to exert a hold over filmmaking to this day.

Countertrends

Considering these trends, the reader is probably ready to agree with the proposition that blockbusters took over Hollywood in the eighties. The industry felt economically compelled to make blockbusters, but these films were actually a very small part of the decade's overall production output. As soon as one moves away from the big box-office hits, the true diversity of eighties production becomes apparent. Many of the decade's most significant filmmakers, for example, worked apart from the blockbusters. These included Oliver Stone, Spike Lee, Martin Scorsese, Sidney Lumet, Woody Allen, Lawrence Kasdan, Barry Levinson, Brian De Palma, David Lynch, Ridley Scott, and John Sayles. Each filmmaker made at least one masterwork in the period that qualifies as one of the decade's classic films—*Platoon* (1986), *Do the Right Thing* (1989), *Raging Bull* (1980), *Prince of the City* (1981), *Crimes and Misdemeanors* (1989), *Body Heat* (1981), *Diner* (1982), *Scarface* (1983), *Blue Velvet* (1986), *Blade Runner* (1982), and *Matewan* (1987). Unlike the high concept blockbusters, which were aimed at adolescent and young adult audiences, these films are more nuanced in their moral and thematic designs and traffic in irony and ambiguity, all hallmarks of a mature artistic sensibility.

Clearly there was plenty of room in Hollywood during the period to bring alternative kinds of pictures to the screen, albeit ones that often had clearly limited box office potential. Clint Eastwood's career illustrates the relative ease with which a filmmaker might move between clearly commercial and more personal kinds of filmmaking. Eastwood would play his popular Dirty Harry character or make a western and then go off and direct unusual pictures such as *Bronco Billy* (1980), a throwback to the Hollywood screwball comedies of the 1930s; *Honkytonk Man* (1982), in which Eastwood plays a consumptive country-western singer; *Bird* (1988), a film biography of the great jazz saxophonist Charlie Parker; and *White Hunter, Black Heart* (1990), in which Eastwood plays a Hollywood film director modeled on John Huston.

Moreover, one of the decade's most significant developments was the explosion of independent filmmaking, with an abundance of pictures being financed and/or distributed outside the major Hollywood studios. If blockbusters represented a consolidation of control by the Hollywood majors, the rise of independent filmmaking represented a countertrend of decentralization in the industry. This trend emerged at mid-decade, and it has characterized American film ever since. In 1980, the major Hollywood studios released 134 films, while there were only 57 films in distribution from other companies. By 1985, however, things had flip-flopped. The majors released 138 films that year, but independents put 251 films into distribution, and that proportion has remained relatively constant ever since (MPAA "2003"). The real proportion of filmmaking occurring outside the orbit of the majors was even more skewed because many of the films distributed by the majors were in fact financed and produced independently.

Prominent independent distributors in the period included Cinecom, Island, Miramax, New Line, Vestron, New World, Hemdale, and FilmDallas, and the majors formed subsidiaries (such as Fox Classics and Orion Classics) to handle alternative films. These companies made possible an extraordinary expansion of filmmaking opportunity, and many of the decade's important films and filmmakers got their start here—Joel and Ethan Coen's *Blood Simple* (1984), John Sayles's *The Brother from Another Planet* (1984), Jim Jarmusch's *Stranger Than Paradise* (1984), Steven Soderbergh's *sex, lies and videotape* (1989), Joyce Chopra's *Smooth Talk* (1986), Spike Lee's *She's Gotta Have It* (1986), Oliver Stone's *Salvador* (1986), Tim Hunter's *River's Edge* (1987), Robert Townsend's *Hollywood Shuffle* (1987), and many others.

By decentralizing the industry, this expansion of production and distribution created opportunities for filmmakers with alternative projects and sensibilities that clearly fell outside the commercial mainstream. These included Paul Schrader, whose *Mishima: A Life in Four Chapters* (1987) is one of the decade's best and most unusual pictures, a radically designed portrait of Japanese author Yukio Mishima. It was shot in Japan, with all dialogue in Japanese and no American actors, yet was distributed by Hollywood major Warner Bros. While very few women directors were entrusted with major productions in the period (exceptions being Randa Haines [*Children of a Lesser God*, 1986], Penny Marshall [*Big*, 1988], and Barbra Streisand [*Yentl*, 1983; *Nuts*, 1987]), smaller budget and independent films afforded numerous female directors opportunities to work. These included Martha Coolidge (*Valley Girl*, 1983), Amy Jones (*Slumber Party Massacre*, 1982), Penelope Spheeris (*The Decline of Western Civilization*, 1981; *Suburbia*, 1983), Susan Seidelman (*Smithereens*, 1984; *Desperately Seeking Susan*, 1985), Amy Heckerling (*Fast Times at Ridgemont High*, 1982), and Kathryn Bigelow (*Near Dark*, 1987).

Why did independent filmmaking expand in the 1980s? Why were there significantly more pictures in production and distribution at mid-decade? The answers lie in one of the era's key developments, which in turn has become one of the most important, transformative events of American film history. This was the introduction of the videocassette recorder and the advent of film viewing at home on videotape. On the one hand, the majors were alarmed by the prospect of home viewers making their own copies of movies—the majors construed this as a copyright violation and erroneously thought that it would lead to a loss of revenue—but they moved quickly to embrace the new technology. VCRs were introduced in the late 1970s, and by 1980 the majors were releasing their films onto home video, in many cases with subsidiary companies created to develop this market.

While the story of home video is too complex to cover in detail here (for more details see Prince 94–116), the key points involve the manner in which it transformed American film during the decade. Home video shifted film viewing away from theaters and celluloid and into the home on an electronic format. Compared with the luminous beauty of film, videotape was clearly a substandard format, offering very poor resolution and the cropping of widescreen cinema images to fit a television screen. But given the convenience of watching a movie in the home, viewers happily accepted these limitations.

By mid-decade more people were watching movies in their homes on videotape than in the theater, and the revenue streams from these markets demonstrated this shift. By mid-decade, revenue from home video was out-pacing that from theatrical exhibition. In 1987, home video revenues were $7.5 billion compared with a $4 billion box office. In 1989, the differential increased to over $11 billion for video against a $5 billion box office (*International* 391). This relationship has persisted ever since; the theatrical market was never again the primary one for the Hollywood industry.

But contrary to predictions at the time, home video did not kill theaters. Instead, there was a boom in theater construction. Screens nationwide rose during the decade from 17,590 to 23,132, the biggest expansion in forty years (MPAA "1996"). The exhibition sector was robust, and the Hollywood majors went on a buying spree, purchasing theater chains. Why did this happen at the very time that film viewing was shifting increasingly into the home? The answer can be found in the way that home video created an extraordinary demand for film product. It was a voracious market, as was cable television, which also expanded in the period. To feed the burgeoning home video sales and rental markets, and to provide films that could subsequently play on cable television, the studios had to get more films into production and distribution. But studio capital was fully extended, and so the independent sector stepped in and fed the expansion of production and distribution that the video markets required. And more theater screens were needed for this extra product. Theatrical release was the launching pad for a film's performance in the ancillary (nontheatrical) markets. Thus, home video, and cable television to a lesser extent, drove the expansion in film production and exhibition that was so striking in the era.

We are now in a period during the second century of cinema where film is disappearing and being replaced by electronic formats; this process began with home video in the 1980s. Moreover, the ancillary markets that came on line then began to drive the business, changing it from a film industry to a communications industry. During the eighties, multinational communications companies bought all the Hollywood majors except for

Disney, and the logic of big budget filmmaking shifted toward synergy, toward getting all the interrelated markets of film, music, book and magazine publishing, and retail merchandising to work together around the release of a highly commercial film. *Top Gun, Gremlins* (1984), *Flashdance, E.T., Footloose* (1984), *Batman, Who Framed Roger Rabbit,* and *Return of the Jedi* were all marketing phenomena, as much a triumph of synergy and aggressive promotion as of filmmaking savvy. These films and many others like them stimulated huge waves of related product merchandising. They were simultaneously films, home videos, soundtrack albums, rock music videos, books, toys, T-shirts, and so on. Thus, it wasn't just film *qua* film, preserved on celluloid, that was disappearing. It was film as a discrete, stand-alone medium. As of the 1980s, film became part of "home entertainment," merely one component of something much broader than cinema itself.

This shift in emphasis may explain one of the decade's most striking developments. Many of the great directors, who were celebrated as auteurs during the golden age of the late 1960s and early 1970s, stumbled in the 1980s and experienced difficulties maintaining their careers. These included Martin Scorsese, Robert Altman, Peter Bogdanovich, William Friedkin, Francis Ford Coppola, Brian De Palma, and Arthur Penn. They all made films in the period, and at least two—*Raging Bull* and *Scarface*—are considered classics, but in general the kind of personal, ironic, and off-beat films they were making a decade earlier seemed increasingly harder to accomplish. Because of this development, many critics of the 1980s have suggested that its blockbusters and synergies were antithetical to the personal, auteur cinema of the 1970s and that the decade gave us instead "movie brats" like George Lucas and Steven Spielberg, weaned on movies and television and for whom the box office was the arbiter of success.

Leaving aside for the moment the question of whether this is a fair assessment of Lucas and Spielberg, the allegation overlooks the many new auteurs who emerged in the period. The auteurs of the 1970s did experience a crisis in the eighties, but the decade proved to be very receptive to the emergence of a new group of singular filmmakers. These included Tim Burton (*Pee-Wee's Big Adventure* [1985], *Beetlejuice* [1988], *Batman*), James Cameron (*The Terminator* [1984], *Aliens* [1986], *The Abyss* [1989]), Joe Dante (*The Howling* [1981], *Gremlins, Innerspace* [1987]), Jim Jarmusch (*Stranger Than Paradise, Down by Law* [1986]), Lawrence Kasdan (*Body Heat, The Big Chill* [1983], *The Accidental Tourist* [1988]), Barry Levinson (*Diner, Tin Men* [1987], *Avalon* [1990]), Spike Lee (*She's Gotta Have It, Do the Right Thing*), and Oliver Stone (*Salvador, Platoon, Wall Street* [1987], *Born on the Fourth of July* [1989]).

The style and tone of these films are different from what the 1970s auteurs were making in their period, but the work is just as singular and uniquely defined in terms of a prevailing creative sensibility. It would be wrong to regard these films as being not the work of uniquely talented directors. Clearly, the eighties was not hostile to auteur filmmaking, but it was true that the "golden age" style of seventies film—scrappy, a little ragged, open-ended, ironic, ambiguous, often despairing—was not as welcomed by the industry. The aesthetic, social, and political factors that sustained films like *Easy Rider* (1969), *The Last Detail* (1973), and *Chinatown* (1974) had shifted, as they inevitably do, to a different constellation of factors nourishing eighties film and the rather different creative profiles of its auteurs. In general, film in the eighties was less politicized from an oppositional, even radical, perspective, and its style was lusher, glossier, and much less ironic and ambiguous than it had been in the late 1960s and early 1970s.

Spielberg and Lucas

For some critics, though, this represents a falling off from the achievements of that earlier period. Eighties film is regarded as being more adolescent, even infantile, in its appeals, and responsibility for this is often attributed to the work of Steven Spielberg and George Lucas and their influence on other filmmakers. Their work in the eighties (and even before, with *Jaws* and *Star Wars* in the seventies) is presumed to personify and to popularize all the detrimental effects of blockbuster filmmaking.

Without question, they were the most commercially successful filmmakers of the period, fashioning a series of tremendously popular pictures—*The Empire Strikes Back, Return of the Jedi, Raiders of the Lost Ark, E.T., Indiana Jones and the Temple of Doom* (1984), *Indiana Jones and the Last Crusade* (1989). These films offer an uncomplicated emotional appeal to their viewers and are generally without irony and moral ambiguity. While the popular audience loved these qualities, critics did not, and many suggested that the films offered a fundamentally adolescent appeal. The films are also very strong on fantasy and special effects, and these elements became prerequisites of blockbuster filmmaking from then on. While *The Godfather* (1972) was a blockbuster in its day, it was a film made for adults. By contrast, the popcorn movies of Spielberg and Lucas were aimed at what thereafter became Hollywood's sacred demographic—teens and older children. The breathless narrative pacing of these films, top-heavy with climax after climax, seemed to equate cinema entirely with the provision of spectacle. The iconic emotion in Spielberg's films of this period is awe—close-ups of stunned characters, staring slack-jawed at visions that overwhelm them, exactly as the films aimed to do with their audience.

Their style was massively influential and not just because their films were so popular. Spielberg and Lucas worked extensively as producers in other people's work, in the process extending their style across a decade's filmmaking. Spielberg's work as producer generally emphasized special effects fantasy and adolescent adventure: *Used Cars* (1980), *Continental Divide* (1981), *Poltergeist* (1982), *Twilight Zone: The Movie* (1983), *Gremlins, Young Sherlock Holmes* (1985), *The Goonies* (1985), *Back to the Future, An American Tail* (1986), *The Money Pit* (1986), **batteries not included* (1987), *Innerspace, The Land Before Time* (1988), *Who Framed Roger Rabbit, Dad* (1989), and *Back to the Future Part II*.

As producer, Lucas's films included *Raiders of the Lost Ark, Twice Upon a Time* (1983), *The Ewok Adventure* (1984), *Indiana Jones and the Temple of Doom, Ewoks: The Battle for Endor* (1985), *Howard the Duck* (1986), *Labyrinth* (1986), *The Land Before Time* (co-produced with Spielberg), and *Indiana Jones and the Last Crusade*. Lucas's effects house, Industrial Light and Magic, designed effects for his own films as well as scores of other prominent movies, thereby putting the Lucas seal on these works. They included *Dragonslayer* (1981), *The Dark Crystal* (1982), *Cocoon* (1985), *Harry and the Hendersons* (1987), *The Abyss, Ghostbusters II, Field of Dreams* (1989), and the *Star Trek* and Indiana Jones films.

ILM's work enabled Lucas to explore his developing interests in digital cinemas and to champion the industry's transition in that direction. In the mid-eighties, Lucasfilm developed a computer-assisted electronic editor (Editdroid, using laserdiscs) and an all-digital sound editor (SoundDroid), and ILM worked on the key films of the period that showcased digital effects—*Star Trek II: The Wrath of Khan, Young Sherlock Holmes*, and *The Abyss*. Indeed, Lucas's most profound influence on American film may lie in the technologies that he has helped to champion, a process that began in the 1980s. The most famous of these, of course, are the digital methods of production and post-production, but additional examples include Skywalker Ranch, which included a state-of-the-art sound recording and mixing facility used by numerous filmmakers and recording artists and which helped lead the general upgrading of audio in films of the period. And in 1983 Lucasfilm introduced its THX-certification program for calibrating optimal picture and sound quality in theaters. Lucas's technical innovations were designed to showcase his own productions, but, with their remarkable upgrades in the quality of picture and sound, they quickly spread throughout the industry.

Thus, on the one hand, a massive number of films in the period exemplified what might be called the Lucas-Spielberg style. On the other hand, both filmmakers fashioned work that went against this style. Lucas co-produced Akira Kurosawa's samurai epic, *Kagemusha* (1980), Francis Ford Coppola's period film *Tucker: The Man and His Dream* (1988), Lawrence Kasdan's film noir update *Body Heat*, and, most remarkably, Haskell Wexler's *Latino* (1985), a pro-Sandinista film that was one of the few pictures in the period to explicitly criticize U.S. support for the contra rebels fighting the Nicaraguan government. In each case, Lucas used his position in the industry to help other filmmakers get their unorthodox projects into production.

The path of Spielberg's artistic growth has been a more gradual and interesting one. His popcorn films have a very calculated quality, at once stylistically exuberant and cautiously conservative, seeking to please their viewers while shying away from anything that might complicate this mix. It is an orientation that can imprison a filmmaker by preventing him or her from growing artistically, and it was a problem for Spielberg early in the period, as his response to the bleak ending of Bob Fosse's *All That Jazz* (1979) indicates. The film's main character, a dance choreographer played by Roy Scheider, has a heart attack and dies, and the very last shot of the film is a close-up that shows him being zipped up in a body bag. Scheider reported that Spielberg told Fosse that he should not end the film this way, that it would lose millions at the box office.[1] Fosse disregarded the advice and kept the ending, which plainly would not please a mass audience but is artistically right for the film. Spielberg's fantasy films in the eighties never dare this much, and, in time, he came to feel constrained by the artistically cautious underpinnings of his popular success.

Thus, after working exclusively in a popcorn movie mode, Spielberg attempted in the second half of the decade to escape this. In 1986, accepting the Irving G. Thalberg Award from the Academy of Motion Picture Arts and Sciences, he made a speech lamenting the poorly written quality of many contemporary films and urging filmmakers to use cinema as a means for exploring ideas and important themes. With *The Color Purple* (1985), *Empire of the Sun* (1987), and *Always* (1989), Spielberg stepped out of the blockbuster mode of special effects fantasy and adolescent thrills in order to pursue more adult-themed filmmaking. *The Color Purple* portrays the harsh life of a poor black woman who suffers physical abuse from her husband. *Empire of the Sun* shows the moral confusion of war through the experiences of a young boy separated from his parents in Shanghai when the Japanese invade in a prelude to World War II. *Always* updates a World War II era story about a pilot, killed in a plane crash, who spiritually watches over the woman he had loved. Each of these movies has evident failings, but they demonstrate that Spielberg aspired to more than a strictly commercial brand of filmmaking. He did not return to popcorn movies until the end of the decade with *Indiana Jones and the Last Crusade*.

His initial foray into a more grown-up cinema served him well as preparation for subsequent efforts. His mature films of the nineties— *Schindler's List* (1993) and *Saving Private Ryan* (1998)—are far more accomplished even if they are, at times, undone by Spielberg's evident inability to trust that the audience will accompany him where he wants to go. If, to this day, there remains a great filmmaker in Spielberg that is still struggling to get out, his eighties films show us a filmmaker enjoying an unparalleled rapport with his audience and then seeking to go beyond this to create a more nuanced and thematically complex filmmaking.

The Reagan Era

Given the extraordinarily high profile that Spielberg's and Lucas's work enjoyed in the period, it is tempting to take their work as a template for the entire period. Their films were massively influential, and yet a fundamental truth of Hollywood cinema is that it is heterodox. It is composed of many different styles and sensibilities because the audience to which films must appeal is variegated. Thus, as I have noted, the eighties boasted numerous auteurs whose work is very different from the Spielberg-Lucas style of blockbusters. Critics, however, who take their work as a template for the decade often connect it to another of the master paradigms used to explain and interpret the 1980s. This paradigm is what we might simply call Reaganism, referring to the political, cultural, and ideological influence of the Reagan administration during its two terms of office. Politically, the 1980s inaugurated an uninterrupted decade of Republican dominance of the White House, with the one-term presidency of George Bush following the eight years Reagan occupied the Oval Office. Although Reagan's policies were fiercely debated during the decade, since that time the myth-making forces at work in American political life have elevated him to the status of a towering figure in presidential history, minimizing the controversies that surrounded his tenure. To what extent did Hollywood film reflect the politics and culture of Reaganism?

The answer is, to a degree. The Reagan era worked a profound transformation of American political and cultural life, moving the country in a rightward direction. Since the Reagan period, and relative to the 1960s, as political scientist Cass Sunstein notes, "what was then in the center is now on the left; what was then in the far right is now in the center; what was then on the left now no longer exists." With his hostility to government as a provider of social programs for the public, Reagan fulfilled long-standing conservative dreams of rolling back the economic and political reforms of Roosevelt's New Deal, and toward this end, during his first term, he instituted a program of sizeable tax cuts that favored the wealthy. He affiliated with the Christian Right and its efforts to infuse a religion-based morality into American politics, and he invoked the specter and fear of Soviet expansion, in the process returning the country to the hard-line anti-communism of the 1950s. His historical legacy becomes very clear when one considers that all these policies characterize the twenty-first-century administration of George W. Bush, provided that one substitutes the contemporary monolithic focus on world terrorism for that on world communism.

American film during the eighties is only somewhat consistent with this ideological template. The clearest correlations lie in the cycle of action-adventure films that demonize the Soviet Union and portray it as Reagan himself did, as an "Evil Empire" seeking to impose its will on the free world. Reagan revived the Cold War of the 1950s, and this group of films can accurately be described as New Cold War productions. In *Red Dawn* (1984), the Soviets invade and conquer America, except for isolated bands of young American guerrilla fighters. The Soviets invade again, with a proxy army of terrorists, in *Invasion USA* (1985), and only action hero Chuck Norris can stop them. In *Rocky IV* Sylvester Stallone's pugilist hero symbolically battles a robotic Soviet boxer and wears an American flag in victory. In *Top Gun* and *Iron Eagle* (1986), brave American jet fighter pilots joust in the skies with the Soviets and their allies. In *Rambo: First Blood II* and *Rambo III*, Stallone's super-warrior rampages through Vietnam and Afghanistan, stomping Soviet forces into the ground. Rambo was the über-mensch of the period, his engorged muscles and phallic weaponry making a symbolic statement about the reawakening of American military power after its period of post-Vietnam dormancy, an idea that was a key theme of Reagan's presidency.

Although Hollywood film throughout the period dramatized the Reagan administration's obsession with communism and the Soviet Union, it was only the belligerent New Cold War films that overtly endorsed the claims of Washington's cold warriors. A larger group of films focused in a less combative way on U.S.-Soviet relations. These included *Moscow on the Hudson* (1984), *Spies Like Us* (1985), *White Nights* (1985), *The Falcon and the Snowman* (1985), *Russkies* (1987), *The Fourth Protocol* (1987), *No Way Out* (1987), *Little Nikita* (1988), and *The Package* (1989). Though less noticed,

Rambo (Sylvester Stallone) was the great Ur-warrior of Reagan's America, here in *Rambo: First Blood Part II* (George P. Cosmatos, Carolco). Jerry Ohlinger's Movie Material Store.

these films may reflect not only the ideologically diverse nature of American film, but also perhaps the industry's mistrust of an overly close alliance with Washington. Bitter memories remain in Hollywood over the period of government blacklisting in the 1950s, a time when Reagan was president of the Screen Actors Guild and instituted a loyalty oath for its members. This may have had an impact on some of Hollywood's production cycles contesting the claims and policies of the Reagan administration, particularly as Reagan's politics inclined increasingly to the right of mainstream Hollywood in the intervening years.

One of the most important administration policies dealt with war and revolution in Central America. Grinding poverty faced by farmers and peasants and a huge concentration of wealth among the landowning class ignited fires of political rebellion in Guatemala and El Salvador and brought a revolutionary government to power in Nicaragua. The Reagan administration viewed these indigenous responses as instances of Soviet expansion, and attempted in the name of anti-communism to overthrow the democratically elected Nicaraguan government, as well as to support the fascist regimes in Guatemala and El Salvador. Throughout the region the United

States supplied money, arms, and military training to be used for a wide-spread massacre of the politically restive peasantry. Thousands of people were tortured and killed by death squads on behalf of the armies the United States was funding.

Reagan's policies brought enormous devastation to the region, and Hollywood film stepped outside of Washington's Cold War template to level heavy criticism at U.S. foreign policy. *Under Fire* (1983) offered a sympathetic account of the Nicaraguan revolution that the United States was trying to destroy (and would succeed in destroying). *El Norte* (1984) showed the poverty and political repression in Guatemala that drove refugees northward to the United States. *Latino* portrayed the United States training the contra army in order to sow sabotage and destruction in Nicaragua. *Salvador* (1986) connected the election of Reagan in 1980 and his well-known anti-communism with the rise of the death squads in El Salvador. *Romero* (1989) dramatized the alliance with the poor of Salvadoran Archbishop Oscar Romero and his defiance of the Salvadoran government, which led to his assassination by death squads. While Reagan was embracing the Christian Right and its moralistic agenda in the United States, *Romero* showed a different kind of politicized Christianity, what was then called "liberation

Raul Julia in the title role of *Romero* (John Duigan, Paulist Pictures). In dramatizing the political activism of the Salvadoran archbishop, the film offers a critical portrait of Washington's foreign policy. Jerry Ohlinger's Movie Material Store.

theology," in which priests sided with the poor and oppressed against their cruel governments.

An additional film in this cycle expanded the focus to South America. *Missing* (1982) dramatized the U.S.-backed overthrow of the democratically elected government of Chile in 1973 by a military regime that proceeded to torture and execute its political opponents. Jack Lemmon plays an American father searching for his son amid the repression, learning finally that the boy was among those killed with U.S. complicity.

Another cycle of films offered a sustained critique of Reagan's economic policies, which rewarded the wealthy and the corporate sector while cutting the social safety net from the poor and the inner cities. In this case, the critique was not as overt as in the Central America films because it was typically projected through the guise of futuristic fantasy. A series of dystopic science fiction films showed the United States transforming into a neo-fascist nation, with ruthless corporate power running the state and funding the police and military, the objectives being the expansion of military empire and the subjugation of the poor living in decaying urban centers. The grim future worlds evoked in *Alien* (1979), *Escape from New York* (1981), *Outland* (1981), *Blade Runner*, *Aliens*, *The Running Man* (1987), *RoboCop* (1987), and *Total Recall* (1990) offer a pointed rejoinder to Reagan's sunny "Morning in America" optimism. Viewed in a post-9/11 world, these films look even more remarkable than they did in the 1980s.

The era's most important cycle of social and politically themed filmmaking was its productions about the Vietnam War. The industry had sought to avoid the topic in the 1960s and most of the 1970s, believing it was box office poison, until the critical and popular successes of *The Deer Hunter* (1978), *Coming Home* (1978), and *Apocalypse Now* (1979) signaled that the period of neglect was ending. Throughout the eighties American screens depicted the fighting in Southeast Asia from a variety of social and political perspectives that were generally free of the antiwar opposition that had been so strong during the Vietnam period itself. While the Vietnam War could not be depicted with the moral clarity that Hollywood's World War II pictures had shown—it had been too controversial and fraught with doubt for that—in general the eighties films took the view that while the war may have been wrong, America's soldiers remained an honorable and patriotic force. Collectively, then, this cycle of films undertook the rehabilitation of America's Vietnam forces which, until then, had remained relatively stigmatized in popular culture.

Films in the first half of the decade—*Uncommon Valor* (1983), *Missing in Action* (1984), *Rambo: First Blood Part II*—focused on the issue of Americans missing in action and depicted heroic rescue attempts after the war. In *Missing in Action* and *Rambo,* these become substitute symbolic victories over the Vietnamese fought by surrogate über-warriors. The latter films rendered the war in comic book terms, and it was in that context that Oliver Stone's *Platoon* premiered with extraordinary force. It offered what appeared to be the most realistic and gut-wrenching depiction of the "grunt's" experience of jungle war yet filmed, and a flood of pictures followed, many offering close-in depictions of combat: *Hamburger Hill* (1987), *Good Morning Vietnam* (1987), *The Hanoi Hilton* (1987), *Gardens of Stone* (1987), *Full Metal Jacket* (1987), *Off Limits* (1988), *Bat 21* (1988), *84 Charlie MoPic* (1989), *Casualties of War* (1989), *Born on the Fourth of July.* Many of the films offered overtly symbolic templates for understanding the war—the hero's ruined body in *Born on the Fourth of July,* the good-evil dualism of the two sergeants in *Platoon*—in a struggle to assimilate via cinema this historical debacle and extract its relevant meaning for contemporary America. In the end, the films offered more in the way of poetry, symbolism, and mythology than they do of history, but whatever their limitations, the outpouring of productions made this Hollywood's Vietnam decade, unmatched in any period since.

Hollywood Genres

Depictions of Vietnam kept the war film alive as a thriving genre with a contemporary salience. But what of Hollywood's other basic genres? The gangster film remained favored by filmmakers, but on the whole the work was not especially memorable. *Atlantic City* (1980), *Gloria* (1980), and *Thief* (1981) were accomplished and interesting variations on the theme, but all were in a minor key mode. After his first two *Godfather* pictures, Francis Ford Coppola's much anticipated return to the genre in *The Cotton Club* (1984) was a disappointment. The trouble-plagued production failed to gel as either gangster film or musical (revolving around the famous Harlem nightclub of the title). Likewise, William Friedkin's return after *The French Connection* (1971) yielded the stylish but relatively incoherent *To Live and Die in L.A.* (1985).

Only one true gangster classic emerged during the period, Brian De Palma's *Scarface* (1983), an update of the 1932 Howard Hawks original, with greatly increased savagery and a memorably operatic performance by Al Pacino. De Palma's picture vividly captured the greed and vulgarity of the unfettered capitalism of the Reagan years and personified it in the picture's empire-building gangsters. Yet when De Palma returned to the genre in *The*

Untouchables (1987), the result was a more calculated commercial under-taking.

Perhaps the genre's perceived lack of credibility led to the decline in the quality of gangster films during the decade. Many filmmakers parodied the genre in various ways in films such as *City Heat* (1984), *Johnny Dangerously* (1984), *Wise Guys* (1986), and *Married to the Mob* (1988). By contrast, direc-tors overseas were using the genre in a far more visionary and imaginative way in pictures like *The Long Good Friday* (1980), *Once Upon a Time in Amer-ica* (1984), *A Better Tomorrow* (1986), and *The Killer* (1989).

In far worse shape was the western. Once a staple of the industry, the western in the 1980s slid into a decline that now seems irreversible. The budget-breaking, over-blown *Heaven's Gate* (1980) became one of the decade's most notorious pictures, whose box office failure ruined its pro-duction company, the once-stellar United Artists. A few good westerns were made in the period—Walter Hill's *The Long Riders* (1980), Steve McQueen's *Tom Horn* (1980), Fred Schepisi's *Barbarosa* (1982)—but production in the genre was sparse and frequently tended toward comedy and parody, a sure sign of decay. Such pictures as *The Legend of the Lone Ranger* (1981), *Lust in the Dust* (1985), *Rustler's Rhapsody* (1985), *Silverado* (1985), *Three Amigos!* (1986), and *Young Guns* (1988) were a series of nails in the genre's coffin. Even *Pale Rider* (1985), directed by Clint Eastwood, was a pallid retread of an earlier classic, *Shane* (1953). Although the genre was still capable of greatness—*Dances with Wolves* (1990) and *Unforgiven* (1992) were just around the bend—the eighties essentially finished the western as a vital and contemporary popular art form.

In better shape, surprisingly, was the musical. Its classical form, from the thirties, forties, and fifties, was long gone, but the musical itself proved to be unexpectedly enduring and showed up in a series of extremely popu-lar films, including *Flashdance, Staying Alive* (1983), *Purple Rain* (1984), *Foot-loose*, and *Dirty Dancing* (1987). Other musicals of the period included *Popeye* (1980), *Xanadu* (1980), *The Best Little Whorehouse in Texas* (1982), *Annie* (1981), *A Chorus Line* (1985), *Little Shop of Horrors* (1986), and *La Bamba* (1987). While the range of quality was uneven, this was an impressive range of output for a genre whose demise had long been predicted. In a period where synergy across ancillary markets was a core industry prin-ciple, musicals offered an inherent strategy for tying in movies, recorded music, and music videos. Perhaps it was this marketing imperative more than anything else that kept the genre on its dancing feet.

The greatest vitality in the period among Hollywood's basic genres was unquestionably found in horror and fantasy/science fiction. Unlike the other genres, horror has been considered somewhat disreputable, one in which few front-rank directors regularly work. This was certainly true at the turn of the decade, especially with the emergence of the ultra-violent slasher films like *The Driller Killer* (1979), *Schizoid* (1980), *Maniac* (1980), *Terror Train* (1980), and *He Knows You're Alone* (1980). These and others offered lurid, graphically detailed violence in stories built around psychopathic mass murderers offing victim after victim. The films aroused great controversy about the effects of watching this kind of lovingly detailed violence, but the controversies, of course, did not dampen the cycle's popularity.

In fact, slasher films spawned several popular monsters in a string of franchise productions, and these characters have become classics in the genre. The most popular were Freddy and Jason. Freddy was the demonic spirit of a child molester who was burned alive by enraged parents and now returns in the dreams of teenagers to torment and destroy them. This he did in the long-running series of "Elm Street" films—*A Nightmare on Elm Street* (1984), *A Nightmare on Elm Street Part 2: Freddy's Revenge* (1985), *A Nightmare on Elm Street 3: Dream Warriors* (1987), *A Nightmare on Elm Street 4: The Dream Master* (1988), and *A Nightmare on Elm Street: The Dream Child* (1989).

In contrast to the wit and perverse joie de vivre of Freddy on Elm Street, Jason was a hulking, silent cipher with a hockey mask on his face in the *Friday the 13th* series. Jason wrought his havoc on slow-witted but nubile teenagers who would hang out at Camp Crystal Lake, although in the first film (1980) he was not the villain. The franchise continued with sequels in 1981 and 1982, followed by *Friday the 13th: The Final Chapter* (1984), *Friday the 13th, Part V: A New Beginning* (1985), *Friday the 13th, Part VI: Jason Lives* (1986), *Friday the 13th, Part VII: The New Blood* (1988), and *Friday the 13th, Part VIII: Jason Takes Manhattan* (1989). Other masked serial killers returned from popular films of the 1970s: Michael Myers stalked through additional *Halloween* films (1981, 1988, 1989) and Leatherface returned in two more *Texas Chainsaw Massacre* movies (1986, 1990).

Many slasher and similarly violent films went straight to home video, a new option for film distribution as of mid-decade. The coarseness and vulgarity of these pictures arguably helped ghettoize the genre, persuading many serious filmmakers to stay away from horror. Nevertheless, a few filmmakers explored the genre for its artistic potential. Stanley Kubrick's *The Shining* (1980), Michael Wadleigh's *Wolfen* (1981), David Cronenberg's *The Dead Zone* (1983), *The Fly* (1986), and *Dead Ringers* (1988), Joseph Ruben's *The Stepfather* (1987), and John McNaughton's *Henry: Portrait of a Serial Killer* (1986) are visionary works of horror by directors who take the subject seriously and use it in an expansive and ambitious way.

Along with horror, fantasy/science fiction was the decade's most popular genre. The second and third installments in the *Star Wars* series, *The Empire Strikes Back* and *Return of the Jedi,* were immensely popular and became huge monuments in the era's popular culture, attracting legions of fans. The films even inspired President Reagan's continuing tendency to see real life in terms of the movies (Rogin; Wills), as when he famously referred to the Soviet Union as the "Evil Empire" (the villains in the *Star Wars* movies belong to "the Empire"). Further testament to the films' hold on the popular imagination was the fact that Reagan's plan to create a missile shield over the United States became universally known as "Star Wars."

The *Star Wars* films projected a very black-and-white moral view, with good heroes and evil villains and little in between, pitted in an epic struggle for the future of civilization. These were the very terms by which Reagan and his cold warriors viewed their conflict with the Soviet Union, and thus many critics have suggested that the *Star Wars* films furnish an ideological template consistent with Washington's foreign policy. Whether this is true or not, it is doubtful that this conjunction mattered much to fans of the films, who responded to the energy, imagination, and affection for old-fashioned storytelling that George Lucas brought to his series.

The success of Lucas's films inevitably inspired a huge wave of similar space fantasies, including new installments in the *Star Trek* series as well as *Battle Beyond the Stars* (1980), *Flash Gordon* (1980), *Tron* (1982), *The Adventures of Buckaroo Banzai Across the Eighth Dimension* (1984), and *The Last Starfighter* (1984). Other significant fantasy films included *Back to the Future* (and its sequels), *Who Framed Roger Rabbit,* and *Batman,* and the sentimentality and sweetness of Steven Spielberg's *E.T.* inspired the whimsical tone of *Cocoon* and its 1988 sequel. Most of these films aspire to little beyond providing pleasant entertainment, but the *Star Trek* films, and the dystopic cycle reviewed earlier, kept alive the intellectual, reflective components of the science fiction tradition as found in literature. So, too, did a few pictures that did not aspire to blockbuster status. These included *Altered States* (1980) and *Iceman* (1984).

Perhaps of greatest significance, the fantasy/science fiction genre in the eighties showcased the industry's cutting edge visual and audio effects. Digital animation debuted in several films before becoming widespread in the 1990s. Computer-animated sequences appeared in *Star Trek II, Tron, The Last Starfighter, Return of the Jedi, Young Sherlock Holmes,* and *The Abyss.* Digital audio sound recording and mixing were used in *E.T., Poltergeist,* and *Star Trek II,* and Lucasfilm used a proprietary digital sound workstation for mixing and editing on *Indiana Jones and the Temple of Doom.* Sound playback in theaters during the 1980s was still in analog format, but in 1986 Dolby Laboratories introduced Dolby SR (Spectral Recording), which reduced noise and provided a cleaner signal on optical four-channel sound tracks. As the decade ended, the industry was on the verge of mastering digital sound and rapidly moving to embrace digital imagery as a key ingredient in conventional filmmaking.

Conclusion

The eighties was a decade of tremendous change that gave the Hollywood industry and American film its modern shape and form. As the decade ended, the film industry had successfully assimilated the new ancillary markets of home video and cable television and had itself been assimilated into the global communications industry. In the process, film as film began its slow vanishing act, as moving image media became all electronic. As a result of these changes, the studios' major capital investments went to special effects blockbusters, which today remain a primary focus of the industry because they appeal to its vital teen demographic and because they are so capable of creating synergies across multiple media markets.

But, as I have suggested, these features constitute only part—albeit an extremely determinative part—of the picture. American film remained vitally diverse in its aesthetic, stylistic, and ideological appeals and expansive enough to accommodate the emergence of important new talents. Indeed, at decade's end, a new wave of African American filmmakers was about to emerge, of which Spike Lee was the first prominent exemplar. In the next few years, films by John Singleton, Matty Rich, Robert Townsend, and Allen and Albert Hughes would bring a new range of voices and issues to American cinema, a range that was simply unprecedented. Before this, no African American filmmakers had secured funding and distribution from Hollywood.

The subsequent chapters in this volume highlight the divergent appeals and subject matter of the decade's films. Joanna E. Rapf examines the depiction of women in *Coal Miner's Daughter, Urban Cowboy, Just Tell Me What You Want, Nine to Five, Atlantic City,* and *Private Benjamin.* Diane Negra considers the political uses of nostalgia in a series of pictures that revisited classic Hollywood formulas and genres, including *Body Heat, Raiders of the Lost Ark, On Golden Pond,* and *Continental Divide.* Warren Buckland examines the importance of Self/Other oppositions in *E.T., Tron, Blade Runner,* and *Poltergeist,* as well as in films outside the science fiction and fantasy genre. Alan Nadel looks at the political tropes of Reaganism as they were manifest in such films as *Return of the Jedi, The Man with Two Brains, Zelig, The Right Stuff,* and *The Big Chill.* Rhonda Hammer and Douglas Kellner explore the ways conservative and liberal films, including *Red Dawn, Indiana Jones and the Temple of Doom, El Norte,* and *The Killing Fields,* translated and transformed the era's political discourse.

Christina Banks and Michael Bliss find themes of redemption and ideals of landscape operative in *The Purple Rose of Cairo, Brazil,* and *Witness.* Leger Grindon finds a spirit of resistance to mainstream political culture in *Platoon, Aliens, The Fly, Hannah and Her Sisters, Ferris Bueller's Day Off,* and *Blue Velvet.* Jack Boozer explores films that mirror national scandals in *RoboCop, House of Games,* and *Wall Street,* and also examines the salience of Vietnam War films and those examining the broadcast media. Deron Overpeck finds contradictions between the ideology about America and the actual social conditions so important in *Big, Working Girl, Die Hard, Alien Nation,* and *Mississippi Burning.* Jennifer Holt also finds a questioning of core values in *Batman, Do the Right Thing, sex, lies and videotape,* and *Born on the Fourth of July.*

These authors propose a variety of templates for interpreting the era's films. This variety testifies to the richness of cinema in the period. The eighties is a decade of incomparable importance to the history of American film. So much about cinema as we know it today is traceable to the events of those years. And, of perhaps even greater significance, the movies of the eighties are beloved by viewers. Those who grew up in that period remember these pictures with great affection and nostalgia. And that's a fine legacy for a decade of film.

NOTES

1. Scheider's remarks are on his audio commentary on the DVD edition of the film.

1980

Movies and the New Woman

JOANNA E. RAPF

A time "to imagine," to groove on rock 'n' roll and dream of a more utopian and egalitarian world, faded as the Reagan era dawned. On 8 December, a month after the former actor and governor of California was elected president, John Lennon was fatally shot outside his home at The Dakota apartment building in New York City. For millions of his mourning fans, it was as if the sixties had ended all over again.

Only three weeks earlier, however, it was a fictional shooting that preoccupied America, when the 21 November broadcast of the television series "Dallas" answered the question that viewers had been asking for eight months: "Who shot J.R.?" The revelation that the shooter was a glamorous, emotionally unstable woman may have had no particular significance, but overall it was a year in which strong female characters made a notable impact.

The election dominated the year's news, and the results reflected several growing trends. A study from UCLA and the American Council on Education indicated that management was the most popular undergraduate major and that college freshmen were interested in status, power, and money more than at any time during the preceding fifteen years. The top issues for voters were the economy, jobs, the reputation of the United States around the world, and the hostage crisis in Iran. Inflation was in the double digits, gasoline was $1.20 a gallon, interest rates were as high as 22 percent, and unemployment was about 7 percent. Ronald Reagan's famous rhetorical flourish in his 28 October debate with incumbent president Jimmy Carter summed up why the country would soon turn to him:

> Are you better off than you were four years ago? Is it easier for you to do and buy things in the stores than it was four years ago? Is there more or less unemployment in the country than there was four years ago? Is America as respected throughout the world as it was? . . . If you answer all of those questions "yes," why, then I think your choice is very obvious as to who you'll vote for. If you don't agree . . . then I could suggest another choice that you have.
> (Schneider 249)

The Iranian hostage crisis, during which more than fifty Americans had been held captive in Tehran since the previous November, played a major role in bringing down the Carter administration. All the president's efforts at securing the hostages' freedom had failed, so in April he called on the U.S. military to attempt a rescue. The mission turned out to be a disaster that ended when a rescue plane and helicopter collided, leaving eight Americans dead and freedom for the hostages nowhere in sight. It was not until the day of Reagan's inauguration that the hostages were released, an achievement for which he took credit in his first address as president.

Reagan was elected on a Republican platform that for the first time opposed the Equal Rights Amendment (ERA), after having endorsed it over the previous forty years. Among Reagan's most visible supporters was Phyllis Schlafly, who headed the Stop-ERA movement. On the heels of a Supreme Court decision in June that upheld limits on federal funding for abortion, the Republican platform also came out in favor of a constitutional amendment to ban the procedure and stipulated that any federal judge appointed by a Republican administration must be explicitly opposed to abortion. Reagan, aware that the country was divided on these issues, inserted a conciliatory paragraph regarding discrimination against women near the beginning of his acceptance speech at the Republican National Convention:

> I know we have had a quarrel or two, but only as to the method of attaining a goal. There was no argument about the goal. As president, I will establish a liaison with the fifty governors to encourage them to eliminate, wherever it exists, discrimination against women. I will monitor federal laws to ensure their implementation and to add statutes if needed.   (Malbin 116)

The Democrats' platform endorsed both the ERA and a woman's right to an abortion. They supported the use of federal funds to subsidize abortions for poor women, and they pledged to withhold party support from any candidate who opposed the ERA. They further agreed not to hold any national or regional party meetings in states that had not ratified the amendment, and advocated increased federal funds for child-care programs. Gay Vote '80, an organization of homosexual activists, also won significant victories in the Democratic platform, with six openly gay delegates to the convention serving on the platform committee.

Carter's loss to Reagan was accompanied by the substantial defeat of Democrats nationally, who lost control of the Senate for the first time in a generation as well as numerous seats in the House of Representatives. Although polls indicated that the ERA, abortion, and gay rights were fairly low on the list of factors that influenced voters, the trend toward increasing conservative values and the influence of the Religious Right was set.

All this suggests that it was not a particularly good year for women, at least offscreen. They were still doing most of the housework and childcare, and those who held jobs earned an average of 41 percent less than their male counterparts. Onscreen, however, certain films reflected the strides women had made in the previous decade. While the most popular films conventionally appealed to the fifteen- to twenty-five-year-old white male demographic (*Airplane!, The Blue Lagoon, Brubaker, Caddyshack, Cheech and Chong's Next Movie, The Empire Strikes Back,* and *The Blues Brothers*), and well-known directors released significant films that do not particularly stand out for their portrayal of independent women (Stanley Kubrick's *The Shining,* Woody Allen's *Stardust Memories,* Brian De Palma's *Dressed to Kill,* David Lynch's *Elephant Man,* Jonathan Demme's *Melvin and Howard,* and Martin Scorsese's award-winning *Raging Bull*), it was also a remarkable year for female roles, notably in the six films that are the focus of this essay: Michael Apted's *Coal Miner's Daughter,* James Bridges's *Urban Cowboy,* Sidney Lumet's *Just Tell Me What You Want,* Colin Higgins's *Nine to Five,* Louis Malle's *Atlantic City,* and Howard Zieff's *Private Benjamin.* In them we find the energy of women who refuse to be victims and who stand up for their rights.

Independence and Nurture in *Coal Miner's Daughter*

Jerry Rodnitzky has remarked that "no matter what kind of music they sang, the country female vocalists were often tough-minded and independent business women. Tammy Wynette, Loretta Lynn, and Dolly Parton were all strong role models who warmed feminist hearts" (76). Dolly Parton showed her true colors in *Nine to Five,* discussed below. In *Coal Miner's Daughter,* Loretta Lynn (Sissy Spacek) grows from a timid girl in a poor Kentucky coal mining family who at the age of thirteen marries a domineering man, soon becomes an overburdened teenage mother, and eventually ends up a strong, self-assured country music star. For this to happen, her husband, Doolittle "Mooney" Lynn (aka "Doo") (Tommy Lee Jones), must learn to nurture their children and Loretta must learn to stand up for herself. In the end, both Doo and Loretta discover that for their marriage to work, compromise is necessary. *Coal Miner's Daughter* is about how a man must change, a fact not lost on essayist Roger Rosenblatt, who wrote that he now looked forward to *Coal Miner's Son-in-Law* (72). However, the film is about a woman changing, too.

Thematically and structurally central to *Coal Miner's Daughter* are the concepts of moving too fast and needing to slow down. As the film begins, Doo is driving a red jeep too fast into the coal mining community in which Loretta lives with her family. Loretta is wearing a red coat, and the two reds standing in contrast to the dreariness of the mines make it obvious that Doo and Loretta are destined to be together. When Doo asks Loretta's father for her hand, her father agrees on two conditions: "Don't hit her" and "Don't take her far from home." Doo does both.

The moment Loretta commits to singing is the turning point in the film. It happens on a hill, away from people, in a conversation between her and Doo. She is at her father's grave (the couple has returned to Kentucky for his funeral), and Doo comes up in a noisy bulldozer. Loretta's words explicitly define the theme of the film, finding the meaning of home: "Mommy's moving away; Daddy's gone; I ain't gonna have no home." In a two-shot, Doo tries to comfort her: "You got *our* home." She rejects the solace and Doo walks out of the frame, leaving her alone. We hear the sound of his bulldozer starting up. In the next shot she joins him and what follows is a long take, a tracking shot that lasts a full minute, going over the terrain with the dozer, as Loretta finally commits: "I want to be a singer, Doo, I want it real bad." "We gotta move right now," he says. The rough movement of the camera mirrors the journey that will take them to the end of the film, first as Doo drives them from radio station to radio station, then as they tour with Patsy Cline, and finally in a luxurious bus belonging to Loretta herself. No journey to success is easy. In an emotional breakdown, when she can't sing in front of a large Nashville audience of her fans, she tells them that things are "moving too fast in my life; they always have." Doo had embodied this, with his fast red jeep and the intensity with which he pushed her career into moving "right now." "Little girl, you've got to run your own life," Patsy Cline tells her, but with success, it's been handlers, advisers, a bus for a home, not her "own life" at all. It's time to slow down. She lets Doo carry her off the stage and take her "home" to recover.

Visually, the balance the two find in their lives is represented by the prospective "home" on the new land Doo has bought. He takes Loretta in a jeep, again driving much too fast, to show her where he plans to build her a house with a bedroom in the front, looking out over the hills with a view reminiscent of the Kentucky of their youth. But Loretta refuses to be patronized: "You never asked me nothing about a new house!" Doo lets his childish male chauvinism come out: "I'm tired of this bullshit." When he suggests a divorce, she says, "I don't want a divorce; I just want a bedroom in the back of the house." Past and present are brought together as the two of them discover "our home," away from coal mines, away from fans, in the privacy of the wooded hills of Tennessee, but with roots reaching back to their coal-mining families in Kentucky. The concluding montage reminds us of what we already know, that Loretta Lynn went back to work onstage with the support of her husband. She sings, "I'm proud to be a coalminer's daughter." In the audience Doo, also proud, is smiling.

Urban Cowgirl: "Lookin' for Love"

Tammy Wynette's "Stand by Me" plays at a moment in *Urban Cowboy* when the romantic leads, Bud (John Travolta) and Sissy (Debra Winger), have separated and are dancing with different partners, yet gazing at each other with a longing to which neither will succumb. Based on an article by Aaron Latham entitled "The Urban Cowboy" from *Esquire* (12 September 1978), the film explores a mythology endemic to the southwest: that dressing up in cowboy regalia and riding a mechanical bull makes one a man. But when a woman enters the bullring, Latham notes, "The cowboys were no longer simply measured against the bull, they were measured against the cowgirls" (qtd. in Kael, *Taking* 30).

Urban Cowboy is supposed to be Bud's story, a classic romance Texas-style: he meets girl, loses girl, gets girl back, and in the process learns something about himself and life—a predictable story. Bud has left his family in rural Texas to work in a refinery near Houston and he meets Sissy at Gilley's roadhouse. A much more interesting character, she embodies the grit of the new woman. There are a number of connections between *Coal Miner's Daughter* and *Urban Cowboy,* released two months afterward. Country music figures prominently in both—there is a Dolly Parton look-alike contest in *Urban Cowboy*; a woman marries, in this case impulsively, is expected to cook and clean, gets slapped by the men with whom she is involved, fights for what she believes is right, almost gets divorced, and discovers something she can do well. When she meets Bud at Gilley's, Sissy is trying to hit a punching bag like a man. She bruises her knuckles and a pleased Bud says, "You're trying to do things a girl can't do," setting up the male/female rivalry that will structure the narrative. When Bud slaps her, she refuses to be victimized and tells him to "go to hell." Bud and Sissy end up in a puddle, and while soaking wet climb into his truck and suddenly decide to get married. Bud and Sissy have a traditional wedding with white gown and cake, and in a ritual reenactment of female submission she is blindfolded as they drive to their new trailer home where he carries her over the threshold.

UC-5174-36A

Urban Cowboy (James Bridges, Paramount), starring John Travolta, explores the mythology of cowboy manhood in contemporary America. Jerry Ohlinger's Movie Material Store.

But Sissy is not submissive. Bud gets mad at her because their home is a mess. She reminds him that she works, too, so that time to clean up and cook is as hard for her to find as for him. Soon she learns to ride the mechanical bull at Gilley's—better than Bud. As she gains confidence, he loses his, a see-saw of control that is visualized in the cross-cutting between Bud, literally falling from a tower at an oil refinery, and Sissy riding the bull at Gilley's. Several shots in this sequence have Bud hanging upside down in the position of a reverse crucifixion. Is he being sacrificed for his macho sins of power and control? The male voiceover is provocatively ambiguous: "Arch your back, hang on," words that could be spoken to either one of them at this point, either by Bob (Barry Corbin), Bud's uncle on the ground below, or by Wes (Scott Glenn), the man running the mechanical bull who will turn out to be Bud's rival for Sissy's affections. Physically and emotionally wounded, Bud is no longer the man he was. He becomes increasingly abusive toward Sissy, eventually kicking her out of their trailer after she rebukes him, "You ain't my daddy; you can't tell me what to do," to which he replies, "I'm the next best thing to your daddy, and you ain't never riding, never."

Another sequence of cross-cutting sets up the conclusion of the film. Bud and Sissy have now become involved with others, she with the villain, Wes, a criminal out on parole, and he with a wealthy Houston socialite, Pam (Madolyn Smith). After a night at Gilley's, the music shuts off suddenly, signaling an uneasy transition, and there is a straight cut to a fan in Wes's trailer. The obvious heat and amber/yellow tones of the film stock suggest Sissy is in a fallen world. In tangled sheets she lies next to Wes, but there is no communication; they do not touch. A cross-cut to Bud being taught to ride a mechanical bull at his Uncle Bob's provides a vivid contrast. This scene is edenic, bright, optimistic, and cheerful, Bob reconnecting with his bull-riding past and passing his knowledge on to his nephew. A revealing cut back to a close-up of Wes's sleeping head comes on Bob's instructive line to Bud: "The treachery of the bull depends on the treachery of the man operating the controls." Remorseful, Sissy leaves Wes's trailer and goes to Bud's. The editing shows her cleaning up, something she has constantly declined to do, interspersed with Bud successfully learning to ride the mechanical bull. Now the imagery is reversed: he rides the bull triumphantly while she washes garbage down the drain. We see her reflected in a mirror, suggesting the duplicity she regrets, and we hear her voiceover, speaking the note she writes to Bud that begins "Sorry about last night," and ends, "I miss you."

Wes turns out to be a macho pig: "You can't expect a man like me to be faithful to any woman." And Bud's new girlfriend realizes he is only using her to make Sissy jealous. In its conclusion this film is less successful than *Coal Miner's Daughter*. Sissy's fiercely independent drive to ride the mechanical bull simply drops out of the plot. We are left knowing that Bud has won the bull-riding contest, has thwarted Wes's attempted robbery of Gilley's, and has his girl back. He is finally able to say, "I love you, Sissy," to which she replies, "I love you, too." In a muffled line as the two embrace, with the camera on her face, we hear Bud mumble, "You can ride the damn bull . . ." but she quickly cuts him off: "I don't want to ride it." Her spunky independence, her desire to do something well, even if it is just being an "urban cowgirl," melts in a concluding embrace, as the soundtrack plays the hit song "Lookin' for Love." In a classic Hollywood romance, the triumph of love is enough. But it covers up some hard-edged social issues—the poverty and unemployment in rural Texas, the plastic sterility of lives in a trailer camp, and the reality of an environment where men may drink too much and compensate for a sense of inadequacy with violence against women—and also some unanswered questions: Is love all that matters? What *does* Sissy want?

"He Didn't Change, I Did": Just Tell Me What You Want as Screwball Comedy

In the opening voiceover of *Just Tell Me What You Want*, written by Jay Presson Allen from her novel of the same name and directed by Sidney Lumet, Bones Burton (Ali MacGraw) reverses the gender roles of *Urban Cowboy*: "He didn't change, I did." Allen claims that her interest in writing for the movies (she started with Alfred Hitchcock's *Marnie*) had to do only with making money and that she was not particularly interested in making political statements about the representation of women. "I don't concern myself with it. It is not an issue that I think about" (qtd. in Francke 95). But as Nick Roddick points out, her films are very much about "women whose control of their lives is not as total as they would have others believe" (qtd. in Francke 95). Following the model of screwball comedies of the thirties and forties, with their delightfully flawed heroes and heroines, *Just Tell Me What You Want* applies to both its male and female leads the idea that people are not in as much control as they like to believe. The film follows the screwball formula almost exactly, with a man and woman battling as intellectual equals, overcoming "wrong" relationships, and discovering that they really belong together. Stanley Cavell calls screwball films comedies of remarriage, and Wes Gehring's five key points about how they differ from romantic comedies all fit *Just Tell Me What You Want* precisely: screwball comedy emphasizes "funny" rather than love—it is not obviously reality-based;

screwball spoofs romance—"love comes across as hardly more significant than a board game"; screwball is filled with eccentric characters, starting with a zany heroine; the heroine frequently finds herself in a triangle with the sought-after male and his often life-smothering fiancée, or vice versa; as it concludes, screwball comedy accelerates while romantic comedy slows down (1–4). The casting of Myrna Loy (aka Nora Charles of *The Thin Man* series) as Stella Liberti, the shrewd administrative assistant to Max Herschel (Alan King), further emphasizes *Just Tell Me*'s screwball connection.

The film begins as Max walks into Bergdorf Goodman's and Bones Burton walks out, establishing that the two are going in opposing directions. She turns around and goes back inside, and after she has smacked Max twice in the head with her purse the frame freezes and we hear her voiceover in ironic counterpoint to a series of visuals that introduce the characters in separate frames. "I want to tell you how I got married. Actually, it is a very romantic story," although the image of the department store assault is anything but romantic. The fairy tale parody continues as she introduces "a fierce and powerful tyrant" (freeze on Max pointing); "me, the damsel in distress" (freeze on Bones in a shower cap); and "a brave young knight" (freeze on the ineffectual young writer Bones will initially marry, Steven Routledge [Peter Weller]). As these ironic shots indicate (and in the true screwball tradition), the story is anything but "romantic." Bones is anything but a "damsel in distress." Max, the fierce and powerful tyrant, is a needy neurotic who describes himself beneath his sexist facade as "a dead Jew." He's an entrepreneur who treats people badly, admires the breasts of his new secretary by complimenting her sweater ("Nice fit"), and avoids serious romantic complications with his long-time mistress, Bones, by refusing to divorce his crazy wife. And the "brave young knight," the heroine's inappropriate partner, is a mediocre playwright with ambitions to make it big in Hollywood who is easily duped by the wilier Max.

From the start, Bones is ambitious. She is tired of being a successful television producer, and she wants to make movies. "It's a locker room out there," instructs Max, insinuating that if you are too old to get laid (over twenty), you don't have a chance. Bones knows her own capabilities, however: "You won't give me the job because you're afraid if I pulled it off I wouldn't need you anymore. That's all it is."

In contrast to the staccato of the opening that presents everyone separately, the closing unites Bones and Max visually, in spite of their sparring dialogue. Lumet likes to use long takes for moments of emotional significance, and this is a very long take indeed. It begins with Bones in Max's hospital room against his wishes. They are both now alone in life. His wife has choked to death on beef Wellington, and Bones's marriage to Steven is obviously washed up. In a dark fur coat against the stark whiteness of the room, the sheets, and Max's pajamas, she is the strongest figure in the frame, and when she sits on the bed, she dominates his prone position. To further her power, she takes the controls of the bed and gradually raises its head up, moving Max's face closer and closer to hers until they almost touch, but with hers slightly higher. Their dialogue has them in intense negotiation, about movies, about money, and about love. When he says he loved his wife and that a young girl sitting out in the waiting room loves him, she replies in a strong, matter-of-fact way, "I love you, too." She is pregnant, and she is going to keep the baby.

"Just tell me what you want," says Max, echoing a refrain he has spoken in each act of the film. Bones replies, "I want you to say you love me." Even though he never says it, the camera makes the feelings obvious; for now, after slow passage, it has crept in to a point where it almost squeezes their two faces together in profile. His last line, spoken to the telephone, is an instruction not to put any calls through: "I'm negotiating." Then, four minutes and twenty-five seconds after this long, subtle shot began, it freezes. With the film's theme music in the background, Bones concludes her narration, "Well, that's how I got married. That's it. Didn't I tell you it was a very romantic story?"

In the earlier screwballs what most of the heroines really wanted was marriage to the right partner. Although like a good screwball heroine Bones says that the story is going to be about how she got married, the story is really about how she ended up with what she wanted: not only the right partner and not to have an abortion, but her own independent movie studio. Old-fashioned romance has nothing to do with the "merger" of these two. The "awful truth" is that Bones and Max are meant for each other, they are like each other, and, as in any classic screwball, the couple that was initially together must overcome all obstacles, including an aborted marriage, to reunite at the end.

Change in the Office: *Nine to Five*

Nine to Five, from a story by Patricia Resnick, takes female resistance to male supremacy to a more farcical extreme than *Just Tell Me What You Want*. All three lead women in this film had already gained fame independently offscreen, as artists, activists, or singers. Lily Tomlin had achieved success on the television comedy series "Laugh-In." She and her partner Jane Wagner have long been outspoken advocates for women's

Judy (Jane Fonda) and Violet (Lily Tomlin), feminist heroes of the satirical *Nine to Five* (Colin Higgins, Twentieth Century Fox). Digital frame enlargement.

rights. Jane Fonda became well known in the 1960s as a protestor against the Vietnam War, earning the nickname "Hanoi Jane." With then-husband Tom Hayden, she championed a number of anti-establishment causes, including the Black Panthers, the American Indian Movement, and environmentalism. Dolly Parton made her first screen appearance in the film, but she was well established as a country music star and media celebrity on TV specials and talk shows.

Nine to Five was produced by IPC, a company Fonda formed with Bruce Gilbert. Her portrayal of the innocent, mousy, divorced Judy, who finally leaves her first job to marry the Xerox salesman, is largely against type. But when, in reaction to the sexism, racism, and exploitation of the employees at Consolidated Companies, Inc., she asserts, "We must do something," we hear the Jane Fonda we recognize. Parton, an astute businesswoman like Fonda, seems to play against expectation in this film as well, as a busty, ditzy blonde, although when she finds out that everyone in the office thinks she is the mistress of the boss, Frank Hart (Dabney Coleman), she reveals to the sexist pig that her baby-doll sexy innocence is largely a facade:

> So that's why everyone around here treats me like some dime-store floozy. They all think I'm screwing the boss. . . . I've put up with all of your pinching, poking, and staring and chasing me around the desk because I need this job. But this is the last straw. I've got a gun out there in my purse. Up until now I've been forgiving and forgetting because of the way I was brought up,

but I'll tell you one thing: If you say another word about me or make another indecent proposal, I'm gonna get that gun of mine and I'm gonna change you from a rooster to a hen with one shot.

With the Equal Rights Amendment such a hot issue, *Nine to Five* was timely. It was released in December, after Reagan's election, and it advocated many of the employment reforms that had been campaign topics, such as flex time and job sharing programs, day care in the workplace, and equal opportunity and pay not only for women but for other minorities as well, including the handicapped. In her review of the film, Pauline Kael called it "a slick-package movie as a vehicle for progressive ideas" and asked, in response to the Dolly Parton speech above, "Didn't any of the feminists involved in this project register that a castrated rooster is a capon, not a hen, and that this joke represents the most insulting and sexist view of women?" (*Taking* 163–64). Not everyone found the comedy of *Nine to Five* degrading, although even the more generous Vincent Canby in his review in the *New York Times* (19 December) suggests the effective satire of the beginning slips into excessive farce; for Canby the film ends "by waving the flag of feminism as earnestly as Russian farmers used to wave the hammer-and-sickle at the end of movies about collective farming" (C20).

But with the nation suffering from an energy crisis, inflation, recession, job shortages, racial tensions (especially in the inner cities), and a loss of prestige abroad, comedy in any form was a welcome relief and an effective way of dealing with some of the current controversial issues involving women in the workplace. *Nine to Five* deliberately indulges in all the workplace clichés of male chauvinism. The prim and proper Judy has to go to work for the first time in her life when her philandering husband leaves her for his secretary. Smart, efficient Violet (Tomlin), a widowed mother of four who can fix a garage door opener and smokes pot with one of her sons, has been with the company for many years but is always passed over for promotion by men she helped to train. Sexy, safely married Doralee (Parton) puts up with her boss's advances only because she needs the job.

Frank Hart talks in clichés about the value of teamwork in business but resists any hint of unionization. He's sorry "the girls" never got to play football or baseball because playing a sport is the best place to learn about teamwork. Violet fetches his coffee, although it is not her place as office manager to do so, but she wants to be promoted. When Frank gives the job to Bob, a man on whom she has five years' seniority, she blows up. Frank's defense is familiar: "Spare me the women's lib crap." Bob has a college degree, a family to support, and the company needs a man in the position because clients do not like to deal with women. Violet is blunt, echoing the civil rights struggles of the 1960s: "You are intimidated by any woman who will not sit in the back of the bus."

The centerpiece of the film is the fantasy sequence. Violet, Doralee, and Judy meet in a bar to talk over what to do about the office. They recognize that "it's the same all over. We live in a pink collar ghetto." Later at Doralee's house, they relax, laugh, and smoke marijuana. Carolyn Heilbrun has written that women laugh together only in freedom, in the recognition of independence and female bonding (129). That is the situation here. Each of the women, now high on pot, indulges in a fantasy of how she would deal with Frank, a fantasy of vengeance that each will later fulfill as circumstances actually lead them to keep him in bondage for six weeks, literally chained in his own house and reduced to watching soap operas like the metaphoric woman in the kitchen. Women's aggressive laughter *at* someone or something is rare onscreen. Since this kind of laughter is connected with power, which the women do not have, it must unfortunately be played out in fantasy. The fantasies not only parody sexist behavior, they parody movie genres that traditionally stereotype women in subservient roles as sexual objects, femmes fatales, or blissful innocents. *Nine to Five* therefore addresses not only the role of women in American society and the workplace but also the role of women onscreen.

Judy's fantasy, shot mostly in sepia tones, seems to echo prison movies, crime movies, big game hunting movies, and film noir. Frank is hunted down by an unruly, angry mob, is shot at by Judy like a moving target in a shooting gallery, and ends up displayed as a trophy head mounted on his own office wall. The color is a little brighter in Doralee's western genre fantasy. The sepia is replaced by the yellowish tinge of an amber-colored filter. Yellow has been associated with Doralee throughout the film, so her western parody is awash in hues of gold and light brown. Rossini's finale from the *William Tell* overture tells us we are in the world of the Lone Ranger as we see Doralee ride Silver up to a hitching post outside the office window. In the office, she turns the tables on Frank's sexual harassment, referring to him as "boy" just as he talked about "his girls," and seducing him. With his resistance, the sequence becomes a rodeo parody, and ends with Frank tied on a spit, like the sexist pig he is.

Violet's fantasy takes on Disney, with its overly bright colors, especially red and blue. In the persona of Snow White, and accompanied by blue birds, Bambi, Thumper, and other Disney characters, she whistles while she works, but her work is poisoning Frank's coffee. Young, animated Disney women, with their perfect skin, flowing hair, and tight-waist dresses, represent an archetype of white innocent femininity. "Disney's trademarked innocence operates on a systematic sanitization of violence, sexuality, and political struggle concomitant with an erasure or repression of difference," write the editors of *From Mouse to Mermaid* (Bell et al. 7). Lynda Haas points out that even the typical mother in films such as *Snow White and the Seven Dwarfs* (1937), *Pinocchio* (1940), or *Cinderella* (1950) "is absent, generously good, powerfully evil, or a silent other. . . . In this way, mothers are either sentimentalized or disdained; in either case, their identity and their work are simultaneously erased, naturalized, and devalued" (Bell et al. 196). Violet turns Disney topsy-turvy, transforming Snow White into a serenely deliberate murderer whose evil deed is cheerfully condoned by the Disney characters who watch it. With the wicked boss now out of the way, bells chime, prisoners are freed, and there is jubilation in the land, as the fantasy ends with a send-up of magic kingdom films and religious epics.

Women's roles in comedies usually denigrate them and allow them to be laughed at as victims. Frances Gray describes the situation:

> Comedy positions the woman not simply as the object of the male gaze but of the male laugh—not just to-be-looked-at but to-be-laughed-at—doubly removed from creativity. Hence the relentless stereotyping of women into roles which permit them to be looked at, judged, laughed at as sexual objects: the dumb blonde, the wise-cracking tart, the naive virgin, the dragon who doesn't realize she is sexually past it. (9)

Nine to Five deliberately inverts these roles. Doralee is the dumb blonde who turns out not to be dumb. Violet is the wise-cracking tart whose wise-cracks are on the mark; we laugh at the object of her barbs, not at her. She even dresses primarily in red. Judy is the naive virgin, dressed in pale blue and pink, who grows into womanhood. And we can take Roz (Elizabeth Wilson), Frank's in-house snitch, as the older "dragon lady," whose motivation for telling on the women with whom she works would seem to be an attraction for her boss. It has traditionally been the role of comedy to challenge social and symbolic systems. The situation in the country as the year drew to a close may have seemed like the beginning of a funeral march for women's rights, but on screen *Nine to Five* reminded audiences of what women could achieve.

A Fantasy on the Boardwalk: *Atlantic City*

Pauline Kael wrote that *Atlantic City* is "a prankish wish-fulfillment fantasy about prosperity: what it does to cities, what it can do for people" (*Taking* 177). Set in the sleazy underworld of gambling and drugs in the New Jersey seaside resort where gambling was made legal in 1976—but which had not yet been glamorized by the likes of Donald Trump—the film deals with a man who must overcome social expectations of machismo and a woman who struggles to establish an independent life for herself. Unlike *Coal Miner's Daughter,* this is not the biography of a woman's rise to fame, but it is about a woman's survival. And unlike *Urban Cowboy,* it is not a romance, although Lou (Burt Lancaster) and Sally (Susan Sarandon) have a romantic fling and it does appear that Lou has found romance, or perhaps contentment, at the end with the gangster's widow, Grace (Kate Reid). Sarandon was not yet recognized as a political activist. But in this film she is not only strong, she is that rare woman onscreen who is not even "lookin' for love" and who remains independent of a male (or even a female) companion at the end as she heads off for Monte Carlo.

The changing face of Atlantic City is the dominant metaphor in this film, with its wrecking balls of destruction and its promise of new construction, its nostalgia for the past and its uncertainty about the future, and ultimately, the unpredictable hand of luck pulling many of the strings. Director Louis Malle peppers the film with sounds and images of the revitalization of Atlantic City, a correlative for the revitalization of the two main characters and markers of the discordant world in which they live. As the film opens, the husband whom Sally left in Canada and her pregnant sister roll into town on the back of a flatbed truck like migrant workers, passing a statue of an elephant so huge it almost fills the frame. At the elephant's feet is a much smaller sign saying "Welcome to Atlantic City," while superimposed over this fantastical image is the director's credit. It is clear that the film is going to take us on a journey between a grotesque facade of glamour and the drab reality underneath. The next shot, establishing the scene, is the imploding of a grand old Atlantic City hotel. As we enter the casino where Sally works, a line of chorus girls is gaily singing, "On the Boardwalk in Atlantic City, things will be peaches and cream." But things will be anything but "peaches and cream." A short while later, high up on the tangled beams of what seems to be a construction crane looking out over the boardwalk toward the ocean, Sally's husband is killed by the drug dealers he cheated out of their cocaine. In the scenes that follow, Malle further dramatizes the contrast between the revival of this resort town and the darkness of its sordid drug scene and petty crime, a repressive underbelly that has trapped Lou and Sally. Lou feels he has failed as a man. Instead of "protecting" his friend Grace when her gangster husband was killed, he ran away, a coward unable to act. Once a gofer for the mob, he now supports himself in a petty numbers racket. Sally works behind the oyster bar in a casino but dreams of being a croupier in Monte Carlo.

Asked to identify her husband's body, Sally is accompanied by the police to the Atlantic City Medical Center's Frank Sinatra Wing, where singer Robert Goulet is celebrating a large donation by the casino. As she makes her way to the morgue and as an official of the hospital accepts a check, the voiceover is ironic: "I have a vision of the future of this glorious island of Atlantic City, shining like a beacon whose light was nearly extinguished. If it wasn't for the casinos, we'd have been dead a long time ago." The juxtaposition between Sally's business at the morgue and the celebration going on at the same time becomes increasingly absurd. We hear applause for Goulet as she looks at her husband's corpse, then Goulet sings the Paul Anka song, "Lady Luck was on our flight . . . And now this welcome sight, glad to see you born again, Atlantic City, my old friend." As he sings, Goulet mingles with a small crowd of dancing chorus girls, patients, doctors, nurses, and attendants in a grotesque and incongruous scene.

Lou finally does succeed in "protecting" a woman. He shoots the men who are after the drugs the dead husband stole. Later, in a motel room outside of Atlantic City, he triumphantly asks Sally, "Did anyone ever take care of you like I did? Do you feel safe?" Sally's triumph is to walk out on him— they are both aware she is going—with most of the drug money. They flip to see who will leave to get pizza. Lou's last line to her: "You win." He watches her from the motel window, a reversal of the usual female role of looking out a window at the world in which she is not a full participant. But Sally, young, ambitious, and now with the money to follow her dream, drives a stolen car down a New Jersey highway on the way to deal her way through Europe—maybe. Both main characters seem to have overcome the obstacles preventing them from getting on in life: Lou has proved his manhood and Sally has money. It's a temporary illusion, of course, like the movie itself.

Sally stands out among the women in the six films discussed in this essay as the only one who has nothing to do with marriage or children onscreen. All three women in *Nine to Five* are or were married, Loretta Lynn and *Urban Cowboy*'s Sissy are reconciled with their husbands at the end, and the subject of marriage and the role it plays in a woman's life are an important part of *Just Tell Me What You Want*, as they are in *Private Benjamin*. *Atlantic City* is unique in giving us a woman who does not need a man. Sally obviously married for convenience; the now murdered husband was a way of getting out of Saskatchewan. Her sister is going to have a baby by him. However, neither husband nor baby matters to her. Her self-determined drive may be a fantasy, but unlike the revenge fantasies of *Nine to Five*, Sally's dream, although connected with a drug deal, is not the result of smoking pot and is not farcical. We don't laugh at Susan Sarandon's character. We admire her tough determination to strike out on her own, alone in a stolen car. The only other film discussed here that ends similarly is *Private Benjamin*.

Private Benjamin: "Don't Call Me 'Stupid'"

Like Dolly Parton, Goldie Hawn is often a dumb blonde in her films, but like Parton, Loretta Lynn, and Jane Fonda, she is a shrewd businesswoman behind the scenes. The new woman in film was gaining power offscreen in a production capacity, as well as onscreen. Hawn was executive producer of *Private Benjamin,* a film that encompasses many of the ideas explored so far in this essay. It begins with a wedding and ends with an un-wedding; the journey in between is one of self-discovery.

In this comedy the men, like Frank in *Nine to Five* and Max in *Just Tell Me What You Want,* are insensitive and chauvinistic, indifferently ordering women around. They do not change. Here, on the night of her second marriage, and before he dies of a heart attack while trying to make love to her on a bathroom floor, Judy Benjamin's new husband, Yale (Albert Brooks),

Goldie Hawn as *Private Benjamin* (Howard Zieff, Warner Bros.), who seeks freedom and self-determination. Digital frame enlargement.

condescendingly requests, "Peanut, get me a Perrier with a twist." Also on the wedding night, Judy's father (Sam Wanamaker), who chooses to watch the recap of a baseball game rather than join the wedding party, similarly expects to be waited on: "Ju, get me a cigarette," and "Get me a match, doll." And Judy's potential third husband, Henri Alan Tremont (Armand Assante), suggests that what he likes about her is that she does not make any sense. He orders her around to such an extent that when he yells, "Sit," Judy sits, only to discover he was directing his order not at her but at his dog.

Brought up as an affluent Jewish girl in a Philadelphia suburb, Judy tells us that all she ever wanted in life was "a big house, nice clothes, two closets, a live-in maid, and a professional man for a husband"—an old-fashioned dream. But Judy grows from a wide-eyed, materialistic victim of patriarchal pressure (get married, be "protected") to a more socially aware, liberated woman. After Yale's funeral, she retreats to a room at the Liberty Bell Motel for eight days, alone for the first time in her life. Desperately adrift, she asks a radio talk show host if he has seen Paul Mazursky's *An Unmarried Woman* (1978). In contrast to Jill Clayburgh's character in that film, however, Judy whines, "If I'm not going to be married, I don't know what I'll do." When she is recruited into the army and finds out it is not the army she innocently had been led to expect, the one with "condos and private rooms," her inability to function effectively leads to her whole platoon being punished. But in the army, and especially in bonding with her fellow female soldiers, she comes a long way in understanding herself as a person, independent of the expectations of her upper-class family. In a scene where Judy is offered the opportunity to leave the army after she has discovered it does not boast the country-club life she anticipated, she sits meekly in her messy green fatigues and combat helmet between three standing figures, her parents and her commanding officer and military nemesis, Captain Doreen Lewis (Eileen Brennan), who hands her the release papers to sign. This time it is her mother who babies her like a puppy rather than treating her as a woman. She pats her on her helmet while talking to her as she would the family pet: "Here darling, here you are. Here, take it." Judy has accepted the demeaning comments from the men in her life, but it is her mother's condescension that seems to motivate her to stand up for herself, which she literally does as she rejects the papers: "I think I'll stay." From this point on, Judy becomes successful in boot camp and her integration into the female community of the army transforms her into a new woman.

Judy can be compared to the Judy played by Jane Fonda in *Nine to Five*. Both undergo a similar transformation, from innocent and inexperienced women who never wanted anything more out of life than marriage to women who bond with other women. Through this, they find independence, although in *Nine to Five* Judy goes back to marriage at the end. Judy Benjamin eventually bonds with the women in her platoon during a war game exercise, including an African American who had earlier found her insensitive. At night, around a campfire, they laugh and share stories, just as the women in *Nine to Five* smoked pot and shared revenge fantasies. Carolyn Heilbrun's above-mentioned observation about women laughing together is well illustrated in this film as the whole platoon dances in the barracks and sings, "We Are Family." Even the sympathetic African American male drill sergeant, L. C. Ross (Hal Williams), joins in.

Like her namesake in *Nine to Five,* Judy Benjamin is again sucked into the patriarchal expectation of husband and children. She falls in love with Henri, a French gynecologist with whom she reunites on a new assignment in Paris. When it is discovered he was once a communist, and she is told she must relinquish either him or her successful career in the army—and a promotion—she chooses him. The world has moved beyond the postwar Red scare of the 1950s, but not at the Supreme Headquarters Allied Powers Europe (SHAPE) where she works.

The decision is dramatic. The narrative has come full circle at this point and, as at the film's beginning, we see Judy worrying about the color of fabrics and other materialistic details. She makes Henri's hair appointments and takes his dog to the vet and his car to the shop. But her acceptance of a servile existence, of negating her life for his, is not automatic this time. The fact that her activity for one day, as she tells Henri, consisted of doing nothing more than rearranging her closet for three hours pushes her toward the realization of how meaningless her existence has become. Then, when she discovers that her fiancé has been carrying on with their maid and that he is still involved with his previous lover, Claire, she begins to have serious doubts about their impending marriage. At their wedding in Henri's chateau, while she stands at the altar with him, listening to their marriage vows in French, a language she does not understand very well, she looks at her prospective third husband but sees Yale's face superimposed over Henri's, reprising the marriage scene with which the film began. With the French vows continuing in the background, she then sees her father's face upbraiding her, and in a final mental picture she is reminded of Henri demanding a prenuptial agreement. Three images of three men who have regarded her as a possession rather than a person override the automatic "I do." Instead, she says to Henri, simply and politely, "I know this is a very awkward time to do this, but I want to break up."

As he tries to stop her from backing out of their marriage, his facile words are unconvincing. She tells him he's "a jerk," and walks from his side at the altar to the door at the back of the room. The last straw is when he makes clear how he really feels by yelling after her retreating figure, "For once in your life, don't be stupid." At this, she goes back and, in front of all their wedding guests, socks him with the full power of her army training. Finally, she rejects demeaning epithets with a simple line: "Don't call me *'stupid.'*" Now ready to be an "unmarried woman," she departs. In *Atlantic City* we knew where Sally was heading at the end and we also suspected she would probably never get there. In *Private Benjamin,* Judy's life and its direction are undetermined. Outside of Henri's chateau, she defiantly turns to face the camera and in a medium shot tosses her wedding veil out of the frame, into the wind. It drifts off, a white gauze floating in the air, a visual image of liberation. Judy smiles, turns, and heads down a road alone, accompanied by a faint roll of military drums and the film's theme song. It is an uplifting ending, both literally and figuratively, a comic assertion of not only enduring but also of triumphing over the old order represented by the staid, antique chateau of Henri's ancestors from which she flees.

Pauline Kael hated *Private Benjamin:*

> The script of this women's liberation service comedy goes from one formula to the next. It's a reworking of generations of male service comedies, with a reverse Cinderella theme: the madcap princess learns to respect the under-privileged members of her ethnically balanced group of recruits and becomes a strong, independent human being. . . . This movie, with its message—unmarried womanhood is the only kind of womanhood—is cuckoo.
>
> (*Taking* 93–95)

Private Benjamin may be "cuckoo," but the idea of "a reverse Cinderella" is what the new woman in the films of the year is all about. She refuses to be a servant, to be a victim, or to be patronized. She may want "to have it all," like Bones in *Just Tell Me What You Want* and Sally in *Atlantic City,* or she may be willing to compromise while maintaining her hard-won independence, like Loretta Lynn in *Coal Miner's Daughter* or Sissy in *Urban Cowboy*. Winning a prince is not her goal. The ideas of the ERA are more important, as exemplified by *Nine to Five*. In another important film of the year, Robert Redford's *Ordinary People,* the emotionally frozen Beth Jarrett (Mary Tyler Moore) leaves the man who was once her prince, but her departure is a retreat from life. Judy Benjamin, on the other hand, exuberantly rejects her prince and sets out alone, like Sally leaving Atlantic City, on the road to a new life.

In *The Second Stage,* Betty Friedan explored some of the questions with which she believed the second wave of feminism should be concerned, and asked: "How do we transcend the polarization between women and women and between women and men, to achieve the new human wholeness that is the promise of feminism, and get on with the concrete, practical, everyday problems of living, working and loving as equal persons?" (41). These films, coming at the end of feminism's first wave, do not necessarily answer the question, but with their energetic and determined heroines and their occasionally sensitive men they set us on the road with Judy Benjamin toward a "new human wholeness."

1981

Movies and Looking Back to the Future

DIANE NEGRA

In a year that witnessed serious assassination attempts on both the U.S. president and the pope, the successful assassination of Egyptian president Anwar Sadat, the birth of the first American test tube baby, and the unanimous confirmation of Sandra Day O'Connor as the first female U.S. Supreme Court justice, discourses of possibility and constraint, progress and recidivism, seemed to characterize American life in particularly marked ways. It is especially interesting therefore to ponder the frequency with which Hollywood films in this year raided the archive of classical Hollywood genres, tropes, and archetypes, recirculating (and occasionally refreshing) the repertoire of ideas and images that had dominated American cinema in its robust mid-century commercial years.[1] It was a notable year in popular film for both franchise formation and continuation. On the one hand, American cinema was showing an emerging propensity for remaking and sequelization—some of the biggest hits of the year included *Superman II*, the James Bond film *For Your Eyes Only*, *Tarzan, the Ape Man*, and *Halloween 2*. The year saw a large number of classical heroes, heroines, villains, and monsters revived, including not only those in the above films but also Cinderella, King Arthur, and assorted werewolves. Yet equally important is the fact that a number of films (including *Raiders of the Lost Ark*, *Body Heat*, *On Golden Pond*, *Mommie Dearest*, and *Under the Rainbow*) referenced the studio period through potent but diffuse aspects of genre and stardom. Popular cinema appeared itself to be highly nostalgic, with many of its fictions reaching back to Classical Hollywood.[2] A survey of films released in a particular year of the decade may provide an opportunity to alternately historicize a period we think we know so well.

In December *New York Times* film critic Vincent Canby bemoaned, "For much of this year we've sat through megamovies based on minicomic strips, through failed comedies at which only the charitable could laugh, and through hideous horror movies about psychopaths. . . . It has sometimes seemed that filmmakers either had lost touch with the nervous, unpredictable, frequently unfair world the rest of us inhabit or had simply accepted it at sleazy face value, without question or curiosity." American films were clearly preoccupied with classical Hollywood, though the relationship sustained with Old Hollywood forms was both complex and mutable. This preoccupation was also heavily gendered, working most frequently to excavate heroic and empowered images of masculinity and to discredit images of active femininity. Already Hollywood was exhibiting a tendency to disingenuously move audiences "back to the future."

This shift might easily be located within a broader cultural turn, bearing in mind that in Ronald Reagan's first term, national life in America itself was broadly turning back toward a classical set of images and archetypes to "explain" American character, concerns, and dilemmas on conservative terms. As Michael Rogin skillfully analyzes, Reaganite storytelling was devoted to certain broad themes presented as inherently and classically "American," yet built into many of these themes was a broadly countersubversive mindset, a stigmatization of dependency, a paranoid fear of contamination, and a psychologically insulated position in relation to violence in all its forms. Popular films exhibit an ongoing preoccupation with the morality of violence, regularly requiring that male protagonists rededicate themselves to violence under conditions when it is justified for civic defense (this theme runs through films as disparate as *Superman II* and *Nighthawks*).[3] In this sense and in others, the fictional content of many Hollywood films harmonized with the emergent political framework, as seen in a selective sampling of the year's biggest box office hits.

American films displayed certain clear ideological tendencies, among them the propensity to recast the terms of couplehood, familialism, and neighborliness. Ironically, this recasting frequently took place in self-consciously revived classical genres or through overt remakes of earlier films. At a time when many of the concepts of self and society that had shaped the civil rights, feminist, and student movements of preceding decades were being pushed underground, cinema often paired conservative and progressive ideological impulses together, and the result could produce a high degree of textual irresolution in regard to the negotiation of gender.

The New Femme Fatale: *Body Heat*

Instructive in this regard is *Body Heat,* Lawrence Kasdan's languid reformulation of the classical film noir, a film whose video jacket advertises a "liberated but illicit relationship." *Body Heat* initially appears

Body Heat (Lawrence Kasdan, The Ladd Co.) revives the classic noir character of the femme fatale, played here by Kathleen Turner. Jerry Ohlinger's Movie Material Store.

to corroborate conservative definitions of erotic intimacy showcasing the performance of male domination as key to female arousal; though Matty Walker (Kathleen Turner) invites Ned Racine (William Hurt) to her home, she flouts his sexual expectations until he takes the dramatic precipitating action of breaking a door with a chair. The passionate couple then bluntly articulate the language of female erotic submission as he tells her, "You're not so tough after all, are you?" and she replies, "No, I'm weak." However, the film handles these incidents with a knowingness that suggests Matty's submissive style is to be mistrusted. And questions of gender and agency come to be significantly complicated as we learn that Matty has elaborately contrived a plan to kill her husband, and has targeted Ned as the kind of man who will best assist her in carrying out her intentions. Although Ned endeavors to play the traditionally gendered role, undertaking the moral governance of their affairs as a couple—he speaks about Matty's husband, Edmund, as not deserving what they're going to do to him and says, as Matty plots to revise her husband's will, "We're not gonna get greedy"—his effort is a failed one. She already has her plans well in motion.

Body Heat expands upon its predecessor texts in several respects, significantly revising the isolation that marked the protagonist couple of earlier film noirs by enlarging (if not deepening) commentary about gender. Particularly troubling is the masquerade being carried out by the femme fatale who has appropriated a high school classmate's identity; the film flags Matty's friendship with Mary Ann as troubling when Ned confuses their identities and is then sexually embarrassed by having propositioned someone he doesn't know. In a further flourish, Matty kisses Mary Ann on the lips, an act of physical intimacy that is encoded as worrisome. In a parallel development, the film underscores Ned's friendship with two male cronies and highlights both the group's robust homosociality and the worry his friends feel about his relationship with Matty, whom they characterize as "very bad news." The contrast is clear: female affiliations are sinister and male affiliations are associated with decency, integrity, and the quest for justice. Thus Body Heat significantly compounds the guilt of its femme fatale protagonist, introducing anxieties into the film that exceed those of classical film noir. At the conclusion, with Matty having attained her high school ambition "to be rich and live in an exotic land," Ned is in jail, placed in a fully feminized position where he can only speculate about the behavior and motives of his former lover. Furthermore, Ned's epiphany that "Matty was the kind of person who could do whatever was necessary" echoes Edmund's earlier self-assessment with regard to succeeding in the new economy. In that conversation, Edmund had casually denigrated his wife and her presumed incapacity to understand the realm of "male" business matters. Thus Ned's observation serves as a historically precise indictment of the film's "bad woman" and furthers our understanding that this film takes on new ideological contours in which female friendship and the fear of female access to new patterns of self-making in 1980s America become sources of deep concern.[4]

▪▪▪▪▪▪▪ Negotiating Gender in Quest Narratives and Family Dramas: *Raiders of the Lost Ark, On Golden Pond, Mommie Dearest*

While *Body Heat* concludes on a note of high (gendered) anxiety, its male protagonist incarcerated and symbolically feminized and its female protagonist enjoying the proceeds from her husband's murder, the two highest-earning films of the year were more emphatic in closing down possibilities for unruly femininity and imposing gender conservatism. They certainly do so in quite different ways, but both adamantly insist on a romanticized female subordination at closure. Michael Ryan and Douglas Kellner have perceptively categorized *Raiders of the Lost Ark* as a "combination of rememoration (harking back to a romanticized patriarchal past), narcissistic individualism, incipient authoritarian leadership and fun" (239).[5] The success and influence of the film should certainly not be understated; in pioneering one of the more durable film formulas of the decade—the internationalist adventure romance—the film also generated a prototype that remains salable up to the present, trading on the appeal of a stock plot in which a male hero, unruly heroine, foreign landscape, and various ethnic mediators would feature. The internationalist romance is heavily steeped in an awareness of "Old Hollywood," for it looks to screwball comedy, film noir, and early internationalist romances such as *Casablanca* (1942) for its generic source material. It may also (as in the case of *Raiders of the Lost Ark*) be set in the past. Indeed, in his rave review of the film for the *New York Times* Vincent Canby deemed it "an homage to old-time movie serials and back-lot cheapies," suggesting that the 1936 setting works specifically to attach *Raiders of the Lost Ark* to the films it remembers. The internationalist romance reiterates American hegemony abroad, but it also potently filters concerns about sex, race, and gender roles in a changing cultural milieu. The question of whether/how the unruly heroine can come to be reclassified as the reward for the hero's struggles looms large in these sorts of texts.

Raiders of the Lost Ark's bar owner Marion (Karen Allen) is first seen drinking a massive Nepalese man under the table, but a moment later she is symbolically dwarfed by the looming shadow of Indiana Jones (Harrison Ford). While the centrality of Marion's participation in the quest for the Ark of the Covenant allows the film to claim a "modern" status for its central couple, it is impossible to overlook the way the film also delights in Marion's subjugation. Plot machinations require that, when Indy discovers she is not dead but held captive by the Nazis, he nevertheless leave her bound and gagged (and furiously squawking). While Marion bears a grudge against Indy for a vaguely defined earlier romantic disappointment, we are prompted to read these concerns as trivial and "feminine" in contrast to the importance of Indy's efforts to secure the Ark of the Covenant. Marion is repeatedly shown that whatever Indy's interpersonal limitations, the other options for her are always worse (from Nazi torturers to poisonous asps). Indeed, the film's punitive treatment of its heroine reaches a point of remarkable culmination when Marion is symbolically gang raped by a group of moldering corpses and reacts with hysterical terror. Through its inclusion of such scenes the film strenuously argues that feisty women are obliged to accept the protection of rational, virile American adventurers.

There is a further use as well for the heroine of the internationalist romance, and it is one that speaks to these films' prioritization of the moral purity of American males. Very frequently in such films female agency is associated with dishonorable or illicit ways of doing things. While Marion demonstrates early in the film that she is prepared to participate in violence (indeed she saves Indy's life by handily shooting an attacker), her relationship to violence is later complicated and problematized. A key scene has her at the controls (though, it is emphasized, she is certainly not in control) of a Nazi plane that she uses to strafe a large group of Nazis while Indy engages in a fistfight at ground level with an enormous German soldier. Marion's actions are instrumental in tipping the balance at a moment when she and Indy are decidedly outnumbered. But in a film where honor is associated with fists and pistols, but not automatic weapons, the film uses her here to exploit on the one hand the stereotype of the technically incompetent woman but also to guarantee Indy's moral purity within the film's codes of violence.

The second highest grossing film of the year, *On Golden Pond*, offers some of the starkest support of my argument that high-profile films of the year typically engaged in some way with the representational/industrial features of the studio period. Its casting of two of the best-known icons of

On Golden Pond (Mark Rydell, Universal) portrays a generational rift between father (Henry Fonda) and daughter (Jane Fonda). Jerry Ohlinger's Movie Material Store.

classical Hollywood, Henry Fonda and Katharine Hepburn, as Norman and Ethel Thayer was a key selling point, and the film also drew upon audience attraction to the spectacle of seeing Fonda onscreen with daughter Jane, who was cast as the Thayers' daughter, Chelsea, visiting from Los Angeles. In one sense, *On Golden Pond* may be readily linked to a cluster of high-profile American dramas of the period which, as Estella Tincknell has pointed out, both "marked the reassertion of the domain of middle-class family life" but also registered anxiety about "feminist-driven changes in society" (138). However, the film also particularizes its account through reverberant casting that heightens its intertextual sense of realism.

In *On Golden Pond* cross-generational affiliations and tensions define the straightforward narrative of an elderly couple returning to their annual lakeside summer cottage in Maine, which serves as the pretext to examine questions of maturity and mortality within family life. Norman, an obstreperous octogenarian, has heart palpitations and occasional lapses of memory, but the film suggests that fundamentally his anxieties about his own mortality can be assuaged through a reconnection to parenting and a "boys together" experience on the lake with Chelsea's new adolescent stepson, Billy. When Ethel tells her daughter, "I should have rented him a thirteen-year-old boy years ago," Chelsea is stung that the father she feels has always criticized and diminished her has so quickly bonded with Billy. When she tells Ethel, "He probably made a better son than I did," Ethel mildly replies, "You're sounding very childish. You made a very nice daughter." But when Chelsea continues, "How come it's so easy? Why wasn't that old son of a bitch ever my friend?" Ethel slaps her across the face and says, "That old son of a bitch happens to be my husband."

I single out this segment because it strikes at the heart of the film's concerns with generation and a conservative restoration of family values. Chelsea's suggestion that her father might value a son more than a daughter has to be counteracted if the film is to stay within its thematic boundaries; the fact that her breach of ideological etiquette is sharply corrected and enforced by a star as venerable as Katharine Hepburn shows the film as implicitly critical of Chelsea.[6] The suggestion has been building that at age forty Chelsea is failing in her adulthood; divorced and about to remarry at the start of the film, she has no biological children of her own and calls her elderly mother "Mommy." Ethel's resonant criticism of her daughter's "childishness" suggests that it is time for Chelsea to undertake the kind of emotional care work that is endlessly modeled by Ethel in her relationship with her husband. (In a line heavily privileged in the film's trailer, Ethel tells Norman, "You're my knight in shining armor and don't you forget it.") In the succeeding scene Chelsea tells her father she wants them to have a healthier, more open relationship, and at her father's prompting she performs the same dive Norman has been coaching Billy to perfect over the course of his visit. Chelsea's symbolic enactment here of the role of obliging (rather than unruly) daughter is rewarded by her father's gift to her of his old college diving medal, and leads him to close the film meditating on a pair of loons at the lake (the film's symbolic device to convey the naturalness of Norman and Ethel's symbiotic relationship). In dialogue that closes the film, Norman observes the birds and says that "it's just the two of them now. Their baby's grown up and moved to Los Angeles or somewhere."

The suggestion that Chelsea is in some way infantile/dysfunctional and that her task in the film is to come into compliance with social expectations for adult femininity resonates within *On Golden Pond*'s meta-commentary on the notion of "Hollywood generations." Jane Fonda's status as both icon of international art cinema in those years when Hollywood struggled to find a family audience and politically radical critic of the Vietnam War marks her place in the film as a reminder of internationalism and systemic/political critique. The film's placement of her as a midlife woman who has lost her way but is crucially reconnecting with the values of a patriarchal culture takes on a larger significance when we acknowledge that Fonda's well-known persona as the embodiment of baby-boomer sexual and political radicalism would surely have informed audience perceptions of the film. In this way *On Golden Pond* is linked to a broader "reintegration" of Fonda taking place at this time, one that tamped down her earlier political activities in favor of ideologically normative definitions of femininity. As Susan McLeland has pointed out (246–49), this reintegration played through Fonda's later transformation to video workout queen and wife of conservative media magnate Ted Turner, but it is also dramatically enacted in a film that simultaneously stages a rapprochement for the fictional Thayer family and the real-life Fondas.

Furthermore, the film makes recourse to an operative tension between the body and the voice that McLeland observes to have been crucial to Fonda's stardom. While the pre-political Fonda incarnated the objectified hypersexualized female body, Fonda's antiwar activism (and notably her 1972 radio broadcasts addressed to U.S. bombers asking them to stop their raids on North Vietnam) saw her, in effect, become de-corporealized; in the public imagination she became a shrill political voice no longer safely grounded within a sexualized female body. In *On Golden Pond* Chelsea's speech through most of the film is associated with the wary antagonism she exhibits toward her father.[7] Yet increasingly the film suppresses her confrontational speech through displays of her lithe, fit body diving into the waters of Golden Pond. The culmination of this is the dive she makes for her father that reenacts her childhood and symbolizes her willingness to take up the role of daughter. Thus after a period of political speech acts that highlighted Fonda's status as a dangerously disembodied voice, *On Golden Pond* emphatically restores her body; the fact that it does so is in keeping with the broader political and ideological account the film gives of family life.

Another parent-child narrative and one of the most heavily hyped films of the year, *Mommie Dearest* also resuscitates an earlier era of Hollywood history, though it does so in a biopic format that, as Annette Brauerhoch has pointed out, strategically mixes elements of melodrama and horror to cultivate a severely judgmental view of Joan Crawford (Faye Dunaway, in a bravura performance).[8] Like *Body Heat,* the film adapts aspects of classical genres to cultivate a cautionary tale about a bad woman that is nonetheless marked by a sense of precise historical timeliness. Anxieties about women's access to material rewards and professional power color the film in significant ways. Yet for all that *Mommie Dearest* castigates the star as a failed mother, there is at work in the film a counter-discourse about Crawford's limited access to power in her industry. As Brauerhoch has noted, scenes that inspire sympathy for Crawford are always quickly succeeded by scenes that sever identification and emphasize the star's vicious tirades and punitive behavior toward her daughter, but there persists an ongoing concern about how this driven, talented woman is subject to the patriarchal power politics of Hollywood. ("I may as well have 'property of MGM' tattooed on my backside," reflects Crawford at one point.) Not only is she released from her contract in a humiliating scenario carefully orchestrated by studio chief Louis B. Mayer (Howard da Silva), the film also reflects on the limitations of her social power despite her fame. When Crawford wants to adopt a child, she is prevented from doing so because she is a divorced single woman, but her boyfriend, Greg Savitt (Steve Forrest), is effectively able to make the arrangement for her. In another scene in which Joan has pushed herself to her physical limits jogging to keep in shape, she eagerly runs to the phone for a phone call from Greg telling her that she has won the lead role in *Mildred Pierce* (1945). Her response of jubilant pleasure is strangely countermatched by Greg's dispassionate style, and he abruptly ends the call even as she rejoices.

At a later stage after the death of her husband (Harry Goz), the chairman of Pepsi-Co., Crawford spectacularly fends off the company's attempt to downgrade her position, profanely and bluntly telling the board of male corporate executives that they won't be able to disenfranchise her. Moments such as these may counterbalance the critiques elsewhere of Crawford's driven, perfectionistic approach and even partly validate Crawford's Machiavellian worldview (at one point she advises her young daughter that in life "you've got to know how to compete and win"). The film is finally unable to convincingly settle the question of why Crawford spends much of the film in a state of vibrating rage, and its stilted, excessive conclusion works too transparently in attempting to do so. At the reading of Crawford's will, her adopted children, Christopher (Xander Berkeley) and Christina (Diana Scarwid), learn that she has elected to leave them nothing, and while Christopher reflects that "as usual, she has the last word," Christina asks portentously, "Does she? Does she?" in intense close-up view. In his review of the film Vincent Canby referred to Crawford's rages as being "full of a kind of mysterious sorrow." What is mysterious to Canby may be decidedly less so to anyone with a structurally informed understanding of gender, ageism, and the social expectations of mothering. *Mommie Dearest* works so hard to try to craft a negative view of the star's bad mothering and callous narcissism that it makes itself available to feminist questions of how structural inequalities are so often symbolically "resolved" through discourses of female failure.

■■■■■■■■■ **Negotiating Gender in Military Comedy,
Horror, and Superhero Narratives:** *Stripes,
Tarzan the Ape Man, Superman II, Continental Divide*

While a cluster of Hollywood hits fretted about femininity in various states of empowerment, another strong representational trend highlighted masculinity and its capacity to metamorphose, mutate, and sustain hegemonic/heroic control. Many of these films were equally as nostalgic for classical film forms and actively drew from classical genres in their approach. Although its Cold War themes would seem to suggest an utterly contemporary focus, *Stripes* recycles material from the military comedies of the World War II era. The film focuses on an unlikely group of enlistees whose experiences in basic training provide grist for broad comedy. After a decade of intense antiwar movies, this film's comedy depoliticizes the experience of military life, working to set aside the traumatic cultural aftereffects of Vietnam and move to a more upbeat, empowered position in regard to American military capacity. In this respect and in others *Stripes* bears out Nicolaus Mills's contention that a key characteristic of American political, social, and economic life in this decade was an inversion of meanings in which loss is cathected into triumph. Indeed, the film's narrative trajectory neatly illustrates Mills's observation that "the counterculture of the 1980s found itself checked by the culture of triumph" (179). The film's buddy pair (played by Bill Murray and Harold Ramis) are at risk for subversion until they discover that even authoritarian structures like the military can accommodate (and will reward) male idiosyncrasy.

John Winger (Murray), a taxi driver, and Russell Ziskey (Ramis), a teacher of English as a Second Language, begin the film as put-upon working stiffs; neither of them does meaningful work, the film signals us to understand, because their clientele are termagant women and childlike, non-English speaking immigrants. Their choice to enlist in the army sets in motion the film's fantasy that within authoritarian, absolutist regimes of discipline, there is still room for idiosyncrasy and male play. John, Russell, and their platoon mate Ox (John Candy) crucially come into their own in sequences where they symbolically defeat figures of female authority and establish a fundamental mastery over women. John and Russell have sex with two female MPs; in John's case foreplay consists of his removal of her gunbelt, as he tells her, "You know what your problem is, baby? Your problem is that you're armed, you're heavily armed, and guys get in trouble with girls that are armed. They don't know how to come on." Ox, meanwhile, is goaded to enter a mud-wrestling contest with a group of women in a bar. At first overpowered and humiliated and resisting using violence against his female competitors, he becomes increasingly successful at tearing off the women's clothes, and his triumph is portrayed as resonant both for him and his mates.

When the hapless platoon is threatened with having to redo their basic training if they are not presentable for drill display at graduation, John provides a pep talk in which he simultaneously talks up and disparages his fellow soldiers, telling them, "We're Americans with a capital A! We're mutts. . . . But there's no animal that's more faithful, that's more loyal, more loveable than the mutt. Who saw *Old Yeller*?" Inspired by this exhortation to heroic attainment despite their "averageness," the group stays up all night training and generates an idiosyncratic yet precise performance at drill display the next day. As a result, they are commended as "go-getters" and sent to Italy to accompany a new urban assault vehicle that the Pentagon wants to unveil to the news media at a military base. The fact that this section of the film culminates with a patriotic display that is gleefully (but not meaningfully) subverted by the platoon's antics is entirely in keeping with the broader ideological project of the text. From this point forward, it will increasingly graft together patriotic rhetoric and discourses of personal idiosyncrasy.

Yet the film's serious Cold War rescue plot significantly fractures as we see Russell mastering the urban assault vehicle's technological features as if it were a videogame, and at a triumphant moment in which the pair regather their platoon we get a clear restaging of a *Star Wars* (1977) getaway scene. *Stripes* treats the prospect of the platoon members becoming serious, competent soldiers as in one sense preposterous but in another sense as strangely plausible in a Cold War geopolitical landscape that is itself fundamentally absurd. In its excessive concluding sequence, John and Russell are celebrated as heroes, and we get magazine cover snapshots of the status they have secured as a result of their exploits. Russell is featured on the cover of *Guts: The Magazine for Real Men* in an over-the-top combat pose, snarling and brandishing an automatic weapon while denigrating the Russians as "pussies." John, meanwhile, has become a celebrated figure of male iconoclasm, appearing on the cover of *Newsworld* with the tag line, "The New Army: Can America Survive?" To close the film, Ox competently leads John and Russell's platoon in drill formation. Yet just as the credits roll, they break into "Do Wah Diddy," a song previously associated with John's ability to innovate military discipline and combine authority with play. The film's comedic conclusion thus broadly distributes the experience of triumph converted from initial loss (here the economic and social circumstances that pushed these unlikely men toward military enlistment in the first place) central to the political psychology of 1980s American culture.

The transition made by *Stripes* into a patriotic discursive formation is also to be found in *Superman II,* which closes with Superman flying with an American flag to be restored to the White House. This film is also marked by a set of narrative inversions in which loss becomes triumph; *Superman II* depicts the momentum of a developing relationship between Superman (Christopher Reeve) and Lois Lane (Margot Kidder) abruptly checked and closure tied to the regaining of the status quo. In a narrative that is clearly working to invent the rules of blockbuster sequelization, the film opens with a recap montage of the entire first film, stages a de rigueur rescue of Lois at the Eiffel Tower, then moves to concentrate on the workplace romance of the couple.[9] When Clark and Lois pose as newlyweds at Niagara Falls to expose a honeymoon racket for a newspaper story, Lois puts two and two together after Superman performs a rescue and Clark Kent simultaneously disappears yet again. Testing her theory, she throws herself dramatically into the falls while Clark is nearby, but the film is adamant that Lois cannot compel Clark's unmasking: he merely uses his heat vision to sever a log that she is able to put to use as a flotation device. In a succeeding scene, however, Clark trips and to steady himself puts his hand into the "flames of love" fireplace in their honeymoon suite, but sustains no injury. Seeing this, Lois blurts out, "You *are* Superman," and speculates that Clark's fall wasn't a true accident but the reflection of an unconscious wish to give her incontestable proof of his real identity. That the couple's conversation (and Lois's ensuing confession of love for Superman) plays out with Clark standing on a raised platform in their suite and Lois on her hands and knees on the floor is one distinct sign of the film's limitations with respect to egalitarian romance.

As Superman is compelled to give up his powers if he is to love an "ordinary" woman, the country is quickly being taken over by a trio of archvillains, who first land in Houston but whose threat is quickly and distinctly nationalized as they remake Mount Rushmore in their own image and force the president (E. G. Marshall) to kneel before them on the floor of the Oval Office. When Lois and Clark attempt to behave as a normal couple, without his superpowers, Clark is thoroughly beaten up by a man who hits on Lois at a Metropolis diner, and Lois tells Clark, "I want the man I fell in love with." After the president calls upon Superman for aid and Lex Luthor (Gene Hackman) emerges to tell the archvillains that if they apprehend Lois Lane, Superman will inevitably respond, Superman is able to reverse the molecular process that deprived him of his powers and contend with the three villains in Metropolis. In interesting comparison to more recent superhero blockbusters, the film finds it necessary to equate Superman's efforts with the moral purity of the presidency. Having been humiliatingly subjected to the authority of archvillain General Zod (Terence Stamp), the president is cast as an emblematic figure whose political authority and fundamental decency need to be reasserted. The symbolic contamination of the presidency registers even more forcibly when Luthor has the opportunity to sit in the president's chair and mimics Richard Nixon's "V for Victory" gesture.

Having dispatched the villains, Superman understands that he cannot be so foolish as to relinquish his powers again. In its conclusion, *Superman II* thus sustains an interestingly mixed set of messages, one of which is the validation of benevolent leadership. Although General Zod marvels that Superman "actually cares for these Earth people," and at one point a group of angry citizens, believing Superman to be dead, attempts a populist assault on the villains, the film is keen to reinstate the inherent and transcendent difference between Superman and mere mortals. The requirement that he maintain his exceptional status makes it necessary for him to bestow an amnesia-inducing kiss upon Lois, one that ensures her ongoing ignorance of his true identity and abruptly casts their relationship back to what it has always been. When Lois sends Clark out to get her a hamburger, he is able to restage the scene of his earlier humiliation, beating up the man who had earlier beaten him. In concentrating in these ways on the restoration of a gendered knowledge hierarchy and on the character and personal sacrifice of a charismatic leader figure, *Superman II* chimes with the neoconservative turn of late-twentieth-century American culture and rewards belief in traditional social norms.

Another update of a classic Hollywood formula, *Tarzan, the Ape Man*, also tests the applicability of classical codes of heroism in regard to "modern" concepts of gender, privileging the notion that a female perspective is guiding the action in this iteration of the Tarzan story, starring Bo Derek and directed by her husband, John Derek. William J. Palmer calls Bo Derek "the ultimate eighties symbol of old-fashioned Hollywood sexploitation" (256–57), an apt tag and one which begins to explain the deep squeamishness some critics felt about a film that was brazenly and misleadingly publicized as a "feminist" Tarzan. While this task in itself could make for interesting creative possibilities, given the ways that (as John Kasson has shown) Tarzan emerged as a figure of masculine rejuvenation in an era of urbanization and rhetorical devotion to the social/economic power of the New Woman, the problem is that the film's "feminism" is tied to an

Tarzan, the Ape Man (John Derek, MGM), starring Bo Derek, looks at classic models of heroism in relation to modern gender relations.

exploitative sense of the heroine as sexual object and "little girl" questing to regain a relationship with her father, James Parker (played, with what might charitably be called gusto, by Richard Harris).

Tarzan, the Ape Man emphasizes innocent sexuality (re)discovered in a natural paradise and at the same time puts across the idea that it adopts an ostensibly feminist approach by highlighting Jane's awareness of patriarchal power and indictment of her father's failings. Early in the film Jane tells Holt (John Phillip Law), a member of her father's expedition, "It's a man's world. Women aren't allowed to be participants." When Holt replies, "It sounds like you don't like us very much," she says, "I don't dislike men. I envy them." *Tarzan, the Ape Man* means to carry through this idea when James Parker tells his daughter as he lies dying at the film's conclusion that "your life is going to be such a marvelous adventure. I envy you." However, the film makes only the most rote gestures at a progressive refocalization of the Tarzan narrative; indeed, the film's rhetoric of female self-discovery and strength quickly gives way to Jane's pleasure in being overmastered by a "white primitive." Given that the Tarzan role in the film is entirely non-speaking, Jane's interactions with him rather oddly consist of her speaking her thoughts/responses to her absent father and to Holt, a gesture that re-inforces her answerability to the patriarchal culture she critiqued at the outset. Thus, questions of gender and power circulate through the film in quite muddled ways and are instantiated even in its promotional imagery, which visualizes a key contradiction; under a *Tarzan, the Ape Man* title we see a nearly nude Jane swinging on a vine.

Ultimately, *Tarzan, the Ape Man* hijacks a rhetoric of female self-discovery as a thin pretext for a sexed-up Tarzan tale in which Jane makes her way through the jungle in a skintight, translucent ensemble, and when taken prisoner by a group of hostile natives, she pleads with her father (also cap-tured) to "be a good daddy, and tell me a story." Scarcely the "erotic adven-ture" the film promoted itself to be (and we should note that Hollywood films that use this tag line are almost without exception exploitative and sexist), *Tarzan, the Ape Man* concludes with an image of "innocent" sexual-ized play as Jane leaves her culture behind and romps with (a still silent) Tarzan in the jungle. In this clumsy iteration of Tarzan mythology, however, notions of female empowerment are called upon to rationalize what is largely a regressive fiction of female dependency and sexual titillation.[10] It is worth briefly observing that a very different sort of "back to nature" plot is centralized in the werewolf horror narrative, which was updated in two films, *An American Werewolf in London* and *The Howling*. United by the con-tributions of makeup effects wizard Rick Baker to both, the films are also alike in the ways they seek to update classical codes through humor and a foregrounding of male sexuality as part of the psychological matrix of horror. They are nonetheless rather different in their ideological predispositions, with *An American Werewolf in London* fundamentally situating the theme of primitive transformation in relation to an anxious conception of Europe and *The Howling* specifically linking its sense of the desire/terror of a humanity turned animalistic in relation to the social economy of Los Angeles (see Negra).

While the majority of contemporary Hollywood interpretations of classical formulas tends toward conservative ideological ends, it is not inevitable that they do so. Instructive in this regard is *Continental Divide,* a restorative romance with heavy national overtones. At a moment when a stagnant economy and (some) feminist destigmatization of the "working woman" were creating conditions for family, couple, and communal life "on the ground" that seemed to be largely unrepresentable in political and filmic discourse, this film shines attention on an unlikely couple both so passionately committed to their work that they struggle to imagine a life together. Where the films examined above customarily seek to recentralize the middle class couple, castigate the bad (single) mother, erotically trivialize the female coming-of-age narrative, and generally pull women into alignment with conservative norms of gender, *Continental Divide* sketches a portrait of Nell Porter (Blair Brown), a self-sufficient ornithologist whose work is encoded as nationally productive (she studies and staunchly defends bald eagles). As the film opens, John Belushi's muckraking Chicago newsman Ernie Souchak has scored another journalistic coup, and as he walks down the street he is congratulated by prostitutes and salt-of-the-earth kiosk proprietors alike. He is a throwback, which helps to mark the film's connection to romance in the newsroom pictures from the classical period admixed with a sense of political righteousness reminiscent of 1970s political dramas. In this way, *Continental Divide* may be classed within a set of films Matthew C. Ehrlich has designated as "journalism movies . . . a distinct genre that embodies myths colored by nostalgia and that addresses contradictions at the heart of both journalism and American culture" (2).

Continental Divide is strikingly and overtly less sanguine about the contemporary political scene than the vast majority of films I have discussed; it even undertakes some direct political/environmental critique. In a significant early scene preoccupied with the symbolics of ascent, Souchak goes to meet an informant, Kermit Hellinger (Bruce Jarchow), and his young son in an alley. (The scene ultimately establishes that Hellinger, a contracts clerk at City Hall who shares evidence of corruption with Souchak, could not have "fallen to his death" as is later claimed because he is deeply afraid of heights.) When Souchak offers Hellinger cash, he rejects it, saying, "Please, what for?" Souchak congratulates him on his moral fortitude, replying, "You're a good man, Mr. Hellinger, just don't run for president." The scene catalyzes an emergent theme in *Continental Divide* that references a deep sense of despair in relation to "good government" and a desire to reclaim a primordial sense of Americanness in nature. While *Continental Divide* trades upon a male-personified city and a female-personified nature in highly problematic ways, the film is quite open in its uncertainties about whether governmental/corporate corruption can ultimately be quashed. The question is neatly evaded, however, when Souchak is obliged to leave his urban territory to write a profile on Nell, with whom he falls in love. By resecuring Souchak to a wilderness heartland the film conveniently relegates him (or at least his emotional commitments and energies) elsewhere throughout much of the action, concentrating on a "fish out of water" story that marginalizes politics. In this sense the majority of *Continental Divide* deals with the perception of national/institutional failings by inviting us to contemplate the glories of nature. Where the film is unconventional, however, is in its unwillingness to have either member of the protagonist couple give up their work for the sake of romance. Although they are married in a general store in Wyoming, Souchak and Nell each return to their "natural habitat" in the conclusion, planning, it would appear, to undertake a (very) long distance commuter marriage.

Conclusion

In this selective sample of a single year of American filmmaking, I have examined the persistent engagement with classical Hollywood themes and tropes, most often as a means of shoring up conservative ideological positions over gender, the family, class, and cultural authority. While it is hardly surprising to find such tendencies in Hollywood output across a year in which, as one recent historical account claims, "Reaganism peaked" (Troy 77),[11] I have also indicated that some films rework Hollywood formulas without necessarily reproducing conservative ideological stances. This is the case, for instance, in *Continental Divide*, a film that centralizes a muckraking journalist but avoids the standard triumphalist closure in which having exposed corruption in one instance, all corruption is symbolically done away with. Likewise, films like *An American Werewolf in London* can be seen to complicate and nationalize classical horror codes, moving uneasily between a sense of the present and a sense of the past, and ultimately concluding with a bizarre message of congratulations to the newly married Prince and Princess of Wales. Even with these exceptions in mind, broadly speaking, whether in the form of family dramas like *On Golden Pond*, a film that I have argued symbolically mediates the disjuncture between classical and contemporary Hollywood, or in the form of nominally updated versions of classical fictions like *Tarzan, the Ape Man*, American popular cinema engaged in a strategic nostalgia that looked to recover past representational and ideological precedents as a way forward for the individual, the couple, and the family.

Yet just as the industry was enacting this evasive relationship to the problems, dilemmas, and complications of the American present, film fictions in this year were likely to demonstrate an internal evasiveness. Nearly all the films I have discussed here feature plots in which transformation, self-discovery, reconciliation, and intimacy happen "elsewhere" (in an isolated summer cottage or mountain retreat or on an international quest for historical treasure, among other examples). The implications of this are bleak for those of us who look for a passionate, engaged American cinema, one capable of speaking to the conditions of mainstream, everyday life.

NOTES

1. William J. Palmer discerns a different dynamic, contending that "one notable trend of both the films of the seventies and of the eighties was their nostalgic attraction to fifties and sixties events, issues and social mores" (x). While not disputing this broad claim, my interest here is in the ways a large number of films of the year seemed to reach back even further than this in a cultural/representational memory bank.

2. Palmer contends that the nostalgia of the 1980s was tied to a wholesale recapitulation of the 1950s, a characterization that seems radically oversimplified.

3. This is particularly evident in the latter, a maladroit buddy film in which New York cop Deke DaSilva (Sylvester Stallone) must learn to "take the shot" as he tracks an international terrorist. The film implies that only the vigilance and justified violence of white American men will keep women and racial minorities safe.

4. The film's recirculation of the film noir femme fatale should be examined in its own right for its influence at the start of a decade that would later spawn a number of high-profile caricatures of female agency, perhaps most notably *Fatal Attraction* (1987). The legacy of this role for Kathleen Turner is also interesting to contemplate given that her partnership with a succession of male heroes through the 1980s may well have functioned to offset the troubling display of female material/sexual agency *Body Heat*'s conclusion does not close down.

5. And interestingly, Kathleen Turner's femme fatale would be rehabilitated through this formula, with the actress experiencing her most high-profile and successful role as romance writer Joan Wilder in *Romancing the Stone* (1984) and its sequel *The Jewel of the Nile* (1985).

6. Just as Fonda's role as Chelsea is intertextually informed by her previous films, Henry Fonda's appearance as Norman Thayer draws force from and is sentimentalized by the social memory of a film career in which, as McLeland puts it, he generated "a series of

portrayals of stoic, honest heroic American icons" (234). These portrayals appear in films such as *Young Mr. Lincoln* (1939), *The Grapes of Wrath* (1940), *My Darling Clementine* (1946), and *Mister Roberts* (1955).

7. In the opposite sense Hepburn's association with feisty, gender-bending roles makes her enforcement of traditionalist femininity here all the more striking.

8. Dunaway's performance, which was variously described as either brilliant or dreadful, was widely viewed as career-ending. After a run in the 1970s as one of the most successful stars in Hollywood, in which Dunaway typically played driven, neurotic, sexually magnetic women, she was rarely cast again in a high-profile film in the 1980s.

9. Very much in keeping with my argument that many of the highest-profile films of the year work to discredit images of active femininity, the early sections of *Superman II* bestir annoyance at Lois Lane's poorly thought-out yet persistent attempts to "get the story." Here, her ambition is also linked to a shallow careerism; as she lies in jeopardy at the Eiffel Tower she lists the names of the prizes she hopes to receive for her reporting, including the Pulitzer and the Nobel. Here and elsewhere in the *Superman* films, Lois's zealousness in pursuing a story is exactly what necessitates her frequent rescue.

10. *Tarzan, the Ape Man* holds the dubious distinction of being ranked in the bottom 100 films on the Internet Movie Database with a dismal 3.0 ranking.

11. In *Morning in America: How Ronald Reagan Invented the 1980s*, Troy pinpoints this summer as the high-water mark in Reagan's political capital in light of the ongoing success of the "Reagan legislative steamroller," his appointment of O'Connor to the Supreme Court that July, and his firing in August of 11,000 striking government air traffic controllers (77).

1982

Movies and Other Worlds

WARREN BUCKLAND

Ronald Reagan was in the middle of his first term in office as president. His prospects for a second term looked bleak. By the end of the year, the U.S. economy was still in recession, with the manufacturing, auto, and housing industries in decline and unemployment over 10 percent. The administration slashed the federal budget for domestic outlays while increasing military spending and cutting taxes, which only ballooned the already-considerable national deficit. Many large private corporations (except in the defense industry) posted disastrous earnings. Such problems sharply diminished Reagan's political impact at home. Abroad, especially in the Middle East and Central America, headaches abounded.

Reagan's solution to domestic and foreign problems was twofold: (1) reduce the federal government's size, influence, and regulation and introduce supply-side economics; and (2) send a message that "America is back" and "America is walking tall," no longer haunted by its defeat in Vietnam. Reagan rhetoric became synonymous with the following cluster of terms: nostalgia, populism, anti-intellectualism, aggressive self-confidence, spiritual uplift, and reassurance, all focused around an attack on liberalism and secular humanism. The result was the reification of a structure at the center of Western thought: the opposition between Self and Other. The Other defines everything that exists outside the Self; the Self is therefore defined in relation to or against the Other; indeed, the Self exists only through the Other. Hegel's maxim sums up this structure exactly: "Man exists only in so far as he is opposed." The Manichean opposition between Self and Other is inherently unstable, which encourages the Self to take control and master the Other. This leads to violence, oppression, and exploitation, in the form of racism, sexism, and colonialism. Reaganite ideology rigidly exaggerated the status of the Self against the Other, whether through government deregulation to "preserve" individual liberty or a foreign policy that perpetuated patriotic nationalism in the form of Cold War ideology (aimed at the Soviet Union and other havens of communism such as Nicaragua). Reagan strongly enforced traditional values such as the legacy of individualism, developing a distorted sense of self-empowerment and self-importance, which prompts a defensive attitude toward any kind of criticism.

Popular films should not be ghettoized within the sphere of public entertainment, because they articulate and represent contemporary issues concerning identity and politics, especially the opposition between Self and Other. This is evident in one of the prominent genres of the year: science fiction and fantasy. Films from this genre are centrally preoccupied with the representation of an Other world and its inhabitants, whose otherness reinforces (or occasionally challenges) the boundaries of the Self, although usually on a more benign level than the patriotic nationalism of 1980s Cold War ideology. Science fiction and fantasy films discussed in this chapter include *E.T., Poltergeist, Blade Runner,* and *Tron.* The other worlds represented in these films were coded either as the future, perhaps in a galaxy far, far away, or as a world within the new technology that was beginning to inhabit our work and home space: the personal computer. The more fantastic and alien the other world is portrayed, the stronger it challenges our sense of Self. Additional films examined here, in their metaphorical representation of Other worlds and the identity of their inhabitants, include *One from the Heart, The Loveless,* and *Chan Is Missing.*

A number of industries bucked the depressing economic and political trends. Hollywood economics were largely unaffected by the recession, and the new electronic industries—focused around cable television, videocassettes, PCs, and video games—witnessed steady or, in some cases, dramatic growth. Collectively, these new industries constitute the entertainment dimensions of the Information Age, an age in which electronic technologies revolutionized "the production and distribution of entertainment and information" (Wasko 1). Cable TV grew due to government deregulation of the industry, but it didn't take off until later in the decade. As for the VCR, Sony marketed the first home video machine in 1975 (the Betamax system), soon rivaled by Matsushita and JVC's VHS format the next year. The VCR (especially the VHS system) soon demonstrated impressive market penetration: two million units were sold this year, more than double the sales of just two years earlier (Wasko 124). This hardware boom was accompanied by a growth in videotape rental, which, due to the expense of the tapes, was more common than purchase. The burgeoning demand for videotapes led to the creation of a new type of establishment, the video rental store, which increasingly appeared on street corners and in shopping malls or were integrated into larger stores. In 1980 only 2,500 video stores existed; two years later over 13,000 were up and running (Wasko 150), most independently owned (Blockbuster did not begin operating until 1985). The recording capacity of the VCR soon created copyright problems for the film industry, signaling the beginnings of video piracy. Yet in the form of videotape rentals, the studios discovered an additional platform for releasing (or re-releasing) its films, which of course meant an additional source of revenue—very important for expensive films such as *Blade Runner* that did not find their audience during the initial theatrical release. (The studios did not receive revenues from the rentals themselves, but from the sale of tapes to rental stores [see Prince 103].) Thus this year stands out for the beginning of the video revolution, which, like other electronic industries, exploded in the mid-eighties.

The PC revolution was also in full swing for both business and home users. In particular, other worlds and virtual spaces were represented not only in spreadsheets and word processing, but also in the craze for computer games. The computer game industry was already worth around $2 billion as home and arcade video games had reached their Golden Age. The 18 January issue of *Time* magazine featured video games on its cover and led with a feature article profiling the arcade culture. (In December *Time* also named the computer "Machine of the Year" rather than choosing its traditional "Man of the Year.") Throughout the country over 1.5 million arcade machines were in operation (Kent 152).

Just before the summer blockbuster season began, Aljean Harmetz reported in the *New York Times* that "there is a feeling throughout the industry that Hollywood has at last 'hit the target,' 'made movie-movies,' and 'loaded the gun with star power'" (C11). By the end of the summer season, she confirmed that it had been "the most lucrative summer in the history of the movies" (C22), with a 17 percent increase in box office over 1981. Universal enjoyed the most success, led of course by *E.T.,* distantly followed by *The Best Little Whorehouse in Texas* and *Fast Times at Ridgemont High.* Paramount's big hits were *Star Trek II* and *An Officer and a Gentleman.* MGM/UA had a good year with *Poltergeist* and *Rocky III,* while Warner Bros.' primary success was Clint Eastwood's *Firefox.* Columbia, however, barely recovered its $40 million budget on the musical *Annie,* and Twentieth Century Fox lagged further behind, experiencing major disappointments with *Megaforce* and the comedies *Author! Author!* and *Six Pack.*

The year also witnessed several strong dramas. In addition to *An Officer and a Gentleman,* a surprise hit, there was also Alan J. Pakula's solemn *Sophie's Choice,* a study of a Holocaust survivor (Meryl Streep) living in Brooklyn; Costa Gavras's political thriller *Missing,* based on a true story in which a father (Jack Lemmon) goes to Chile to search for his son; Alan Parker's poignant study of divorce, *Shoot the Moon*; David S. Ward's adaptation of John Steinbeck's *Cannery Row*; Barry Levinson's directorial debut, *Diner,* a nostalgic look at the rites of passage of five young men in 1959 Baltimore; Fred Zinnemann's final film, *Five Days One Summer,* a love story starring Sean Connery about a man who takes his young mistress with him on a mountaineering adventure to Switzerland; and the psychological thriller *Still of the Night,* with strong performances from Streep and Roy Scheider. Many 3-D movies from the 1950s were reissued, while *Friday 13th Part III* was shot in 3-D and released on over 800 screens. Yet the revival was short-lived, as interest in 3-D soon shifted to video games.

Women directors also made an impact, including Kathryn Bigelow's first full-length film, *The Loveless,* and Susan Seidelman's debut, the independently produced *Smithereens.* The latter follows the downward spiral of Wren (Susan Berman), who rejects comforting but bland lower-middle-class values in favor of the offbeat, nihilistic lifestyle of punk culture. This Other world is full of demoralized characters on the margins of society, yet it is from this position that Wren dreams of fame and fortune without comprehending the reality of her situation: she is talentless, powerless, penniless, alienated, isolated, marginalized, and self-destructive. Seidelman made the film for $80,000 soon after graduating from New York University (as well as directing, she also co-wrote the screenplay and edited and produced the film). *Smithereens* earned a reputation at film festivals (including Cannes, where it became the first independently produced American film to be accepted in the main competition) before receiving a limited commercial release. Two other women directors also gained a foothold in the film industry this year: Amy Heckerling, with her hugely successful teen comedy *Fast Times at Ridgemont High,* and Amy Holden Jones, who produced and directed the reflexive send-up slasher movie *Slumber Party Massacre,* written by feminist author Rita Mae Brown.

There was also a mini-cycle of mainstream gay-themed films, which as a group received little press attention at the time; these included Arthur Hiller's *Making Love,* Robert Towne's *Personal Best,* Blake Edwards's *Victor/ Victoria,* and James Burrows's *Partners.* All attempted to offer positive images of homosexuality. Yet Vito Russo has argued that these films failed because they "were too straight for gay audiences and much too gay for conservative straights" (271). One problem with these films, according to Russo, is that they negate the Otherness of homosexuality: "You can't plead tolerance for gays by saying that they're just like everyone else. Tolerance is something we should extend to people who are not like everyone else. If gays weren't different, there wouldn't be a problem, and there certainly is a problem" (272). Nevertheless, the fact that these films emerged at all during Reagan's first term, which coincided with a rise in Christian fundamentalism and the Religious Right, again demonstrates "that resistant liberal forces existed in American culture at odds with the dominant conservative value system" (Ryan and Kellner 259).

In comedy, Eddie Murphy made his film debut in *48 Hrs.* The year also witnessed Peter Sellers seemingly brought back to life in *Trail of the Pink Panther;* he had died two years earlier, but the film features deleted scenes from his previous *Pink Panther* movies. Similarly, Carl Reiner's comedy *Dead Men Don't Wear Plaid* kept alive the images of many classical Hollywood stars by skillfully editing together clips from their 1940s film noirs with Reiner's black-and-white footage starring Steve Martin.

Finally, a survey would not be complete without mention of the films listed as the worst of the year. In addition to Francis Ford Coppola's *One from the Heart,* which made several such lists (more accurately, it was regarded as a talented director's misfire), the generally acknowledged bombs of the year include Frank Perry's *Monsignor* (about a priest, played by Christopher Reeve, who seduces a nun); Matt Cimber's *Butterfly* (the scandal surrounding Pia Zadora's Golden Globe award makes the film a historical curiosity), Hal Needham's tacky *Megaforce*, Richard Donner's shallow social commentary comedy *The Toy,* and the completely pointless sequel *Grease II* (Pat Burch returned to choreography after directing this film). Such films are just as important as the recognized winners in defining the year, for they provide a counter-balance to orthodox, standard film histories that only focus on successes.

E.T. the Extra-Terrestrial

By far the biggest success of the year was *E.T.* "Without warning," wrote Vincent Canby at year's end, "Steven Spielberg's 'E.T. the Extra-Terrestrial,' designed to be a nice, unassuming family film, became the kind of runaway hit that happens once or twice in a decade" (H17). Many reviewers pointed out that the film is infused with and represents a childlike idealism and optimism. It updates the classic animal stories in which children befriend wild animals. It articulates clear, binary oppositions between the child's worldview versus the adult worldview, and mythology (fantasy, magic, belief) versus science (abstract-rational thought). While these two realities co-exist in the film, the first terms are obviously favored over the second. *E.T.* conforms to the childhood fantasy of an imaginary friend who has special powers and shares the same experiences as the child: both Elliott (Henry Thomas) and E.T. share a sense of loss regarding home and abandonment by parents.

E.T. the Extra-Terrestrial (Steven Spielberg, Universal) was the year's biggest box office hit, offering an appealing view of the difficulties of childhood. Jerry Ohlinger's Movie Material Store.

Although the film dwells in the realm of the child's worldview, dominated by fantasy, magic, and infantile belief, it nonetheless represents Elliott's transition from the mythological to the adult worldview. This transition involves an acceptance of loss—a loss of imaginary friends and illogical beliefs in favor of abstract rational thought. But the sense of loss is compounded in *E.T.* because Elliott is inflicted with the added traumatic loss of his father. *E.T.* does not restore the original nuclear family; instead it allows one of the affected children to be transformed and come to terms with his loss. That *E.T.* represents a child's worldview at first appears to be a self-evident fact. However, Robin Wood argues that there is a distinction between a childlike nature (the child as symbol of new growth and regeneration) and the childish (regressive sentimentalism in which the child is perceived as an escape from the corrupt and problematic adult world) (175–76). He writes further that *E.T.* wavers between the two concepts before finally committing itself to childish regressive sentimentalism, adding that the film does not so much present a child's fantasy world but a male adult's fantasy about childhood (178).

E.T.'s status as Other is one of the film's dominant themes. Sarah Harwood notes that E.T. "arrives without recognizable gender or language. . . . He has no history and no clear point of origin. The children's attempt to locate him within the framework of their knowledge fails dismally" (161). It is Elliott's younger sister, Gertie (Drew Barrymore), who teaches E.T. to speak and who raises questions about "his" gender identity. She dresses him up in women's clothes, leading Elliott to stipulate that E.T. is male. And when Gertie and E.T. watch "Sesame Street" on television, E.T. begins to repeat the letters of the alphabet, clearly pronouncing the letter "B." "Good," Gertie praises him, and then continues to teach him. E.T. remembers this initiation when he departs at the end of the film, repeating the first lesson to Gertie, "B. Good" (sounding also like an exhortation to behave).

These processes of establishing language and gender at least partly negate E.T.'s Otherness by assimilating him into the familiar world of American suburban society. Wood unearths the political consequences of this process of assimilation: "[A] nation that was founded on the denial of Otherness now—after radical feminism, after gay liberation, after black militancy—complacently produces a film in which Otherness is something we can all love and cuddle and cry over, without unduly disturbing the nuclear family and the American Way of Life" (180). In other words, *E.T.* represents a nonthreatening, domesticated image of the Other (everything that exists outside the Self as defined by the film: a white, middle-class, suburban lifestyle), although Wood does not give due notice to the film's depiction of the non-nuclear family held together by the mother.

Michael Ryan and Douglas Kellner are far more optimistic than Wood regarding the film's politics. They argue that Reagan's aggressive pursuit of a conservative economic program in the public sphere led to a displacement of liberal values and ideals from the public to the private (social and domestic) sphere. In this view Spielberg's family fantasy films are a symptom of this displacement: "The public world had been purged of empathy, feeling, and community [to the extent] that the private idealizations of these traits take on such exaggerated forms in the popular imaginary of Spielberg's films" (262). *E.T.*'s idealization of a harmonious and romantic sentimentalist private sphere accounts for its popularity, according to Ryan and Kellner, which also demonstrates that Reagan's economic and political policies were out of sync with the beliefs of many Americans: "The immense popularity of [Spielberg's] films, especially *E.T.,* suggests that resistant liberal forces existed in American culture at odds with the dominant conservative value system" (259).

Poltergeist

"The Other" again intervened in the nuclear family in *Poltergeist*. This time, the Other is not benevolent and tamed but threatening: it is codified as an occult force that haunts and eventually leads to the destruction of the family home. Steven Spielberg wrote and produced but did not direct *Poltergeist*. Instead, he handed over the directorial reins to Tobe Hooper, known for his body horror films such as *The Texas Chainsaw Massacre* (1974). The tension between Hooper's worldview and Spielberg's is palpably evident on the film's surface. In his review of the film, Chris Auty noted that "the project's originator and producer (Steven Spielberg) and its director (Tobe Hooper) come from . . . different traditions—the former from Disney, suburbia, and TV; the latter from Gothic and the campus scene (University of Texas)" (205). Spielberg reworked elements from *Close Encounters* and *E.T.* (the suburban setting, a middle-class household with its mundane routines) while Hooper created the moments of gore, fright, and explicit shock (disintegrating flesh, bodies surfacing from a graveyard, characters covered in blood and mucous). Spielberg did manage to add some of his own (less scary) effects, such as objects in the kitchen moving by themselves, reminiscent of Gillian's house in *Close Encounters* when the aliens take away four-year-old Barry (Cary Guffey). In *Poltergeist,* the poltergeists take the five-year-old daughter, Carol (Heather O'Rouke). Many reviewers highlighted the uneasy mix of the two distinct visions in the film, a mix that creates an uneven mood and tone.

Robin Wood finds two other tensions that pull the film in opposite directions. First, "its interest and the particular brand of reassurances it offers both lie in its relation to the 70s family horror film—in the way in which Spielberg enlists the genre's potential radicalism and perverts it into 80s conservatism" (180). Wood calls the seventies the golden age of horror, in which the repressed Other surfaces in full view with terrifying consequences and cannot be destroyed (this being its radicalism). While Spielberg (with Hooper's help) draws upon this terrifying Other in *Poltergeist,* it is safely contained in the end—the triumph of conservatism over radicalism. Second, family members at first appear to be the cause of the Other's wrath, but in the end they are innocent because the problem is caused by a few greedy housing developers who built houses on an old graveyard without removing and reburying the bodies. The spirits of the dead are therefore upset with the suburbanites unknowingly living on their sacred ground.

Blade Runner

Blade Runner, based on Philip K. Dick's novel *Do Androids Dream of Electric Sheep?* was barely a critical and box office success on its initial release. Many reviews were in fact hostile. Writing in the *New York Times*, Janet Maslin saw only the special effects and an incoherent narrative. She concluded that director Ridley Scott should not "expect overdecoration to carry a film that has neither strong characters nor a strong story. That hasn't stopped him from trying, even if it perhaps should have" (C10). Gary Crowdus in *Cinéaste* identified the film's debt to film noir and concluded that it is "little more than a tired genre item dressed up in a futuristic setting" (60). And Tom Milne in the *Monthly Film Bulletin* noted: "The sets are indeed impressive (especially the rubble-strewn desolation of Sebastian's apartment block, the skyscraper-high neon ads that line the streets, and the steamy claustrophobia of a permanently rainy Chinatown), but they are no compensation for a narrative so lame that it seems in need of a wheelchair" (194).

A relatively new director such as Ridley Scott, trying to find his way after the immense success of his second film, *Alien* (1979), could have

Harrison Ford in *Blade Runner* (Ridley Scott, The Ladd Co.), which has become a science fiction classic, although at the time it was widely regarded as a mediocre film. Jerry Ohlinger's Movie Material Store.

found himself not eating lunch in Hollywood again after such a chorus of disapproval. Production problems were reported on the set, partly caused by Scott's perfectionism, especially his need to shoot numerous takes. In addition, the film provoked another debate concerning violence in contemporary films, especially since audiences were expecting a variation of *Star Wars* (1977) or *Tron*, neither of which are as sadistic, dark, atmospheric, or slowly paced as *Blade Runner*. Instead, Scott's film seems to combine the violence of a Sam Peckinpah film with the metaphysical ambiance of Jean-Luc Godard's *Alphaville* (1965) and Stanley Kubrick's *2001* (1968).

Although many reviewers interpreted *Blade Runner*'s densely textured imagery as a self-contained element, we can in fact read the film's production design and cinematography as strongly motivated, for they successfully transform the Los Angeles of the future into an uncanny other world—a dark, decaying, and overpopulated metropolis, in which the signifiers of the future are grafted (or retrofitted) onto the present and familiar Los Angeles. Cultural critics such as Ryan, Kellner, and Wood have found the film to be predominantly critical of advanced capitalism, whose excesses lead to an exploited workforce of replicants and a polluted environment—to the point where Earth is almost uninhabitable. This dystopic vision is rendered palatable to a 1980s audience because it is projected into the future and articulated in a science fiction setting. Wood writes:

> The society we see [in *Blade Runner*] is our own writ large, its present excesses carried to their logical extremes: power and money controlled by even fewer, in even larger monopolies; worse poverty, squalor, degradation; racial oppression; a polluted planet, from which those who can emigrate to other worlds. The film opposes to Marx's view of inevitable collapse a chilling vision of capitalism hanging on, by the maintenance of power and oppression, in the midst of an essentially disintegrated civilization. (183)

In the midst of the film's social critique, and belief that capitalism will simply intensify rather than collapse under the weight of its own contradictions, is a metaphysical reflection on what it means to be human. One of the strengths of the film lies in its ability to blur the boundaries between a series of reassuring oppositions: human/nonhuman, reason/feeling, nature/culture, hero/villain. Once the film breaks down these oppositions, the metaphysical question "What does it mean to be human?" comes to the fore.

The first and fourth oppositions are worthy of further discussion. The distinction between human and nonhuman is clearly one of the film's main themes, and is articulated by the replicants being able to "pass" for human—except that, crucially, they have no emotional responses and have artificial personal histories. The job of Rick Deckard (Harrison Ford) as blade runner is ostensibly to identify and "retire" replicants who have illegally returned to Earth. But Deckard is a burnt out, morally ambivalent hero, a shadow of his former self, especially when compared to the villain, the leader of the replicants, Roy (Rutger Hauer), who is far more charismatic and more full of life than Deckard. Wood writes: "The replicants (I am thinking especially of Roy and Pris) are dangerous but fascinating, frightening but beautiful, other but not totally and intractably alien; they gradually emerge as the film's true emotional center, and certainly represent its finest achievement" (185). The opposition between human and replicant is further eroded when Deckard falls in love with another replicant, Rachael (Sean Young).

Wood labels the film an incoherent text, a reading Ridley Scott would no doubt uphold, for he follows Philip K. Dick's strategy of purposely making the story inherently ambiguous, especially concerning the status of its hero—is Deckard a replicant or not? But whereas Dick and Scott view ambiguity as a necessary response to metaphysical questions about humanity, Wood sees the film's incoherence as emerging from its revolutionary critique of capitalism. He seems to think that the film's critique, disguised in science fiction and projected into the future, is insufficient to soften its radical message. He feels the film has to be compromised by reactionary values in order to be accessible to a mass audience. One element of the film's reactionary politics is that it has to fabricate a happy ending based around the formation of the heterosexual couple: "The film is in fact defeated by the overwhelming legacy of classical narrative. It succumbs to one of its most firmly traditional and ideologically reactionary formulas: the elimination of the bad couple (Roy, Pris) in order to construct the good couple (Deckard, Rachael)" (188).

What the mainstream critics and audiences at first missed was that *Blade Runner* presented a visceral image of a very specific and previously unrealized other world—which has subsequently been called "cyberpunk." Scott Bukatman identifies cyberpunk broadly as a sub-cultural label, "referring now to hackers, electronic musicians, ravers and anyone else who professed to employ high technology (or its image) from the margins of society" (52). He argues that cyberpunk creates a new identity (which he calls a terminal identity), "a new position from which humans could interface with the global, yet hidden, realm of data circulation; a new identity to occupy the emerging electronic realm" (45). More specifically, cyberpunk names the merging of the counter-cultural punk movement of the 1970s with the rise of computer technology in the 1980s. *Blade Runner* appeared at the time this merging took place, although critics and audiences did not initially come to terms with the radically new world the film depicts. The film is now credited as influencing the iconography of all subsequent SF films.

One reason *Blade Runner* did not find its audience in the theaters is that it had to compete with other science fiction and fantasy films, including *Star Trek II: The Wrath of Khan*, *The Thing*, and (on a different level of fantasy) *Tron* and *E.T.* Another reason is the poor response at previews and hasty attempts to fix them: the tacked-on happy ending, Deckard's hastily written and indifferently delivered voiceover, the removal of Deckard's dream image of a unicorn that indirectly suggests he is a replicant. The film did, however, find its audience in the relatively new media outlets of cable television, videocassettes, and laser discs. Warner Bros. was keen to recoup its investment in the film (whose total budget was around $28 million), and soon began to saturate the home viewing market. The growing interest in the film—indeed, it gained the status of a cultural icon of the 1980s—resulted in Warner Bros. issuing a director's cut in 1992, based partly on the prints screened at sneak previews ten years earlier (see Sammon 330–71.)

Tron

Disney's *Tron*, written and directed by first-time director Steven Lisberger, suffered from the opposite perception problem that plagued *Blade Runner*. While the latter's dark metaphysics dominated its perceived entertainment value, *Tron*'s serious message was lost in its lightweight, Disneyesque presentation. Whereas Deckard suffered from an existential crisis that affected his very sense of self, the main characters in *Tron* talk and act like Buck Rogers. Both films share the representation of other worlds, and even the same conceptual artists and designers of those other worlds (most notably, Syd Mead and the comic book artist Moebius). But whereas we still recognize *Blade Runner*'s futuristic, uncanny space, *Tron*'s representation of an Other world is so complete that audiences and critics felt lost. Syd Mead commented on the difference between the two films: "The big difference was that *Tron* was a completely artificial construct linked to a classic story of netherworld/ID driven intent versus the 'surface world' of technical possibility and *Blade Runner* was an elaborate comment on where we could be going as a technically enhanced society struggling with matching human ambition, with ever-new tools [that] can either pervert or promise a possible future" (qtd. in Cook).

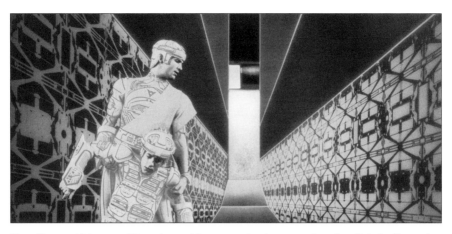

Tron (Steven Lisberger, Disney) provides an early showcase for the digital effects that Hollywood would fully embrace in the next decade. Jerry Ohlinger's Movie Material Store.

Tron transplants a computer programmer, Kevin Flynn (Jeff Bridges), inside a computer, where normal rules of spatial distance, geographical orientation, and even the solidity of objects do not apply. Flynn certainly isn't in Kansas anymore but, unlike Dorothy, the path to the wizard (or M.C.P.— Master Control Program) is not a simple yellow brick road. The Other world represented in *Tron* is cyberspace, and at the time no one had a map.

The film thematizes the new computer and video game revolution, which becomes both the subject matter of the film and also the means to the creation of its images. It combines live action with both optical and computer special effects to create an imaginary, spectacular, if rather cold and antiseptic, image of the inner space of a computer. These images are infused with a narrative conflict concerning "the rebels" battling the "Evil Empire"—in this instance, big business stealing and profiting from the video games that Flynn creates—with the inevitable outcome that the rebels win. But the more serious message behind this cliché is that computers themselves are not damaging; it is a matter of who is controlling the computers and in whose interest (a message also prevalent in *Blade Runner,* in which Deckard says that the replicants are not inherently good or bad). The film, therefore, addresses the fears of a society that saw an increase of computers entering the home and work place on a daily basis.

Special effects began to play an increasingly important role in realizing those other worlds on the big screen, as John Culhane pointed out in a *New York Times* feature essay "Special Effects are Revolutionizing Film," which focused primarily on *Tron*. At the end he noted in passing that "two young animators, John Lasseter and Glenn Keane, are planning a 30-second scene from Maurice Sendak's modern children's classic 'Where the Wild Things Are'" (14). Lasseter, working in Disney's animation department, saw *Tron* and was inspired by its combination of live action and computer animation to create his own hybrid (this time between conventional hand-drawn cartoons and computer animation), in which the computer created the environment and colored in the cartoon. Culhane concluded: "If the experiment works for 'Where the Wild Things Are,' it could conceivably work for a host of other fantasy environments" (14). *Tron*, therefore, represented the modest beginnings of Lasseter's revolutionary use of digital animation to create other worlds, realized later in the *Toy Story* films (1995, 1999, announced for 2008), *A Bug's Life* (1998), and *Cars* (2006).

One from the Heart

A less alienating but still completely Other world is represented in Francis Ford Coppola's *One from the Heart*. Set in Las Vegas, the film depicts the city by deliberately flaunting its artificial status. As if the city itself weren't artificial enough, Coppola reconstructed Las Vegas in his Zoetrope studios, never once leaving the sound stages to shoot on location (apparently in response to the enormous problems he encountered on location while filming *Apocalypse Now* [1979]). The film's plot is deliberately simplistic and artificial, quoting Hollywood conventions and clichés from musical and romance genres as it follows the breakup and reformation of the relationship between Hank (Frederic Forrest) and Frannie (Teri Garr) over a Fourth of July holiday.

One from the Heart presents the Other world of the Hollywood studio picture *as* Other; Coppola makes no attempt to hide the conventions and clichés; in fact, their artificiality actually becomes the film's subject matter. The film is claustrophobic to the extent it never leaves its artificial setting; there is no Other to offer contrast to and oppose the artificiality. This studio-bound Hollywood movie (which also references the fantasy films of Michael Powell and Federico Fellini) is aimed at cinéphiles, and never caught on with audiences who were more used to experiencing Lucas and Spielberg's sincere, sentimental, and less ironic reworking of Hollywood clichés. The $27 million budget sunk Coppola's Zoetrope studios, which only managed to recoup $2 million at the box office.

For many reviewers, the film represents the excesses of auteurism, which they characterized as all style and technology with no message or moral. Yet through *One from the Heart* Coppola initiated a series of electronic

cinema processes encompassing preproduction, production, and postpro-
duction, including video assist (a live video picture of the camera's image,
which could also be recorded); electronic storyboards (a process of heightened previsualization in which either hand-drawn images are videotaped
and sequenced, or rehearsals are videotaped); an electronic control room
(in which the director communicates with the set and records and edits
shots together on videotape); and electronic distribution and exhibition.
Some of these processes (especially the first two) have now become standard practice, while the last is slowly becoming a practical reality.

The Loveless

At the opposite end of the Hollywood spectrum to Coppola
was the unknown, fledgling director Kathryn Bigelow. In August 1981 she
(and co-director Monty Montgomery) took her debut independent feature
film to the Locarno Film Festival. Made for under $1 million, the film stars
Willem Dafoe (in his first leading role) as Vance, a leather-clad biker who
stops in a small southern rural town with his gang to get a bike fixed. The
film explores the extreme contrast and hostility between the locals and
outsiders, who represent a completely alien way of life to each other. One
characteristic it does share with *One from the Heart* is that critics perceived
it as only style and surface with very little story holding it together: "Suggesting that its 50s setting is far more important than content or characters, *The Loveless* displays to maximum advantage its lovingly assembled
props and wardrobe. The camera gloats over Coca-Cola vending machines,
music boxes, cars, old advertisements and pin-up calendars, all carefully
arranged so that bright-red lipstick will set off a blue steel wall and a red-
and-black tattooed arm will similarly complement some motor cycle
machinery" (Baumgarten 203). Similarly, J. Hoberman wrote: "The ele-
gantly composed action is largely a matter of outrageously mannered
hanging out to the strains of an incredibly precise rockabilly score. . . . *The
Loveless* is a virtual museum catalogue of pop memorabilia. Every prop
from playing cards to switchblade knife is a genuine antique fetishized in
clinical close-up" (56).

The film had a protracted release, finally opening in Los Angeles in September 1984, three years after its first screening (under the name *Breakdown*, which was changed to *The Loveless* prior to theatrical release). The
difficulties Bigelow encountered with this (and other) films may not be due
simply to their focus on surface detail, but on Bigelow's art house reworking of traditional Hollywood male genres. *The Loveless* is an homage to and

redefinition of the biker teen movie, epitomized in the classical Hollywood film *The Wild One* (1953) and further developed in Kenneth Anger's underground film *Scorpio Rising* (1964). *The Loveless* therefore combines (and mediates between) the aesthetics of the classical Hollywood film and the underground film.

Bigelow explains the deliberate lack of cause-effect logic in the film: "*The Loveless* was a psychological bikers' film. We wanted to suspend the conventional kind of plotting where everything spirals into problem solving after problem solving, and create a meditation on an arena, on an iconography, using the bikers as an iconography of power" (qtd. in Lane 65). Like Coppola in *One from the Heart,* Bigelow is not simply using the iconography of traditional genres, but taking one step back to create a meditation on the iconography of genres, a "meta" position that makes both *One from the Heart* and *The Loveless* appear to be cold, emotionless films.

The Loveless foregrounds one of the most common characters in Bigelow's films: the androgynous female. It is common for critics to point out that *The Loveless* foregrounds Vance, the male character, but Lane argues that the film is really about Telena, even though she appears in only three scenes. Although *The Loveless* is Bigelow's most explicitly independent art house movie, Lane points out that it anticipates Bigelow's more commercial films such as *Blue Steel* (1990) "in that it undeniably questions the equality of gender politics, as well as the place of women within the generic scripts which are conventionally available to them" (67).

Chan Is Missing

Chan Is Missing represents Wayne Wang's debut entry into low budget independent filmmaking in the United States. The film cost a mere $22,000, which came from the American Film Institute and the National Endowment for the Arts. It was screened in the New Directors/New Films Festival, an annual event organized by the Film Society of Lincoln Center and the Museum of Modern Art in New York, showcasing the work of several foreign and independent American filmmakers. Like many low budget independents, *Chan Is Missing* was shot on location (in San Francisco) on 16 mm b&w (and transferred to 35 mm for distribution). It has a rough look and an almost unintelligible soundtrack, is full of digressions, and focuses more on character than action. Like many independent filmmakers, Wang worked in several positions, including producer, co-writer, director, and editor. It is notable for being one of the first Asian-based films made in the United States and, despite its low budget status, it caught the attention of both critics and art house filmgoers, who recognized its authentic articulation of the diasporic experience and its conflicts, centering around the tensions between assimilation and resistance of Asians into U.S. culture and society. In the *New York Times,* Vincent Canby wrote: "In 'Chan is Missing,' [Wang] is exploring the loyalties of Chinese-Americans divided between ancient traditions and those of a new country that, even for Chinese who have been here for several generations, never permits complete assimilation" (D19).

Wang, who grew up in the United States and Hong Kong, never felt he fit in either society. His hyphenated identity and sense of alienation in both his homeland and host land is strongly articulated in *Chan Is Missing.* Mixing comedy and mystery genres, the film focuses on two cab drivers, Jo (Wood Moy) and Steve (Marc Hayashi), searching for their friend Chan Hung, who has disappeared with $4,000 of their money. The film follows their fruitless quest to find him as they interview his friends, relatives, and acquaintances, each of whom give a completely different description of his personality and behavior. Chan is never found, although Jo and Steve do retrieve their money. The process of discovering the different, multifaceted, and often contradictory personality traits of a character who is never seen on screen is one of the film's main themes.

This theme has multiple meanings when viewed in terms of the identity politics of diasporic or displaced people. Hamid Naficy argues that diasporic filmmakers create accented films—accented not only in the literal sense (their speech indicating their geographic and class status), but more broadly, in that they articulate the experiences of the displaced filmmakers. More specifically, accented films are autobiographical because they articulate the filmmaker's feelings of dislocation, alienation, displacement, loss, estrangement, and nostalgia—in other words, their irrevocable experiences of Otherness. Chan's fluid, contradictory, multiple identities reflect one of the key features of accented films: "In the best of the accented films, identity is not a fixed essence but a process of becoming, even a performance of identity. Indeed, each accented film may be thought of as a performance of its author's identity" (6). Wang thematizes or allegorizes the diasporic fluid identity by the extreme device of not depicting the title character, but only representing his identity through the multiple perspectives of those who (appear to) know him. The film questions the idea of a fixed and stable identity, an experience that forms part of the daily life of displaced people: "As partial, fragmented, and multiple subjects, [displaced] filmmakers are capable of producing ambiguity and doubt about the taken-for-granted values of their home and host societies" (13).

Its low budget and on-location shooting confer upon *Chan Is Missing* a semi-documentary feel. As with many independent films, including *Smithereens*, this budgetary limitation becomes expressed in a positive way, grounding the film in a precise location by offering an authentic view of San Francisco's Chinatown and an insider's depiction of the experiences of its inhabitants.

Conclusion

It would be facile to automatically read these films as a mere symptom of Reaganite ideology. Their status is more complex than that. In a complex society, no single determinant, such as economics or politics, however prevalent, completely influences and controls what happens in that society. Each film needs to be taken case by case, to determine to what extent it perpetuates this exaggerated opposition between Self and Other, or to what extent it offers a liberal humanist critique. (Some films, of course, can offer both, or can present a liberal perspective before being recuperated into the conservative ideology.) For example, *E.T.* confirmed Hollywood's increasing reliance on the blockbuster as the standard mode of film production—of spending more and more money on fewer films in the hope of reaping huge profits by becoming the biggest grossing film of all time. Yet the film's popularity does not necessarily mean the film automatically endorsed the conservative politics and exaggerated Self/Other opposition of the Reagan administration. Indeed, as noted, Ryan and Kellner read *E.T.* as a liberal critique of Reaganism. *Blade Runner* is more radical in its critique, since it offers a dystopic vision of capitalism's excesses. Even *Tron* depicts the evils of corporate greed and the small, young entrepreneurs successfully fighting back. Out of the four science fiction films discussed here, only *Poltergeist*'s politics is overtly ambivalent.

Whereas *One from the Heart* demonstrated the excesses of auteurism, *The Loveless* and *Chan Is Missing* signified the beginnings of a new type of auteurism—independent minority filmmakers entering both film production and the critical spotlight, a process that increased substantially after Reagan's presidency. Both Bigelow and Wang managed to enter the Hollywood mainstream and make big budget films—although with varying degrees of success (Bigelow's *Point Break* [1991] and *K-19* [2002]; Wang's *Maid in Manhattan* [2002]). Gay-themed films, ignored and marginalized at the time, are now visible in the mainstream—in both the cinema and on television, demonstrating that gay identity politics has become a theme of mainstream media. Yet this move into the mainstream is a double-edged sword, for it often neutralizes the radical values of identity politics, absorbing it into entertainment (just as independent production companies—such as Miramax and Revolution Studios—have become subsidiaries of Hollywood studios) and turning it into a benign Other. The opposition between Self and Other (plus all the baggage that goes along with it—self-importance, special status, constant positive reinforcement) is never overcome, but is simply articulated to different degrees on various levels of reality.

ACKNOWLEDGMENTS

I wish to thank Alison McMahan for her comments on an earlier draft of this essay, and Mark Steensland for providing me with documents on *The Loveless*.

1983

Movies and Reaganism

ALAN NADEL

It was a year of Dickensian dualities, a year of looking forward and looking back, of suffering economic growth and economic
decline, of tax cuts and tax increases, of supporting Central American
governments and Central American insurgents. Americans witnessed an
increase in home sales and an increase in homelessness, military humiliation in Beirut, and military triumph in Grenada. At the beginning of the
year, President Reagan's chances for reelection seemed slim, raising serious
questions—in light of his age, his performance in office, a skyrocketing
national debt, a toppling shift in the international balance of payments,
rampant corruption in his administration, and the worst recession since the
Great Depression—as to whether Reagan would even run again. By the end
of the year, however, despite unemployment rates in excess of 9 percent,
the economy was in a clear growth trajectory and Reagan had announced
his plans to seek a second term.

The year reconfigures not only the Republican Party but also the
national ideology. Instead of representing fiscal conservatism, the Republican Party would henceforth stand for unregulated national debt; instead of
supporting an international policy of containment, it would favor pre-
emptive intervention (in such places as Grenada, Panama, and Iraq). Rather
than representing the conservative restraint in deviating from tradition and
altering precedents, the GOP would promote an activist agenda aimed at
amending the Constitution. Further, the party would start junking the
Keynesian economic system that had provided the foundation for American
prosperity over the preceding forty years. In its place, it would advocate an
economic philosophy that equated democracy and freedom, a priori, with
free markets, social welfare with the dissolution of the social safety net, and
national well-being not with the standard of living—which measures the
equitable distribution of basic benefits—but with the right to limitlessly
inequitable distributions of wealth.

The top box office hit was *Return of the Jedi,* grossing over $300 million,
more than the combined gross of the year's next three most successful

films. As the culmination of the first Star Wars trilogy (following *Star Wars* [1977] and *The Empire Strikes Back* [1980]), the film, with an avid audience waiting, did not need particularly strong reviews to become an instantaneous mega-success. Other than in technical areas, however, *Return of the Jedi* received very few award nominations and, perhaps in compensation, the Academy of Motion Picture Arts and Sciences gave it a Special Achievement Award for "visual effects."

The Academy's competitive award categories, however, were dominated by the second highest grossing film, *Terms of Endearment,* a blend of comedy and drama that follows a mother-daughter relationship through a series of episodes evoking the changing values, styles, and relationships that marked the transition from the 1960s to the 1980s. The only other box office hit to receive serious recognition was *The Big Chill,* a film with an inspired sound track full of late sixties and early seventies hits, and an all-star cast including Kevin Kline, William Hurt, Glenn Close, Meg Tilley, Jeff Goldblum, and Tom Berenger. The film looks back on the 1960s from the perspective of a very affluent group of friends, a decade out of college, who have gathered over three days for the funeral of a college friend who has committed suicide.

The other top films at the box office included *Risky Business,* a kind of reckless teen movie that made Tom Cruise a star. Matthew Broderick also made his mark in *War Games,* a modest, albeit extremely successful film about a high school computer whiz who accidentally hacks into the U.S. nuclear defense system, almost starting and then barely averting World War III. Another surprise hit, *Flashdance,* chronicles a female construction worker's attempts to build upon the innovative dance style that she has developed working nights in a girlie bar into the basis for an audition with a ballet school. Its catchy score, combined with the glitzy editing and stylish backlighting that typify many television commercials, turned what was in effect a succession of music videos not only into the third most successful film of the year, but also into an important film style trendsetter. Promoting dance—self-taught and self-styled—as escape from white blue-collar drudgery, the film was a thematic successor to *Saturday Night Fever* (1977). So was another box office (if not critical) hit, *Stayin' Alive,* in which John Travolta reprised the role of *Saturday Night Fever*'s Tony Manero.

Other significant films included two that were well received, and for which there were high expectations, *The Right Stuff* and *Silkwood.* Both films depicted true events, the race to put a man on the moon and the death of a whistle-blower who exposed serious safety violations at a nuclear facility.

Despite good reviews, much hype, and several award nominations, neither performed as well at the box office as had been expected.

Three imports, *The Dresser, Educating Rita* (both Great Britain), and *The Year of Living Dangerously* (Australia) were acclaimed for actors' performances. Another small production garnering critical attention was *Tender Mercies*, directed by an Australian, Bruce Beresford, about an alcoholic country singer, played by Robert Duvall, who puts his life back together. Like *The Dresser* and *Educating Rita*—both essentially two-character films—*Tender Mercies* focuses on a small group of people. The film can be viewed as a country-and-western version of *Terms of Endearment* in the way that it depicts a family encountering tragedy and redemption. Excepting the epic scope and cosmic revenues of *Return of the Jedi*, the bulk of the major films had an introspective quality, often tainted by untimely death: the death of Karen Silkwood, the deaths of the daughters in *Terms of Endearment* and *Tender Mercies*, the suicides of the Indonesian reporter in *The Year of Living Dangerously* and of Alex, whose funeral is the initial event of *The Big Chill*. Even *The Right Stuff* is informed much more by the deaths of test pilots and the hazards of space flight than by the triumph of the space age. And, given that the Jedi return only after Yoda dies, the films whose titles best capture the film spirit of the year may well be *Risky Business, War Games, The Year of Living Dangerously*.

Reaganism: The Retro-Fitted Empire and the Jedi with Two Brains

A great many films reflect a sense of duality and revision, from the absurdist Steve Martin comedy *The Man with Two Brains* to Woody Allen's dark, postmodern examination of revisionist history, *Zelig*. The revision of gender roles is evident in *Flashdance*, as well as such films as *Heart Like a Wheel*, the biopic about a female drag car racer, and *Mr. Mom*, a comedy about a laid-off executive who becomes a homemaker while his wife supports the family. *The Big Chill* reconfigures not gender so much as political values, suggesting ultimately that the only thing worth retaining from the late sixties and early seventies is the music; "Joy to the World," completely divorced from the peace movement, becomes a Yuppie anthem in the film.

The revision of national narratives, such that both the Democratic and Republican parties take giant steps to the right, owed much to President Reagan's ability to substitute a cinematic notion of America for a material one. This is the theme, in fact, of *Trading Places*, a film that uses artificial

Produced during the decade's long bull market, *Trading Places* (John Landis, Paramount), featuring Dan Aykroyd and Eddie Murphy, offers a deft satire of capitalism. Jerry Ohlinger's Movie Material Store.

cinematic conventions to resolve the class bifurcation and racial scapegoating that characterized the Reagan presidency. At the end of *Trading Places*, the ultra-rich, ultra WASP Winthorpe (Dan Aykroyd) and the black street hustler Valentine (Eddie Murphy) combine not to right the injustices perpetuated by the corrupt commodities dealers, the Duke brothers, but to get rich by employing the Dukes' dishonest tactics against them. As Valentine says in the film, "The way to get even with rich people is to make them poor people." The exchange of close-ups at the end of the film, between Valentine, on a tropical beach, and Winthorpe, on a yacht anchored several hundred yards away, allows them to speak comfortably across a quarter-mile gap. Because the camera can stand close to each of them, it disguises the fact that even in their success, they cannot have a plausible face-to-face relationship. Without raising their voices significantly, they appear to be toasting one another, when in fact their toast is a tribute to the cinematic apparatus, as if to suggest that cinematic editing could broach the racial divide promoted by Reaganism, as easily as the scenario could demonstrate that the inequities of Reaganomics could be remedied by equal access to the shady tactics of the marketplace.

To put it another way, an effective transformation occurred in the third year of Reagan's first term, wherein historical precedent rested more effectively upon imagery than material conditions. The "Morning in America" campaign that promoted a positive self-image was, as the phrase suggests, more the effect of spectacular lighting than of actual circumstances. In its combination of past and future, in its faith in a technological return of non-technological supremacy, in its representing itself as the supporters of rebellious freedom fighters and of legitimate governments, the Reagan presidency was as much a manifestation of *Star Wars* as it was an allusion to it. This, after all, was a year that gave us four installments of *Star Wars*: President Reagan's reference to the Soviet Union as the "Evil Empire" in a speech on 8 March (Orlofsky 164; Goldinger and Thompson 269–77); his introduction on 23 March of the Strategic Defense Initiative, commonly referred to as "Star Wars" (Goldinger and Thomspon 305–16); the 25 May opening of *Return of the Jedi*; and the invasion of Grenada on 25 October (see Goldinger and Thompson 847–53).

That invasion premiered the return of the United States as an invasive military force, abandoned with the end of the Vietnam War in the mid-1970s. *Return of the Jedi* opened before that invasion but after the aggressive "Star Wars" rhetoric that anticipated the shift in U.S. global mentality. *Return of the Jedi* appropriately seems to look forward and backward, combining destiny with nostalgia, envisioning America as both anti-empire rebel and neo-imperialist enforcer. This tendency to move forward by looking backward has led many critics and historians to identify Reagan with the film *Back to the Future* (see Cannon; Jeffords; Nadel; Wills *Reagan's*). In many ways the year's films and politics, coalescing around *Return of the Jedi*, the end of a trilogy about an imperial/anti-imperial fantasy, reflects even better the admixture of plasticity, duality, and nostalgia that would characterize the remainder of the Reagan presidency. Both the film's odd position as conclusion and middle (with three chronologically earlier installments in the series yet to be made) and its situation in an epic of perpetual warfare characterize the peculiar tension of Reagan policies that would promote and initiate military presence and military action as it moved toward the end of the Cold War. In many ways, the excessive spending on defense and the military hyperactivity that defined Reagan's foreign policy was lodged in a *Star Wars* narrative, a point vividly illustrated in his "Evil Empire" speech.

Certainly, that reference to *Star Wars* was not intended to suggest that the United States was a weak, marginal entity nobly facing the superior Soviet state, even though that is the position to which the allusion implicitly assigned the United States. Nor would Reagan have wanted to differentiate inaccurately the United States from the Soviets by suggesting that the United States, not the USSR, represented the forces of insurgency, also implicit in the allusion. Rather, he was placing the emphasis on "evil": *they* are the *evil* empire, he was saying, and *we* are the *good* empire. This allusion to the film was apt to the extent that it identified the United States with the anti-imperial forces, the agents of democracy, at the same time as Reagan intensified rivalry for global domination by flaunting American global superiority.

In *Return of the Jedi*, we thus account for the re-alignment that makes the evil empire's destruction a *fait accompli*. At the outset of this film, we have our western hero, Han Solo, frozen in time, and the initial action of the plot must secure his release so that he can return to combat. Like many John Wayne characters, as well as some Jimmy Stewart roles and, famously, Alan Ladd's Shane, Solo is both the loner, as his name implies, and also the representative of civilization at the brink of the frontier. Solo is thus the spirit of the Rebel force as Luke is its spirituality, so that the battle over the control of Solo's body at the outset will parallel the struggles later in the film over the control of Luke's soul.

Both struggles are in a state of crisis because the evil empire is about to complete a force field—an offense to complement a "strategic defense initiative" of the sort that Reagan announced two months before the premiere of *Return of the Jedi*. Quickly named "Star Wars" by the media, the initiative, like Reagan's "Evil Empire" comment, aligned the United States with both the rebel forces and the empire they were trying to defeat. Not surprisingly, success must come from both offensive and defensive actions: the military assault led by Solo and the spiritual resistance maintained by Luke. Reagan said as much in his speech to an Evangelical Christian group on 8 March, when he stated that a nuclear freeze would be "merely the illusion of peace. The reality is that we must find peace through strength." "The struggle now going on in the world," he went on to explain, "will never be decided by . . . military might. The real crisis we face today is a spiritual one; at its root is a test of moral will and faith" (Goldinger and Thompson 275, 276).

In order to resist the dark side, Luke is guided by one, then two dead patriarchs. At first Obi-Wan Kenobi had introduced Luke to the Force, and then Yoda had instructed him in mastering it. Although Kenobi had died in the first movie, his spirit provides Luke with empowering guidance. In *Return of the Jedi,* the even more ancient and more sage Yoda dies, but not before he tells Luke that Luke will only be a true Jedi after he confronts Darth Vader. In both cases, however, death is primarily a matter of lighting, as both mentors seem to guide and empower Luke from beyond (or actually in front of) the grave. Kenobi also tells Luke that he cannot escape his destiny, that he must confront Vader again, but also acknowledges that Vader is Luke's father, although previously he had told Luke that his father was dead. When Luke accuses Kenobi of having lied to him, Kenobi responds, "What I told you was true, from a certain point of view. Luke, you're going to find that many of the truths we cling to depend greatly on our own point of view."

Thus in Kenobi and Yoda we have two versions of Reagan, both empowered in death. Yoda presents us with the congenial, grandfatherly Reagan, the persona exuding timeless confidence, while Kenobi projects the aspect of Reagan deft at the political manipulation of image, explaining—as Reagan did to the Evangelicals—that truth resides not in material outcomes, but in point of view. The fuzziness of these patriarchs is inextricably connected to their visual presence as vaporous and plastic representations in a world otherwise full of clear, vivid images and shapes, shot in a deep focus that, assisted by computer graphics, seems to extend into the farthest reaches of the universe. While even the numerous furry creatures are visually sharp, Yoda's plastic shape bends in and out of the shadows of a cave in a steamy marsh, and finally dissolves beneath a blanket. Shortly thereafter, Kenobi appears as another blurry figure composed, it seems, of flickering smoke or fog.

Both of Luke's ghostly patriarchs caution against pessimism, against, as they put it, the dangers of the dark side. In essence, the light sabers that are the true weapons of Jedi warriors suggest a merger of renewed phallic power, becoming huge and erect when a fight is in the offing, and the triumph of light over darkness, the virtue of clinging to a point of view that defeats the evil empire with the sunrise forces of morning (in America).

In his final confrontation with Vader, Luke not only resists the dark side but also gets Vader to see the light. Vader then saves Luke's life in the process of sacrificing his own. But that sacrifice, like those of Luke's other patriarchs, is only symbolic, for at the moment of his own funeral, the ghost of Vader returns to join Kenobi and Yoda as empowering presences, the proof that the success against the evil empire comes from finding that "many of the truths we cling to depend greatly on our own point of view." Vader's funeral scene literally converts mourning to morning, complete with the festive ritual celebrations performed by the primitive Ewoks.

This theme that truth is a point of view is echoed in C-3PO's manipulation of the Ewoks. As crude, less civilized, and less-than-human creatures with cannibalistic tendencies, the Ewoks resemble the natives in B-jungle pictures. In this film, so self-consciously steeped in the history of adventure movie conventions, the visual representation of the Ewoks evokes, somewhat nostalgically, Tarzan movies. When they first move in on Luke, Han, Chewbacca, and the droids, the Ewok leaders appear from behind the bushes carrying spears and wearing necklaces and crowns made of teeth; unlike the cuter Ewoks, these leaders have prominent dark red lips, associating them more closely with iconography of African "savages" than that of extra-galactic teddy bears.

Like those natives, they are more swayed by superstition than by good judgment, and hence they easily confuse technology with magic. When they see C-3PO's gold surface, they bow and chant, and then, to the sound of jungle drums, they prepare a feast in C-3PO's honor. When C-3PO convinces them that he will use his magic to destroy the tribe, the Ewoks become submissive. Thus, as in the classic American jungle movies to which this sequence so heavily alludes, the heroes are able to exploit the backwardness of the natives in order to turn them into allies. In this case, the technology that facilitates C-3PO's anthropomorphic accomplishments also enables him to transcend them and to impersonate a deity, despite the fact that, as he explains, "it's against my programming."

The confusion of the natural with the supernatural informs the film consistently as it both exalts technical marvels and evokes or memorializes a simpler past—a time when Darth Vader was a Jedi warrior on the side of the Force, when Kenobi and Yoda were young, when spiritual values were stronger than Death Ships. The ghosts of these fictive times create the mandate for a resistance to new technology that takes the form of newer technology. The Strategic Defense Initiative thus represents a technology necessitated as a protection against the possibility of a technology as universal and omnipotent as the Strategic Defense Initiative. As the overwhelming majority of scientists argued, the science informing Reagan's sense of a Strategic Defense Initiative was cinematic.

A National Politics with Two Brains

A fitting bookend to the conclusion of *King's Row* (1942)—in which Reagan plays an amputee who finds agency in an optimistic narrative that defied the limitations of his physical state—can be found in the Steve Martin movie *The Man with Two Brains*. Like Reagan's autobiography, that film, too, could take its title from Reagan's famous quote in *King's Row*, "Where's the rest of me?" as it suggests what the story confirms—that the second brain is not inherent but rather supplemental, the thing that will complete the lack that the brain surgeon feels because, despite Dr. Michael Hfuhruhurr's (Steve Martin) "superior" brain, despite the abundance of brains he works on and manipulates, something is missing. In this case, Michael, the world's most brilliant brain surgeon, is incomplete because his wife, Rebecca, has died. Despite the miracles he can work on the brains of others, he, himself, remains in an empty, disconsolate state of mind. He can repair any brain but his own. The second of the two brains, in other words, is the brain that can allow his to function adequately.

His inadequacies manifest themselves in a susceptibility to phony narratives. Hence, when his car accidentally strikes Delores (Kathleen Turner), a ruthless fortune hunter who effects the death of her current rich, elderly husband only to learn that he had just written her out of his will, Michael is easily manipulated into falling in love with her. Performing brain surgery on her, despite warnings to the contrary ("No doctor should operate on a person he's just hit"), he assumes the role of her savior. In reality, however, he is her victim. She as easily seduces him into marrying her as she convinces him, even after the wedding, that she is not yet ready for sexual consummation. Thus, like the amputee in *King's Row*, he and his marriage are only half of what they are supposed to be. And although he may be of two minds about that disposition, he only has half a mind to do anything about it. Hence, Delores puts him through a series of tantalizing but unfulfilling scenarios while satisfying herself sexually with a muscle-bound gardener (Russell Orozco). The audience also is of two minds. It is torn between empathizing with the well-meaning boob who is clearly being taken advantage of, and feeling frustration about his allowing himself to be manipulated and misled. While not suggesting a direct allegory of Reaganism, Michael manifests a dogged—and doggedly counter-intuitive—optimism that allows him to ignore even the most blatantly inappropriate conduct and not see that Delores is toying with him, lying to him, taking advantage of him.

This tendency to be oblivious reaches its absurd limits when Michael asks the portrait of his first wife to "just give me a sign . . . any kind of a sign," if there is anything wrong with his affection for Delores. At that point, the house starts trembling, lights flash, and the picture rotates while a woman's voice faintly but desperately cries, "No. No," and the wall fissures. Instead of recognizing the sign, much less heeding it, Michael says again, "Just any kind of sign; I'll keep on the lookout for it. Meanwhile, I'll just put you in the closet."

This form of counter-intuitive behavior—the same sort that informed Reaganomics and led Bush (George I) to call it "voodoo economics" in his 1980 campaign for president against Reagan—is echoed in the mix of pseudo-science and crackpot miracle-working suggested by the cranial screw-top method that Michael uses to perform brain surgery and, later in the film, that Dr. Alfred Necessiter (David Warner) uses to transplant the "thoughts and data from a dying brain" into a living brain without surgery.

Necessiter's process, moreover, makes the present the living repository of the past; it is in one sense a form of nostalgia in that it idealizes a current receptacle for the past, a space in which everything lost can return in a new context. Necessiter is able to do for memory, in other words, what the psychiatrist in *King's Row* was not able to do for Reagan's legs. This sentimental reconstitution of the past is a trait that Michael shares with Reagan, a person who, many have noted, relentlessly sentimentalized an anecdotal, small-town America that existed more vividly in movies such as *King's Row* and *It's a Wonderful Life* (1946) than in the places about which Sherwood Anderson, for example, or Sinclair Lewis wrote.

This is why Michael responds to the brain that speaks to him as a disembodied presence in the room where Necessiter hoards his stockpile. With a question that could serve as a grotesque parody of "Where's the rest of me?" the brain asks Martin, "Will I be able to play the piano again?" And when the brain tells him she is afraid, this brain evokes Michael's obtuse optimism: "Things are never as bad as they seem." The movie—as movies are prone to—proves him right. With the brain in the jar, Delores's body, Necessiter's technology, and Michael's genius, they are able to bring both Michael's sadness over the death of his first wife and his bad marriage to his second wife to a happy ending. The diminished potential for Michael's happiness (not to mention the dim prospects for the brain in a jar) is saved through a new coalition ("This may be the one thing that saves our marriage") based on a resurrection of the sentimental past in the context of an array of cinematic clichés and voodoo science. When the man with two brains thus happily confronts the post-transplant second body—the one based on that of the disavowed wife—he finds that his new version of happiness turns out to be a compulsive eater: "You're not disappointed that I'm so fat?" she asks, to which he responds with the same denial that made this marriage possible: "What fat?"

If *The Man with Two Brains* stands as a metaphor for the willful blindness and double vision that enabled Reaganism optimistically to present a vision of morning in America, part of the implicit sagacity in the presentation drew from Reagan's age and its connection to an older, more powerful narrative of America. That narrative functioned as a form of revisionist history that depended on cinematic technology. That technology and its imaginary control of time and space allowed Reagan and his quintessential Americans to insert themselves simultaneously into an enactment of an idealized past, just as Reagan, who had seen the films of the liberation of Nazi concentration camps, began to announce that he had been present at their filming.

In that regard, therefore, *Zelig* seems almost as important as *Return of the Jedi,* combining as it does revisionist history with a malleable identity. This unique Woody Allen film blends still photographs and actual newsreel footage with grainy black-and-white simulations of those media, as well as contemporary color interviews with New York intellectuals and with actors representing aged versions of the fictional characters portrayed in the contrived footage ostensibly from the 1920s and 1930s. The result is a Ken Burns-style mocumentary that juxtaposes documentary material and "talking heads" commentary, unified by an authoritative voiceover narrator and a selection of period music.

The subject of this mocumentary is Leonard Zelig (Woody Allen), a celebrity in the Jazz Age and the Great Depression because of his astonishing chameleon-like qualities. Zelig, who through a childhood trauma had lost all sense of his own identity, was able to assume not just the personality but the persona, physical traits, and often talents and abilities of whomever he met. Thus sepia photos reveal him in the batter's box at a Yankees game or—looking like a Negro—among the members of a jazz combo. He appears in one photo with Eugene O'Neill and in another performing opera. In Chinatown "in the rear of a Chinese establishment a strange looking Oriental who fits the description of Leonard Zelig is discovered. Suspicious, the detectives try to pull off his disguise, but it is not a disguise, and a fight breaks out. He is removed by force and taken to Manhattan Hospital. In the ambulance, he rants and curses in what sounds like authentic Chinese. . . . When he emerges from the car . . . he is no longer Chinese but Caucasian." When interviewed by Dr. Eudora Fletcher (Mia Farrow), he assumes the persona of a psychiatrist. "It's not that he was making any sense at all," the contemporary Dr. Fletcher tells us. "It was just a conglomeration of psychological double-talk that he apparently heard or

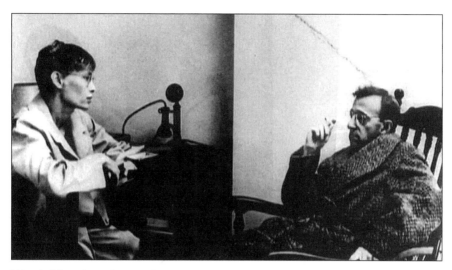

Woody Allen plays a human chameleon in his mocumentary *Zelig* (Orion Pictures), shown here with his therapist (Mia Farrow). Digital frame enlargement.

perhaps was familiar with through reading. The funny thing was that his delivery was quite fluid and really might have been quite convincing to someone who didn't know any better."

Within the first ten minutes of the film, we thus identify a number of Leonard Zelig's cogent traits. He is an accomplished actor, noteworthy not for his histrionic ability but for his unshakable credibility. Rather than create particularly remarkable characters, he performs characters that are remarkably convincing. Delivery rather than logic determines the efficacy of his performance, at least, as Dr. Fletcher points out, for "someone who didn't know any better." The Reaganesque Zelig, in other words, had perfected a style that triumphed over its own double-talk.

Like Reagan, Zelig also engaged in revisionism so effective as to blur the lines between image and reality, for Zelig inhabits not only his array of false personae but also their historical environs, such that he is able to convert imaginative projection into historical presence. But that presence in turn derives its power from film, a point illustrated both thematically and formally. The character of Zelig is, after all, a product of the film *Zelig*, a film that demonstrates the capacity of cinema to insert a fictional presence into a historical past, creating a disruption that alters the way we see that past. In many ways, moreover, Zelig is the essential moviegoer, the person able to identify with the projections of an imaginary elsewhere. He is also, as the film makes clear, the historical subject produced by that identification, the consensus of his environment, his associations, and his culture, as cinema projects those influences. If Zelig is able to remake history in his own image, therefore, it is because everything about him, including his notion of history, is cinematic.

In this regard, *Zelig* is an effective gloss on the success of Reagan's revisionism that merged past and future in a way that transcended contradiction, fact, or physical limitation. Reagan's allusions to *Star Wars* were credible because film provided more than a reference point for Reagan's policies; it provided their source. This anchor in the enduring truth of cinematic representation, it could be argued, gave Reagan the "Teflon" quality that prevented any of his circumstances or statements from sticking to him. The very instability of this quality, moreover, became a staple of Reagan's identity. Zelig similarly acquired a stable public identity based on his instability. Reagan's identification as the Teflon president, in other words, paralleled Zelig's identification as the "human chameleon."

As chameleon, Zelig became not only a popular figure with access to myriad celebrities but also, as the French saw him, "a symbol of everything." And indeed he was—a symbol of everything and of nothing. In the film, he goes through a series of conversions beyond those of his chameleon identity. He becomes a sideshow freak, a missing person, a cured chameleon, and a public spokesperson for anti-chameleon values. He then becomes the subject of national scandals and the target for countless lawsuits, and once again a missing person, only to re-emerge as one of Hitler's henchmen who then escapes from a Munich rally, steals an airplane, and sets a record for flying across the Atlantic upside down. This new feat earns him a full presidential pardon and recognition as "a great inspiration to the youth of this nation."

Zelig is thus about the appropriation of the past by cinema and by history, a point underscored by the inclusion in this mocumentary of footage from what is supposed to be a 1930s Hollywood biopic of Zelig's life. In understanding that the documentary is an inherently redundant genre (e.g., footage illustrates what the narrator articulates and what the "talking heads" affirm [or question]), Allen is expressing the connection between redundancy and the visual composition of cinema, in which something is always passing for something else. *Zelig* turns the story of its hero's passing into the storyboard of itself so that his life, like all cinematic production, is a chronic retelling, the self-referential quality of which is made relentlessly apparent by the film's visual composition, which highlights the relationship between natural and visual texture. Grainy shots juxtapose with the soft lighting of "contemporary" interview sites. In sepia and silvertone black-and-white shots, characters display a conscious self-consciousness to show that they are simultaneously participating in an activity—dancing, golfing—

and in a demonstration of that activity, which is, in turn, a demonstration of documentary convention. All the visual juxtapositions thus compose a catalog that, in their fabrication, demonstrates how history is not a re-cuperation of the past but a performance of conventions. Like Zelig, history itself enacts a fictional morphing and imposturing of the past.

The visual appropriation of the documentary thus becomes identical with its narrative appropriation: the fictional adaptation of the real life of the fictional Leonard Zelig, which was appropriated in its day by the popular media and the general public in several different incarnations, each based on the way in which Zelig appropriated his associations with the public. Novelist Saul Bellow summarizes Zelig's role by explaining that "it was his very disorder that made a hero out of him." But the story of Zelig is as representative as it is anomalous. "It was really absurd in a way," critic Irving Howe states. "He had this curious quirk, this strange characteristic, and for a time everyone loved him and then people stopped loving him, and then he did this stunt with the airplane, and then everyone loved him again, and that's a lot what the Twenties was like, and you know when you think about it, has America changed that much? I don't think so."

The mocumentary, then, resurrects the lost historical figure, Leonard Zelig, as both unique and typical, using him to represent the values of an era and also of something enduringly American. Zelig thus becomes a template for the past, a template that enables us better to comprehend our relationship to it. And to the extent that the fictional story of this fictional character, through the medium of (fictional and documentary) cinematic representation, effectively achieves that goal, our connection to the past is grounded in the amalgam of doctored photos, technically convincing simulations, and fabricated testimonials, supported by the solicited and coached commentary of noted experts and intellectuals. In this context the "expert" commentary by figures such as Bellow, Howe, Susan Sontag, and Bruno Bettelheim asserts Zelig's existence and, simultaneously, their own fictionality, because the merging of Zelig and Sontag puts them on the same plane in the same way that the doctored photographs allow Zelig and Hitler to share the same temporal and physical surface. The film thus affirms the credibility of media representation and the fictionality of Sontag. Just as the images bleed into one another, so too do the referents and the fictional status of Sontag's (or Howe's or Bellow's or Bettelheim's) expertise, a point foregrounded when the real Professor John Morton Blum is identified as the author of a fictitious critical book on Zelig.

Zelig thus exalts the process by which media formally subordinates history and expertise to its fictional goals. Even if this point is meant to be (or succeeds in being) satiric, the uncomfortable relationship between history and representation provides the informing anxiety with which the film wrestles. That anxiety pervaded the Reagan era, as it, like *Zelig*, engaged the legacy of the Great Depression. Zelig's fortunes parallel the nation's, first as a celebrity of the Jazz Age, then as a moral outrage of the thirties, culminating with an ugly identification with fascism. Zelig's ability to turn it all around—literally an *upside-down* flight *back*—allows him to be saved by the actions of President Roosevelt. What proves to be the moment of salvation for Zelig, however, Reaganism turns into the beginning of an American tragedy, for Reaganism vested its credibility in discrediting the New Deal and the growth of the government responsibility, regulation, and size that it initiated. To claim, as Reagan famously did, that government cannot solve problems because government is the problem is to rehistoricize more radically than *Zelig* and, from this year on, far more effectively. Metaphorically, Reagan has to undo Zelig's escape from Hitler to the New Deal by flying upright and full speed in the opposite direction. What both of these improbable flights—toward FDR and away—have in common is their reliance on the effectiveness of cinematic contrivance, their ability simultaneously to enlist and to discredit experts. In both cases, mastery of the medium gives chameleons a stable identity and allows them to serve as models for what the past needs to retain and to disavow.

Nostalgia and Disavowal

A number of the year's films—*Strange Invaders, The Right Stuff,* and *The Big Chill*—serve as templates for the era. The first two promote a nostalgia for the 1950s, in the context of a vision of the future generated from that period. The third provides a renunciation of the cultural revolution of the late 1960s that challenged the values of the 1950s.

Strange Invaders opens with a pastoral shot of the back of a small white house, blocked by trees, with the title "Centerville, 1958" superimposed in white block letters. This is followed by a series of dissolves: the back of the house becomes the house's front on a tree-lined side street, along which a blue (pre-tail fin) sedan passes. That shot dissolves into one of a woman working in a lush garden, and then one of the intersection in a very small town. A 1956 Chevrolet waits at a stop sign while a dog crosses the street and a 1956 Ford turns onto the street. This shot dissolves into one of a road in front of a small farm. Another sedan of pre-'57 vintage drives by. During this sequence, in the same block white letters, the following statement rolls by: "It was a simple time, of Eisenhower, twin beds, and Elvis from the waist up—a safe, quiet moment in history. As a matter of fact, except for the Communists and rock 'n' roll, there was not much to fear. Not much at all . . . until that night."

This description of 1958 combines history and mythology. Although Eisenhower indeed was president, twin beds were not the popular sleeping style and Elvis's body had a lower half. The statement, in other words, describes the 1950s not as lived in America but as seen on American television, a medium that precluded the lower half of Elvis's torso or the furniture in which it might be put to use for purposes other than music. The safety and quiet of the period, too, were the products of television, that medium that provided comfort by idealizing a small-town notion of American life as the ideal repository for the nuclear family at exactly that moment when the population base of the small town was rapidly eroding, and farmland was being turned into suburban developments.

Because tailfins defined auto style in 1957 and 1958, just as rock 'n' roll defined music, their absence is significant. As a repository of pre-1958 values and styles, Centerville marks the 1950s as the culmination, not the commencement of the ideal American life. If the tailfin broke with the stolid, lumpy, confinement of fifties culture, even more significantly it indicated the broader possibility of a radical break with tradition and proved that media had the capacity to popularize with unprecedented speed and ubiquity. The tailfin was to automobile design what rock 'n' roll was to music.

The opening statement, in presenting communism and rock 'n' roll as comparable threats, makes clear that stylistic changes (such as those in music) entailed a political dimension. Connecting the threat of communism with rock 'n' roll emphasizes the music's subversive qualities, its perceived ability to undermine normal American life. The fear of communist subversion has been thematized in many 1950s sci-fi movies, most notably *Invasion of the Body Snatchers* (1956) and *I Married a Monster from Outer Space* (1958), films of the sort to which *Strange Invaders* alludes. If the opening statement invokes the televisual version of 1950s life, the film that follows refers to the sci-fi movies of the 1950s. *Strange Invaders* does not begin in the 1950s, but in a specific cinematic version of that period.

Like *Zelig*, its "reality" is steeped in media-produced versions of the past so that the film's nostalgia is not for the historical past but for its representations. In this light, the strange invaders who arrive one fateful Sunday night while the inhabitants are watching "The Ed Sullivan Show" are more conservative than subversive in that they inhabit all the residents of Centerville while those inhabitants still feared rock 'n' roll, before they could be changed by tailfins, before they could abandon their small-town values not for communism but, as history has shown, for the far more volatile fluidity of suburbia. These strange invaders, by changing nothing—neither hair styles nor cars nor fashion nor values—would preserve the more conservative aspects of 1958 until their revival in the second half of Reagan's first term. Centerville would effectively bridge the gap in American life between that fateful night in 1958 and the dawn of "Morning in America" by preserving the small Illinois town (not far from Reagan's birthplace) just as it was in that moment when Reagan used television to make the transition from actor to spokesman.

This, one could posit, is why in the film the federal government collaborated with the invaders to preserve their secret and keep Centerville isolated for the twenty-five-year span of their inhabitancy. The government agency headed by Mrs. Benjamin (Louise Fletcher) allows the invaders to operate their experimental colony unimpeded for twenty-five years in exchange for valuable information. One of the colony's members, Margaret (Diana Scarwid), however, has married an Earthling, Charles Bigelow (Paul LeMat), and they subsequently had a child, Elizabeth (Lulu Sylbert), before getting an amicable divorce. Now that the aliens are planning to shut down the colony and return to their home planet, they wish to take the girl with them. Margaret, however, wants her to remain on Earth. The preference for Earth over the native habitat of these clearly advanced people is never explained, although the movie offers a suggestion on aesthetic grounds in that by human standards the aliens are extremely ugly, sporting huge eyes, no chin, and reptilian skin. Beyond lies the implicit explanation that America is not only the greatest nation on Earth but also the greatest place in the universe. As Margaret explains to Charles, "I was supposed to find out how things work here, but instead I found a way—the way I wanted to live, and when it didn't work out with you and me, there was still Elizabeth."

That the other aliens do not share Margaret's preference for the American "way" merely attests to their villainy. So too does the fact that the Centerville aliens come to New York dressed as 1950s midwesterners, some disguised as Avon ladies, in order to kidnap Elizabeth. When they succeed, Charles returns to Centerville to try to rescue Elizabeth, assisted by Betty Walker (Nancy Allen), a writer for a *National Enquirer*-type newspaper, and Willie Collins (Michael Lerner), a man who sent a photo of the aliens to her publication after the inhabitants of Centerville abducted his family. These aliens, using electronic lasers, capture humans by turning them into balls of light that emanate a blue glow similar to that emitted by a black-and-white television set. At the end of the film, however, when the alien ship leaves, the captured Americans—those originally inhabited in 1958, those captured during the course of the film, including Willie, and those turned into blue lights in between—are all returned to life, looking just as they did at the moment the aliens captured them. The end of *Strange Invaders* thus marks several returns at once: Elizabeth is returned to her father; Margaret is returned to the aliens; the aliens peacefully return to their home planet; the citizens of Centerville return to life and to their physical condition of twenty-five years earlier; and Willie is returned to life while his family, still in its vitality, is returned to him. Even Charles's dog is returned. Far from being a perverse place, Centerville becomes the site of conservation and rejuvenation. It restores departed friends, family, and pets just as they were before the rise of rock 'n' roll, suburbia, divorce, the sexual revolution, and the Vietnam War. *Strange Invaders* thus rereads the sci-fi films of the 1950s to suggest that they represented a kinder time, when even the manufactured fears were more benign.

The Right Stuff and the Wrong Stuff

As the film's title implies, *The Right Stuff* is also about sorting out the right material in the post-World War II period, focusing, like *Strange Invaders,* on the impact of outer space. Like *Zelig,* it has the qualities of a staged documentary in which actual footage—of the space race or President Kennedy—is intercut with simulations. Like *Zelig,* it also engages the relationship between celebrity and history.

The term "the right stuff" refers to a kind of fortitude that combines mental stamina, physical courage, quiet self-assurance, extraordinary expertise, and unequaled skill. It is the *arête* of test pilots, something "they don't talk about to each other; to outsiders they say less." The embodiment of the right stuff is test pilot Chuck Yeager (Sam Shepard), the first man to break the sound barrier. In 1957, when the Russians launched *Sputnik,* however, the space race started to redefine the meaning of "the right stuff," converting it from a quality to an image. The image of the astronaut as a public figure at the forefront of the Cold War therefore precludes Yeager because he is not a college graduate, and so is unacceptable to the government agenda's of using the astronauts as both role models and spokesmen. As the film repeatedly makes clear, the space race depends less on technology than on funding, and funding depends less on sound science than on effective public relations. Thus, the first seven astronauts become instant celebrities with extensive press coverage. Each earns a large sum by, for example, selling an autobiography (to be ghost-written by a professional reporter) to *Time* magazine. Their press conferences become large publicity events for a space program that still lacks the capacity to launch a manned rocket, that is, to turn the nominal astronauts into actual astronauts. In such a situation, the "right stuff" includes the kind of bravura and self-promotion inimical to the code of test pilots.

Like the automobile tailfins (so meticulously hidden in *Strange Invaders*) that appeared at exactly the same moment as the space race, the space program itself becomes more image than science. Like the astronauts, the program is a "zelig" morphing into the shape of its historical moment. The film attempts to distinguish the real right stuff from the ersatz. As a medium of the ersatz, however, it cannot succeed, despite the manner in which it cuts between the promotion of a national agenda and national heroes. Nor is the problem solved with the film's periodic depictions of Yeager's career from 1947 to 1962, during which time Yeager continues to test the massive jets that constantly push the window of speed and altitude. Wearing denim and leather when off duty, riding horseback in his spare time, living in the rugged western terrain that made parts of California so suitable for filming westerns, Yeager epitomizes the no-nonsense western hero popularized most famously by John Wayne, playing roles for which Ronald Reagan always longed, roles invoked by famous pictures of Reagan riding on horseback at his California ranch.

The last sequence in the film vividly contrasts the two versions of the West developed in the film, that personified by the strong, silent Yeager and that personified by a loud self-promotional Texan, Lyndon Johnson. It impels this contrast by cross-cutting between scenes of a huge party hosted by Vice President Johnson to mark the migration of NASA to Houston and Yeager's attempt to fly a jet more than twenty miles above the Earth's surface. At the climax of the sequence, shots of the jet's failure and free fall alternate with shots of fan dancer Sally Rand entertaining the astronauts, their wives, and thousands of drunken Texans. The sequence concludes with a glimpse of Rand's semi-nude body and then the shot of an ambulance rushing to the crash site to find Yeager, having ejected from the plane, dirty, burnt, and battered, but walking swiftly, with strength and confidence, out of the smoking wreckage on the frontier landscape surrounding Edwards Air Force Base. First seen as a small figure in the distance, then in close-up, looking like a true western hero, Yeager remains the rightful owner of the right stuff, while the astronauts seem very much publicity figureheads.

By the time the film appeared, the distinction implied by the conclusion of *The Right Stuff* was history. Reagan's acting ability had contributed to the demise of that distinction when in the 1950s he became a successful spokesman for General Electric, drawing on his persona as the host of "General Electric Theater" on TV to become an effective speaker before business groups, then becoming credibly associated with the western genre based not primarily on his film credits but on his role as host of the TV western "Death Valley Days." These transitions in Reagan's career took place in roughly the same timeframe as the search for the right stuff to develop the NASA program, that is, when the impact of television (in over 50 percent of households in 1955) would integrate manufactured imagery and dramatic representation into the flow of the home and the practice of everyday life, so that televisual presence would merge with celebrity.

Thus the image of John Glenn—now a U.S. senator and possible opponent for Reagan in 1984—as created by writer-director Philip Kaufman and portrayed by actor Ed Harris, was seen as potentially instrumental in Glenn's candidacy. Like *Zelig,* therefore, the film was a form of self-commentary in that it identified the moment in which its own story would become a form of mediation. Expertise in both films becomes a type of fictional representation, and fictional representation becomes hard to distinguish from expertise. In the end, therefore, *The Right Stuff* is a template that privileges the image of the cowboy—the enacting of which was a leisure activity that Reagan and Yeager (whose names are almost anagrams of one another) shared—over the image of the astronaut. One possible result of applying that template was concluding that Reagan better projected the image of a leader than did Glenn.

In different ways, as seen from a future informed by the restoration of a Jedi empire, both *Strange Invaders* and *The Right Stuff* put forth a conservative agenda by indicating what values ought be preserved, what traditions draw upon, as America confronts the space age; they are the western values of the strong, silent cowboy and the sentimental family values of the anecdotal small town.

To these, *The Big Chill* provides a complementary gloss on what needs to be disavowed. The film reunites six University of Michigan alums a dozen years after graduation for a weekend following the funeral of Alex, another member of their clique, who had committed suicide.

All the rest have achieved remarkable financial success in an astonishingly short time. Meg (Mary Kay Place), just about eight years out of law school, after spending a period as a public defender, has become a successful L.A. corporate lawyer. Michael (Jeff Goldblum), after briefly teaching in Harlem, has become a feature writer for *People* magazine. Karen (Jo Beth Williams) is married to a successful businessman, and Sam (Tom

The Big Chill (Lawrence Kasdan, Columbia Pictures), with an ensemble cast including Glenn Close and Kevin Kline, reflects on the continuity of 1960s-era liberal values in the 1980s. Digital frame enlargement.

Berenger) stars in a hit television adventure show. Sarah (Glenn Close), an M.D., is married to Harold (Kevin Kline), who owns an athletic shoe company that is about to go public. Even Nick (William Hurt), who was rendered impotent by a Vietnam injury, became, while still in his twenties, a successful San Francisco radio personality giving on-air advice to callers. Hearing a tape of one of his shows, Nick realized that after listening to "someone in real pain" for about forty-five seconds, he was giving advice "like I know them and understand and have something useful to say about their lives, and the worst part was they believed me." Nick quit the next day and went on to become a successful, Porsche-driving, high-end drug dealer. All these people in their mid-thirties have incomes easily between the 90th and 99th percentile of American households. As a composite, they exemplify the cutting edge of that demographic group that began to emerge this year: the yuppie. Hard-working and relentlessly materialistic, this group of fast-trackers may in many cases have differed with Reagan philosophically but nevertheless gained significantly from his tax cuts and his shifting the tax burden away from corporate and personal income tax and onto payroll tax.

To enjoy the economic upswing that began this year, therefore, they had to divorce their social beliefs from their self-interests. They needed to reevaluate the period between the dawn of the space age and the initiation of the "Star Wars" Strategic Defense Initiative. *The Big Chill* allowed exactly that. For each of the members gathered at Harold and Sarah's mansion, Alex allegedly represents some best version of themselves. As Sarah says over a pasta dinner, while tearfully regretting that Alex is not there, "I feel that I was at my best when I was with you people," to which Sam responds, "I know what you mean, Sarah. When I lost touch with this group, I lost my idea of what I should be. . . . Maybe that's what happened to Alex. At least we expected something of each other then. I think we needed that." Alex is thus both the center of the group—the reference point they all lost—and its most marginal member, the one least able to survive without the others. The film thus seems to oscillate indecisively: Alex epitomized the right stuff or he epitomized the lack of it.

Perhaps that is the reason the film carefully avoids—as though they were *Strange Invaders*'s problematic tailfins—articulations of Alex's actual views. For all of their allusions to their former "radical" selves, these yuppies shun the specifics of politics either past or present. Apparently television star Sam once spoke before thousands of students, but even at that time the deceased Alex was unimpressed: "You remember—Alex used to call me Sam the Sham," Sam reminds Karen. "Don't say that," she responds. "It was real. I remember standing on campus with thousands of people listening to you. You really moved them." The nature of the event— a homecoming rally? a student strike? an election debate for president of the Inter-Fraternity Council?—remains unclear, nor do we have any hint as to the content of Sam's moving speech. Even Harold's shoe company, "Running Dog," casually commodifies a Marxist slogan.

This vagueness seems intentionally generic. Whatever Sam had said, it was in some way political and on that ground alone it must be disavowed in a Reaganesque world that puts political interrogation at odds with material success. Thus, when Sam says that now he is "reaching millions of people every week and, aw hell, you know it's just garbage," Karen once again dismisses the importance of articulating political positions: "That's not true. You're entertaining people. God knows we need that now."

The film never explains why entertainment is more important now, or what distinguishes that historical moment from the time when entertainment was less important than public statements that moved thousands (even though Alex found them insincere). For the film to attempt such explanations would be to open up the possibility that politics could matter, the possibility that political beliefs could be connected to one's sense of identity, rather than being a hobby or emotional souvenir. As Sarah says at that pasta dinner, "I'd hate to think that [our commitment] was all just fashion." When Meg adds, "Sometimes I think I just put that time down, pretended it wasn't real, just so I could live with how I am now," Harold asks Nick to help him "with all these bleeding hearts." The film carefully avoids completing the cliché "bleeding heart liberals," for even that positioning represents a level of commitment untenable in *The Big Chill*. Omissions such as these make clear that the film regards commitment as a fashion, whether or not the 1969 Sarah did.

Even more telling is the conclusion of the pasta dinner, when Harold plays a Motown LP, "Ain't Too Proud to Beg," and everyone starts dancing in what becomes a montage representation of the cleanup after dinner. This is one of many instances in the film when a dominant song organizes a sequence of disparate events. At the outset, for example, the film cuts among the group of Alex's friends, each implicitly responding to the news of his death; each friend is shown in close-up, followed either by cuts or pans to close-ups of something they are doing with their hands—putting down a glass, filling an attaché case, digging through papers on a messy desk—and then a pan up to the face as the camera slowly pulls back. These short sequences are punctuated with cuts to very close shots of hands dressing portions of Alex's corpse for the funeral. With slight variations, we go through this pattern several times, while the song "I Heard It Through the Grapevine" plays virtually in its entirety. At the recessional from Alex's funeral, "You Can't Always Get What You Want" is used similarly to unite shots of people leaving the funeral, riding in several separate cars. These sequences, like many others in the film, are distinctive because the music is not being used to underscore—or even to narrate—the film; rather, the shots are being sequenced to illustrate the song. They are conforming, in other words, to the conventions of the music video, that medium that, thanks to the meteoric rise, this year, of the MTV network, would set the fashion for music entertainment. The film's proliferation of music videos—often used even to frame dialogue—thus manifests exactly what Sarah feared, that it "was all just fashion."

What makes Sam a sham, therefore, from the film's perspective, is not a lack of political commitment but the fact that he once believed politics could mean more than entertainment, that he did not understand the importance of mainstream media, a misunderstanding clearly corrected—for the audience at least—by the fact that the film reduces his existence into an image in a series of music videos. Nevertheless, even now he is not certain about the value of entertainment: "Well I try. I mean I try at least once every show to put something of value in there . . . but I don't know. . . ." "You do," Karen assures him, "I can see it. I feel my kids have really got something from 'J.T. Lancer.'" Politics has shifted for these yuppies from a national agenda to a television script, one of many indications that they don't really miss Alex at all, for in order to enjoy the tax cuts aimed at people in Sam's and Karen's bracket, it was necessary to avoid asking who would pay off the astronomical national debt and from which social services money would be diverted in order to meet the debt's interest payments. While a nation's overall standard of living might depend on specific political decisions, enjoying the yuppie lifestyle required merely reciting the Reagan mantra that government cannot solve every problem because government is the problem, and then accumulating wealth by whatever means available.

As a result, the film can allow Nick to use insider trading—an illegal tip supplied by Harold—to finance his exit from the drug trade and, implicitly, to shake his drug habit, in the same way that *Trading Places* allowed illegal commodities information to rectify problems of poverty and racism. For many, especially those who don't have the capital to benefit from insider trading tips, drug addiction is not merely a consumer option or a career choice that can be dropped with the same facility that Michael can move from a Harlem school to the staff of *People*. Alex's funeral therefore ultimately allows the owners of these big, chilled, 1983 egos to turn Alex's suicide—his rejection of them—into their rejection of him. Before he died, Meg had told him that he was wasting his life, summarizing the lesson of natural selection that all these yuppies come to learn in the process of rationalizing their narcissistic greed: Alex's lack of commercial success demonstrated his lack of adaptability.

Lack of adaptability, in the world of Reaganism, is a mortal sin. Each of the films I have discussed deals with some version of natural selection. It is this process that allows the Jedi, finally, to triumph. It underlies the metaphor of selective breeding involved in the matching of the right brain to the right body in *The Man with Two Brains* and that produces the little girl in *Strange Invaders* endowed with her father's human genes and her mother's extraterrestrial powers. It is the concept being tested by the Dukes that sets events in motion in *Trading Places*. Adaptability is what *Zelig* is all about, and natural selection is the principle behind the concept of "the right stuff." The assumption that they have been chosen by nature to be so successful, I believe, underlies the smug sentimentalism of *The Big Chill*'s yuppies. The last episode of the film, in fact, involves an act of selective breeding, wherein Sarah gets her husband to impregnate their friend Meg, who has been searching for the ideal father for her as-yet-unconceived child. Implicitly this child, the result of superior breeding, will compensate for the loss of Alex, whom they all loved, even though he did not have the mettle to survive. *The Big Chill*'s yuppies never acknowledge another possibility—that Alex's death did not signify an absence of the right stuff but a symptom of Reaganism. Perhaps Alex killed himself when he realized that being Zelig would not solve every problem; being Zelig was the problem.

1984

Movies and Battles over Reaganite Conservatism

RHONDA HAMMER AND DOUGLAS KELLNER

In November Ronald Reagan was reelected as president of the United States in a landslide. It was perhaps the high point of Reaganite conservatism, and many popular films of the period articulated conservative discourses associated with Reaganism. The former Hollywood movie actor frequently used film phrases and quotations to promote his conservative agenda, as when he called the Soviet Union "the Evil Empire." Further, his spaced-based missile defense program was popularly referred to as "Star Wars," drawing on discourse from George Lucas's immensely popular films. Reagan also would directly quote Dirty Harry's famous phrase, "Make my day," to threaten a veto against Democrats in Congress in 1985. He later used allusions to Rambo to justify his aggressive foreign policy, and in 1983 claimed "the Force is with us," appealing both to Hollywood movie fans and his conservative Christian base.

Ninety-eighty four is the title year of George Orwell's famous novel, leading to speculation in academia and the popular press as to whether Orwell's prophesies had been correct.[1] Appropriately, one may detect in U.S. films of the year, across a diversity of genres, Orwellian and dystopic visions of totalitarianism, technological surveillance and domination, social conformity, escalation of government repression, and suppression of human rights and democracy. At the same time, Reaganism was strongly contested in both the political and cultural spheres. The films of the year contain much opposition to Reaganism and conservatism, and Hollywood films were a contested terrain between conservatives, liberals, and radicals represented in cinematic culture.

It was an unusually rich year for U.S. film culture, exhibiting an eclectic mix and diverse breadth. A partial list of films represents the work of some of the most accomplished and respected auteurs of the era, including *Amadeus,* Milos Forman's portrayal of the Mozart-Salieri rivalry; *A Passage to India,* David Lean's epic presentation of E. M. Forster's novel; *The Killing*

Fields, Roland Joffé's portrayal of the Cambodian tragedy during the early 1970s; Ismail Merchant and James Ivory's adaptation of Henry James's novel *The Bostonians*; Sergio Leone's masterful epic *Once Upon a Time in America*; Francis Ford Coppola's impressive reworking of the gangster film in *The Cotton Club*; Norman Jewison's serious examination of U.S. race relations in the military circa World War II in *A Soldier's Story*; Woody Allen's homage to the New York entertainment industry in *Broadway Danny Rose*; Wim Wenders's disconcerting *Paris, Texas*; Barry Levinson's interrogation of baseball and sexual politics in *The Natural*; Robert Zemeckis's high adventure *Romancing the Stone*; and Robert Altman's critical dissection of Richard Nixon's disintegrating psyche in *Secret Honor*.

These films indicate the global nature of contemporary cinematic culture, drawing on major directors, actors, and talent from throughout the world. The year was also especially rich for independent film in the United States, including John Sayles's critical version of the science fiction film *Brother from Another Planet*; Rob Reiner's clever deconstruction of the rock music genre *This Is Spinal Tap*; Jim Jarmusch's fiercely independent *Stranger Than Paradise*; Alex Cox's searing look at the American underclass, *Repo Man,* a reworking of the codes of youth film and science fiction film; and Gregory Nava's multicultural epic *El Norte*. It was also a good year for documentaries, with Robert Epstein's probing *The Times of Harvey Milk* winning an Academy Award and much praise bestowed on John Scagliotti and Greta Schiller's *Before Stonewall* and Martin Bell's *Streetwise,* both featuring riveting portraits of groups (gays and homeless street kids) not usually visible in Reagan's America.

Throughout Hollywood productions of the period, there are a number of recurring themes in major and minor films that articulate the key events and sociopolitical and economic relations of the time. Indeed, many of these films resonate, and can be reread, within the history of major political conflicts of their period. In general, films can display social realities of the time in documentary and realist fashion, directly representing events and phenomena of an epoch. But films can also provide symbolic-allegorical representations that interpret, comment on, and indirectly portray realities of an era, as well as its dreams and nightmares. Finally, there is an aesthetic and anticipatory dimension to films in which they provide artistic visions of the world that might transcend the social context of the moment and articulate future possibilities, hopes, or nightmares.

We draw on history and social theory to analyze the films of 1984 and use the films in turn to illuminate historical trends, conflicts, possibilities, and anxieties. From this diagnostic perspective, Hollywood films provide important insights into the psychological, sociopolitical, and ideological make-up of U.S. society at a given point in history. Reading films diagnostically allows one to gain insights into social problems and conflicts, and to appraise the dominant ideologies and emergent oppositional forces. Moreover, diagnostic critique enables one to perceive the limitations and pathologies of mainstream conservative and liberal political ideologies, as well as oppositional ones (see Kellner, *Media Culture* 116–17). Our approach thus involves a dialectic of text and context, using texts to read social realities and context to help situate and interpret key films.

Film and History

While Reagan was cruising toward a second term, another conservative, Prime Minister Margaret Thatcher of Great Britain, was firmly entrenched in office, and in Canada, the long-established Liberal Party was defeated in a conservative sweep led by incoming prime minister Brian Mulroney. At the same time, with wars in Central America, fierce debates over the U.S. deployment of nuclear weapons in Europe, and increased military spending in the United States and Soviet Union, the Cold War was heating up.

American films of 1984 articulated firm anticommunist and anti-Soviet attitudes. *Red Dawn* depicts a Soviet invasion of the United States met by guerilla resistance in the form of midwestern teenagers. *Moscow on the Hudson,* the story of a Russian musician (Robin Williams) defecting to the United States in Bloomingdale's during a trip to New York, portrays Soviet society as a bleak, dreary dictatorship, with no freedom of speech or even adequate consumer goods (in the first scene Russians are shown queuing up for toilet paper). And James Cameron's *The Terminator* can be read as a fear of faceless, robotic totalitarian monsters taking over and destroying the United States.

Hollywood's anticommunism was hardly restricted to films referencing the Soviet Union. The defeat of the United States in the Vietnam War continued to haunt the American psyche, and films portrayed a distrust of communists in Vietnam, China, and elsewhere. *The Killing Fields* recounts the horrendous genocide perpetrated by the Pol Pot regime in Cambodia that forced millions to relocate into the countryside and killed countless others who refused to conform to a rigid communist ideology. *Missing in Action* continues the "return to Vietnam" cycle, begun in *Uncommon Valor* (1983), while *Indiana Jones and the Temple of Doom* presents extremely racist representations of "Orientals."

Anti-Chinese sentiments and fears were further aggravated by the signing of an agreement by the United Kingdom and the People's Republic to return Hong Kong to China in 1997 when Great Britain's ninety-nine-year lease would expire (although the Chinese agreed to maintain Hong Kong's capitalist system). Moreover, economic prosperity in both Asian communist and capitalist domains was rising as the United States and other Western nations were in decline. There were increasing fears of Japanese economic domination, especially in the automotive and electronics sector; many people also perceived not only Japanese cars as superior to American models but also the Japanese corporate culture. In *Gremlins,* rapidly proliferating monsters, apparently from the East, terrorize small-town America. *A Passage to India* shows the East as highly exotic and completely Other to the West, with dangerous seductive and destructive cultural aspects.

Meanwhile, guerrilla movements, many of them espousing socialist and revolutionary ideals, continued to threaten U.S. hegemony in the Americas. The Reagan administration supported right-wing dictatorial regimes in Central and South America, with the CIA aiding government forces that operated death squads in El Salvador, while also sustaining right-wing terrorist units, known as "contras," to overthrow the legitimately elected socialist-oriented Sandinistas in Nicaragua. *El Norte* indirectly represents the effect of Reagan's policies in its depiction of the murder of a Guatemalan peasant, killed for his association with a labor organization, whose children are forced to flee to the United States. A sequel to Stanley Kubrick's *2001* (1968), *2010* provides a cautionary warning that U.S.-Soviet confrontation in Central America could lead to nuclear war and argues for detente and cooperation among the superpowers in a story of how U.S.-Soviet cooperation in space saves the world from catastrophe.

In March, Islamic terrorists kidnapped the CIA station chief in Beirut and attacked the American embassy there, leading the Reagan administration to withdraw the Sixth Fleet from international peacekeeping forces due to escalating dangers to U.S. installations. George Roy Hill's *The Little Drummer Girl* is one of a cycle of films of the epoch that presents terrorists as utterly venal and amoral, reproducing discourses of the Reagan administration that link terrorism and communism as the worst menace to freedom and democracy in the world.

In one of the worst industrial disasters in modern times, a toxic gas leak from the U.S. transnational Union Carbide Plant in Bhopol, India, killed 2,000 people and injured over 150,000. During the fierce Iran-Iraq war of the 1980s, Saddam Hussein employed chemical weapons, in part thanks to the loans and technology provided by the United States (Kellner *Media Spec-*

tacle). Fears of technology out of control are addressed in *Gremlins*, spoofed in *Ghost Busters*, and on display in *The Terminator* as well as the anti-nuclear films mentioned above.

However, it was not only chemical spills and weapons that posed serious threats to global peace and survival. French scientists isolated the AIDS virus, which had reached pandemic scope. Although over 7,000 cases had been reported in the United States, President Reagan refused to acknowledge its presence until his wife induced him to recognize the problem in 1987. No Hollywood films of 1984 explicitly address AIDS, but fears of sexuality out of control are evident in the "slasher" horror cycle, discussed below.

Reagan's secrecy on AIDS, foreign policy, and other matters reflects what many have identified as a tendency to evade and misrepresent certain dangers to the country while exaggerating others. Some have argued that the success of Reagan's reelection campaign was due in large part to his positive presentation of his administration's right-wing policies and his ability to exaggerate fears of communism and terrorism (Kellner *Television*). Employing the kinds of rhetoric made infamous in Orwell's *1984*, Reagan, in conjunction with a massive media propaganda operation, managed to convince a majority of Americans that it was "morning again in America" (his feel-good campaign theme). The central missions of his campaign were to reassure Americans that the United States had returned to the position of leader of the free world and that his policies had produced national prosperity, democratic freedom, and economic strength.

Although there was a marginal economic recovery, the Reagan presidency had in reality contributed to the long-term weakening of the U.S. economy. In his first term in office Reagan's fiscal policies nearly doubled the national deficit, which reached a record $200 billion this year. The rising deficit was due in large part to massive increases in military spending as well as tax breaks for large corporations and the wealthy. Funding for social programs, health care, and education were also slashed during Reagan's watch. Consequently, disparities between the rich and the poor were accelerating, foreclosures and property loss were on the rise, interest rates were high, unemployment was widespread, and greater numbers of Americans were living in poverty—41 million by year's end.

A cycle of "Save the Farm" movies put on display one of the sectors harmed by Reaganomics. In *The River*, Tom Garvey (Mel Gibson) is forced to leave his family and join scabs who cross picket lines so he can earn money to save his family's farm. *Places in the Heart* goes back to the 1930s for a story of a family farm in crisis, while *Country* shows a contemporary family in danger of losing its farm. By contrast, independent films, like *El Norte,* put on display the poverty and suffering of marginalized peoples, while the documentary *Streetwise* depicts the growing homelessness of the period and *Repo Man* shows the expanding urban underclass (see below).

As noted, Hollywood films supported but also criticized the dominant political values of the period. In the following analyses, we discuss films that articulate the regnant conservative values associated with Reaganism, opposed by some films that undermine or contest the conservative hegemony.

Militarism, Patriarchy, and Reaction in Reaganite Cinema and Its Contestations

During the 1980s, families of missing vets and veterans groups focused attentions on U.S. soldiers who fought in Vietnam and who Ross Perot and others claimed were being held in prison camps in Indochina. *Missing in Action* shows an American superwarrior returning to Vietnam to rescue American prisoners. This time "good" Americans triumph over "evil" Vietnamese, a formula that provides a compensatory fantasy of victory over communism denied in the Vietnam War. The film shows a communist regime as repressive and tyrannical and thus vindicates those who claimed that the United States was fighting for democracy and freedom in Indochina—arguments made explicitly in the mid-1980s by the Reagan administration.

The second highest grossing film of the year, *Indiana Jones and the Temple of Doom,* offers an imperialist and racist representation of Asians. Produced by George Lucas and directed by Steven Spielberg, the story features the search for a magical stone stolen from a village in India that is being appropriated as part of a vicious sacrificial religious cult, called Kali, which threatens to destroy Christianity and the Western world. Developing world people are presented as either vicious killers and barbaric sadists out to destroy Indy and his friends, or as helpless slaves, children no less, whom Indy must liberate. This paternalistic fantasy thus legitimates neo-imperialist domination by "good" westerners who supposedly save subjugated people from "bad" totalitarians. One of Indy's sidekicks, an Asian boy called "Short Round" (Jonathan Ke Quan), who often refers to Indy as "Dr. Jones," presents a figure of the "good" Third Worlder, adoringly devoted to his White God Master. Much of the film is shot from his point of view, which functions to invite children and people of the developing world to identify with Indy's heroics.

Indiana Jones and the Temple of Doom (Steven Spielberg, Paramount), starring Harrison Ford, uses the style of 1930s adventure serials to offer an imperial vision of America's role overseas. Jerry Ohlinger's Movie Material Store.

Temple of Doom follows the form of 1930s serials, featuring one rapid and violent adventure sequence after another, at breakneck pace from beginning to end. The central feature of the film is its racist-tinged spectacle. The story opens in a 1935 Shanghai nightclub, where American cabaret entertainer Willie Scott (Kate Capshaw) is backed by a chorus line of Asian women in blonde wigs performing Cole Porter's "Anything Goes," in a depiction of U.S. cultural hegemony. The opening scenes in Shanghai utilize the stereotype of the depraved, treacherous "Oriental" who swindles Jones out of a statue that he has procured and then proceeds to try to murder him. Indy, Willie, and Short Round escape, and after a wild chase through Shanghai's streets, they commandeer a plane and bail out, without parachutes, in a remote mountain region of the Himalayas. Once in India, the racism on display intensifies: peasant villagers are depicted as starving and helpless primitives unable to take care of themselves. The Kali cult represents easterners as superstitious, violent, and bloodthirsty, lusting after human sacrifices, and as oppressive exploiters of slaves. Even the humor is racist: at a royal dinner, live eels, insects, and chilled monkey heads are served to the disgust of the westerners, especially the squeamish woman.

People of the developing world are thus depicted in the film as backward, superstitious, and helpless, in need of White Fathers and Protectors. Indiana Jones, by contrast, is shown as completely self-effacing and benevolent. Although he tells the woman accompanying him that he is pursuing the magic stone for "fortune and glory," at the end he returns it to the villagers, noting that it would be just another stone in a museum but is the center of village life in India. This image of the selfless and generous westerner is especially cruel and callous in the face of the actual exploitation and violence inflicted upon the developing world by the West.

In *Temple of Doom,* escapist fantasy and hero myths are thus put into the service of imperialist ideologies. Sexual representations are equally retrogressive. Whereas the heroine Marion Ravenwood (Karen Allen) in the original Indiana Jones movie, *Raiders of the Lost Ark* (1981), showed at least some agency and was provided a modicum of egalitarian status, Willie in *Temple of Doom* screams and whines incessantly at the sight of an insect or the breaking of her manicured nail. She and Indy constantly bicker, and she is repeatedly rescued by him and/or swoons over him.

John Milius's *Red Dawn* offers a compendium of the period's anticommunist anxieties. The film appeared during a period of intense debate over Reagan's support of the Nicaraguan contras, accompanied by a military build-up and hostile posture toward the Soviet Union. *Red Dawn* presents a coalition of Latin American revolutionary groups and Soviet troops, spurred by Russian grain shortages and a U.S. grain embargo, who invade the United States and initiate World War III, thus embodying Reagan's warning that if we didn't fight the communists in Nicaragua, we would have to fight them in Texas.

The film opens with titles on screen narrating a right-wing nightmare of communists taking over large sectors of the world while the United States is completely isolated. Ponderous Germanic music accompanies images of clouds and sky, and the camera zooms down to a mountain vista—all aggressively fascist images culled from the work of Nazi filmmaker Leni Riefenstahl. This opening homage to her 1935 film *The Triumph*

In *Red Dawn* (John Milius, United Artists), the archetypal film of the new Cold War, the Soviets invade America and must contend with a group of unruly high school guerilla fighters (Patrick Swayze, C. Thomas Howell, Charlie Sheen). Jerry Ohlinger's Movie Material Store.

of the Will clearly signals the ultraconservative nature of Milius's vision, as does the teenage guerilla fighters' ritual drinking of a deer's blood as proof of one's warrior manhood, which refers to the Nazi fetishizing of powerful animals and blood. The ritual elaborates an idea that human life is primitivist, a struggle for survival. The Nazi glorification of nature appears at those moments when Milius's camera meditates on nature as a still, immense, and glorious presence, although the young teenage guerrilla fighters will have to learn to survive its rigors as well as partake of its energies.

Milius sets up the communist invaders as barbaric hordes and faceless killing machines by introducing them as they murder a black high school teacher and his students in cold blood during a lecture on Genghis Khan. Later the villainous leaders are shown as stereotypical Cuban and Soviet communists, although, as we shall see, a more complex figure of the Cuban communist, Colonel Bella (Ron O'Neal), is also developed.

Red Dawn employs comic book caricature, pedestrian shooting and editing, cheap studio sets, and schlocky music to depict the ways that the communists have set up a police state, drawing on the earlier codes of the anticommunist genre that was a staple of Hollywood film during the late

1940s and early 1950s. There are images of individuals torn from their houses, marched through the streets, and interned in concentration camps. Other scenes portray in rapid montage book burning, the local movie theater playing Russian films, posters of Lenin, and gun owners rounded up into concentration camps with faces framed in close-ups behind barbed wire. In a nod to the National Rifle Association, the plot suggests that the Russians were easily able to arrest gun owners, after the citizens of the town were forced to register their firearms. Indeed, a bumper sticker is shown with a slogan immortalized by Charlton Heston: "They can have my gun when they pry it from my cold, dead hand!"—and indeed, in one image we see a gun being pried by a communist invader from a dead hand.

The militarist-masculinist scenario of *Red Dawn* is enacted through scenes that transform a small group of teenagers into partisan resistance fighters, and in doing so the film attempts the daring feat of recuperating for the Right the figure of the heroic revolutionary freedom fighter. This was an icon that played a central role in sixties leftist mythology in the form of Che Guevara, the Viet Cong, and others, but which the Reagan administration was trying to seize for the Right in its attempt to present U.S.-funded Nicaraguan terrorists as "freedom fighters." Yet in making the Cuban communist Colonel Bella the emblem of a bold revolutionary, Milius undercuts his right-wing comic book anticommunism, as when the Cuban notes that he was used to being on the side of insurgents and not the occupying forces. In a scene with a Russian officer, Bella tells him that he was once "an insurgent. Now I'm a policeman."[2] In a key scene near the end of the film Bella recognizes the valor of the teen guerrilla leader, Jed (Patrick Swayze), and allows him to slip away, one warrior acknowledging the other.

Yet *Red Dawn* puts on display the awful burdens of both occupation and resistance, showing the ways both sides are forced into compromises and must live with constant fear of death and the need to kill. From the beginning, the supposedly democratic American teenage freedom fighters are highly authoritarian, as when in a key early scene, Jed refuses to allow democratic voting and beats up a liberal high school student who opposes him. We are supposed to sympathize with Jed's "strength" and to see democracy as the ploy of weak, self-interested liberals. The student's father, mayor of the town, collaborates with the communist occupiers, and the son eventually betrays the teen resistance group, positioning politicians as craven cowards with no patriotic ideals.

Russians are depicted as rapists while the teen guerrillas are presented as completely chaste and ascetic. The young women quickly lose their femininity and become warriors accepted into the resistance fraternity. In fact, when one of the women breaks down and tells a hardened U.S. soldier who has joined them how she is desperate for love, she is narratively punished by being shot and killed. Milius's film thus focuses on libertarian masculinism, male bonding, and survivalism.

Nominated for seven Academy Awards, Roland Joffé's *The Killing Fields* is a much more sophisticated and serious film than *Red Dawn,* although it puts on display some of the same strong anticommunist impulses while exhibiting the fissures and contradictions of liberalism. Drawing on *New York Times* reporter Sydney Schanberg's Pulitzer Prize–winning story "The Death and Life of Dith Pran," the film focuses on the relationship between Schanberg (Sam Waterston) and his Cambodian interpreter Dith Pran (Dr. Haing S. Ngor).

Joffé uses the techniques of epic realism in portraying the aftermath of the disastrous U.S. intervention in Vietnam and the secret U.S. bombing campaign in Cambodia. The film opens with a picture of a young boy on a water buffalo in a rice paddy, and a collage of images unfold of a beautiful and peaceful Cambodian countryside that is soon to be ravaged with the horrors of war. Chris Menges's superb cinematography and Jim Clark's editing capture the confusion, chaos, and destructiveness of war, and the haunting sound track combines Western and Asian music with heightened natural acoustics and strange and disconcerting electronic effects.

Schanberg arrives alone in an airport while his photographer, Al Rockoff (John Malkovich), is asleep and hung over in a seedy hotel room. When the two go to an outdoor café for breakfast a terrorist bomb explodes nearby, transforming Rockoff from a babbling eccentric into a highly professional photographer, as he snaps up and begins shooting the carnage. Schanberg's translator Dith Pran breathlessly arrives and tells of reports of U.S. bombing of a civilian village with heavy casualties. He and Schanberg improvise their way to the site, but U.S. embassy and military officials, with reporters in tow, arrive first and cover up the atrocities. The honorable media are thus positioned as the voices of truth against manipulative and mendacious officials, although one U.S. embassy official, played by Spalding Gray, is sympathetic.

Reports circulate that the feared Khmer Rouge is advancing quickly toward the capital where two million refugees have fled, and suddenly journalists, politicians, the military, and civilians are all caught up in the chaos of war. Joffe uses quick jarring cuts, eccentric framing, discordant and operatic music, and slow, sweeping shots of devastation, displaced masses, and mounds of skeletons to capture the horrors and confusions of war.

In an early chaotic evacuation scene, Dith Pran stays behind with the Western journalists, insisting, "Sydney, I'm a journalist too," while U.S. embassy and military figures, his wife and child, and other Cambodian dependents are evacuated under heavy gunfire. At first, the Khmer Rouge are shown as shadowy figures fighting the regular Cambodian army, or as terrorists blowing up a Coca-Cola factory, but as the Khmer Rouge encircles the capital, Phnom Penh, fear begins to mount. Initially, their young troops are received as an army of liberation, but the mood soon changes as atrocities mount and mass arrests are made, forcing the journalists to seek refuge in the French consulate. A ploy to manufacture Dith Pran a fake British passport fails, and he is left behind after the other journalists are allowed to leave.

Reaction shots of the faces of the journalists record the unspeakable horror that they witness and make the horrific events credible. The film changes focus and rhythm as Dith Pran is arrested and incarcerated for his work with the Americans and becomes witness to the atrocities of the Cambodian Year Zero, in which millions were brutally driven to the countryside, incarcerated into "re-education" camps, or murdered in a bloodbath that took between two and three million lives. In the chaos of the Khmer Rouge revolution, Dith Pran practically starves in labor camps, is forced to watch children brutally indoctrinated, and in trying to escape stumbles into a pit of skulls and skeletons in the notorious Cambodian "killing fields." The high percentage of very young soldiers in the Khmer Rouge and the indoctrination camps for children evoke reminiscences of Nazi youth denouncing their parents, and indeed one child exposes Dith Pran's cherished vegetable garden, which is then destroyed. According to one film character, half of the Khmer Rouge were under fifteen, putting on display the often hidden realities of children conscripted into developing world armies.

During the latter third of the film, focus shifts between Dith Pran's agonies and efforts to escape and Schanberg's receiving journalistic awards for his Cambodian reporting and his desperate attempts to find news of Dith Pran. A mixture of cunning, skill, courage, perseverance, luck, and chance enables Dith Pran to escape and be reunited with Schanberg after four terrible years.

The Killing Fields celebrates "good" individuals while criticizing brutal war and the totalitarianism of the Pol Pot regime. But it bifurcates Cambodians into either good opponents of the Khmer Rouge and allies of the protagonists or evil communist butchers. By contrast, the Western journalists have highly differentiated personalities, although all are positively portrayed as courageous seekers of the truth who bond together to try to tell the world about the horrible events in Cambodia.

While the film makes clear the responsibility of U.S. bombing in triggering chaos in Cambodia, it tends to blame the catastrophe on the actions of Richard Nixon alone, rather than investigating the complexities of the political situation and the ways that post–World War II U.S. militarism and an imperialistic foreign policy in Southeast Asia contributed to the disaster. One news report shown in the background, for instance, interprets the events as the "purest expression of Nixon doctrine," as if war were an emanation of Nixon rather than U.S. policy over several administrations.

The film does not, however, comprehend the Khmer Rouge, which is presented as pure evil, although a few good Cambodians are able to extricate themselves and show acts of kindness to Dith Pran. Cambodia is as strange, unknowable, exotic, and foreign in the film's final images as it was in the beginning, since the events were shown to be overwhelming, chaotic, a force of nature and horror, without intelligible logic—a point Joffe, who saw the war as an inexplicable chaos of irrational events, emphasizes in his remarkable commentary on the film's DVD release.

The Killing Fields is ultimately a male love story celebrating a great friendship and the camaraderie and bonding of the male journalists. Although Dith Pran is married, obviously his work and relationship with Schanberg is of primary importance to the film. Curiously, a whole genre of gangster films of the year can also be read as male love stories, including *The Pope of Greenwich Village, The Cotton Club,* and *Once Upon a Time in America,* the last of which celebrates the close relationship of a group of Jewish street hoods who become gangsters and are more devoted to each other than to the women in their lives. The tagline of the film was: "As boys, they said they would die for each other. As men, they did." As we see below, problematical relations between the sexes and male anxieties and hostilities toward women are one of the subtexts of a wide range of this year's Hollywood films.

■ The American Horror Show

In 1982, *Time* magazine named the computer the "Machine of the Year" (in place of its customary "Man of the Year"), and 1984 saw a famous Apple computer ad using the backdrop of George Orwell's novel to show computers liberating individuals from the tyranny of totalitarian organizations. Great hopes were being invested in the computer revolution, robotics, biotechnology, and genetic engineering, but they were also a site of tremendous fear and anxiety.

Science fiction and horror films put these underlying fears and anxieties on display, using the modes of fantasy, symbolism, allegory, and high-tech

Hollywood spectacle. James Cameron's *The Terminator*, for example, portrays a wide set of anxieties focused on technology, societal violence, and personal identity. In the film's dystopic vision, the future is a post-nuclear holocaust wasteland where machines dominate and wage war on people. The remaining humans fight back against machines that have produced androids to destroy them. In order to prevent the birth of a boy who is to become a resistance leader against machine control, an android assassin (Arnold Schwarzenegger) travels from the year 2029 to contemporary Los Angeles with a mission to kill all women named Sarah Connor. To assure the boy's birth, another resistance fighter, Reese (Michael Biehn), returns from the future to destroy the Terminator and save Sarah Connor.

The film offers a complex, dialectic vision of technology, showing both fear and belief in its regenerative and transformative powers. The rebuilding of the Terminator's injured body parts anticipates genetic engineering, as do *The Brother from Another Planet* and *Starman,* which also feature aliens able to regenerate organs and body parts. The aliens in the latter film are portrayed as paragons of goodness and benevolence, whereas Cameron's Terminator appears as a completely malevolent killing machine who represents the fear that technology will displace and destroy humans. Likewise, the post-nuclear holocaust theme articulates anxieties concerning weapons of mass destruction.

Arnold Schwarzenegger plays the Terminator as a fierce, cold killer who represents fears that androids could take over and replace humans as the sovereign of the universe. *The Terminator*'s showdown between Sarah, Reese, and the Terminator takes place in an automated factory that itself represents the replacement of human labor power by machines. As Reese explains to Sarah, the Terminator "does not feel pity, remorse or fear and will not stop until you are dead." In this regard, the Terminator behaves like a kind of serial killer, a character type that had many progeny during the period. A series of "stalk and slash" films showed middle-class American teenagers shadowed and brutally murdered by a set of monsters. These films often use the point of view of its endangered protagonists stalked by vicious killers and then cut to close-ups of the victims. Often employing unnerving, repetitive music, punctuated by jarring and discordant sound effects, the films attempt to disorient and shock their spectators.

The formula for the slasher films is simple. In Carol Clover's words, the killer is usually "the psychotic product of a sick family, but still recognizably human; the victim is a beautiful, sexually active woman; the location is . . . a Terrible Place" (23). In *Friday the 13th: The Final Chapter,* directed by Joseph Vito (who also made *Missing in Action* this year), we are first given a reprise of the series mythology, showing the aftermath of Jason's murder of seven teens and two bikers. Jason's body is taken to the hospital morgue, and just before two interns have sex, Jason awakens to kill them both. The rest of the film, however, is distinctive in that it puts on display male sexual anxieties to an extent rarely visible in Hollywood cinema. Teenagers in a van pass an overweight girl hitchhiking who gives them the finger when they do not pick her up. She is eating a banana that withers and goes limp as Jason stabs her from behind, providing a visual symbol of male sexual anxiety.

Once back in the cabin, the teenage boys begin pairing after having picked up identical twin girls hiking in the woods. A sexually insecure boy couples with one of the twins and after sex asks her with great concern whether he was a "dead fuck." She convinces him that he was great, and he jumps out of bed to brag to a buddy who is watching old black-and-white "nudie" stripper films. Of course, the male teen who has just had sex is stabbed by Jason, who then slaughters the nerdy teen who is watching the old porno films while masturbating.

Combining the dysfunctional family motif of *A Nightmare on Elm Street* with the murdered-teens-in-the-woods theme of the *Friday the 13th* series, *The Final Chapter* features a single mother with two children living in a cabin next to the libidinal teens' cabin. A young boy, Tommy (Corey Feldman), takes great adolescent pleasure in watching the teens next door have sex, but he is greatly disturbed as he spends his time making masks of horror murderers. His divorced single mother (Joan Freeman) looks on at the teen revelry with barely disguised sexual wistfulness, making her seem a repressed and pathetic older woman without a man. Her daughter, Trish (Kimberley Beck), plays what Clover has called the last girl standing, a staple of the slasher cycle. Whereas in classic horror films like *Psycho* (1960) and the standard run of sexist Hollywood movies in which the female in distress is saved by a male hero, in the slasher film the last girl standing successfully battles the monster figure and saves herself and sometimes destroys the monster.

The monster, Jason, represents a sexually dysfunctional male with an unresolved Oedipal complex, who compensates for impotency by using highly phallic instruments to pierce and murder his victims. Clover points out that the identification of male sexual sadism was one of the great achievements of contemporary feminism and that the slasher films tend to naturalize and mythologize pathological male violence (226). Indeed, the slasher films portray male violence as emanating from nature and mythologize the killers in the genre, who become increasingly supernatural. It is as if male violence is part of the order of nature, and women can only survive by taking the male role of aggressor and exerting violence themselves. As Clover notes, the female characters are not rescued by a man, but fight back and usually defeat the killer monster on their own.

The Final Chapter has a bizarre twist, however, on the usual scenario of the last surviving girl becoming a warrior and killing or at least defeating the monster. This time the young boy Tommy shaves his head, taking on the appearance of the youthful Jason, whom the boy discovered in newspaper photos. Tommy then joins Trish in the battle against Jason, in which she whacks Jason with an ax. Jason slumps over and appears to be dead, but his hand twitches and he rises to attack both brother and the sister. Tommy then becomes crazed and repeatedly stabs him while screaming madly. This frightening conclusion suggests that the psychotic killer could be reborn in the young boy, continuing the mayhem (and the genre) indefinitely (indeed, at least five more movies in the series have appeared since then).

Domestic Concerns: Contestations over Gender, Race, and Class

Horror films thus problematize gender representations, ranging from frightening portrayals of male monsters, male anxieties, and strong independent women in the slasher films. While Susan Faludi is largely correct that 1980s films represent the backlash against women replicating the anti-feminism of the Reagan era (113f), there seem to be exceptions to the stereotyped emotional female. These include the strong women in the "Save the Farm" trilogy who battle against adversity to save their families, the young women of the slasher films, the female warriors in *Red Dawn*, Sarah Connor in *The Terminator*, and even the mother in *Gremlins*, who obliterates little monsters in her kitchen with a knife, a microwave, and an assortment of kitchen appliances. Yet the women warriors assume largely patriarchal roles, and in the family farm films the women are ultimately recuperated in traditional domestic positions of the ideal mother and wife.

Many independent films, however, contest dominant Hollywood representations and portray oppositional social movements. Gregory Nava's *El Norte* displays the interrogation of class, race, gender, and national identity in a film that combines epic drama with magical realism, a style in which symbols and images imbue nature with a magical quality. It depicts the oppression of a Guatemalan village that forces a brother, Enrique (David Villalpando), and his sister, Rosa (Zaide Silvia Gutiérrez), to flee to El Norte,

El Norte (Gregory Nava, Island Alive) combines epic drama with magic realism as Enrique (David Villalpando) and Rosa (Zaide Silvia Gutierrez) leave their Guatemalan home for a life in the United States. Jerry Ohlinger's Movie Material Store.

"the North," i.e., the United States. The second part of the film details their attempt to sneak across the border from Mexico, and the third part represents their lives in the United States. *El Norte* demonstrates the oppression of developing world people and the life of undocumented workers from their own perspective, using native languages, actors and actresses, and locales. It also brilliantly demonstrates discrepancies between the ideology and fantasy of life in the United States compared to its realities. The Guatemalans have images of a life of ease and luxury derived from magazines like *Good Housekeeping*. When arriving in the United States, they see that living conditions for the poor hardly approximate the lovely images in the magazines. Contrasts between rich and poor are also brought out through the scenes depicting their first jobs: busing in a luxury restaurant and cleaning wealthy people's houses.

The film makes its political points through realistic depictions of oppression, comedy, and clever asides. It depicts how indigenous peoples are brutalized by native armies in the first part, and the poverty of Mexican urban slum-dwellers and would-be emigrants to the United States in the second and third parts. *El Norte* also exposes the ways in which immigrant labor is exploited; one immigrant points out that without their cheap labor, the economy would collapse. Yet the difference between U.S. affluence and poverty in the developing world is also underscored through humor, as in one scene where Rosa cannot figure out how to use the complicated auto-mated washing machine and washes the clothes by hand instead. The sen-timentality of Rosa's death scene—after it is revealed she was dying of a disease transmitted by rabid rodents when she crawled through sewer pipes to enter the country illegally—is undercut through contrastive irony that shows Enrique carrying on about how good things are in the United States and then planning to abandon his sister for a job in Chicago. The ironic framing of the melodramatic ending thus allows sharp critiques of U.S. val-ues of individualism and everyone-for-themselves attitudes, while affirm-ing values of love, family, and loyalty.

Several documentaries portrayed the lives of marginalized groups. Inspired by a *Life* magazine story of Seattle teenagers who live on the streets, Martin Bell's *Streetwise* provides a harrowing look at the hopeless-ness of life in the expanding underclass in Reagan's America, especially young girls who are doubly abused by their families and the pimps who put them on the street to prostitute themselves.

One of the Seattle street kids is gay and suffers multiple harassment as even marginalized youth use hateful terms like "fags." Another major doc-umentary of the year, *Before Stonewall,* portrays the history of gay and les-bian subculture from World War II to the present. The film takes its title from the 1969 riots in a gay New York bar at time when gay men and les-bians were largely invisible. The film discloses that until the movements of the 1960s and 1970s, queer people were marginalized, oppressed, and hardly recognized in the mainstream culture. Engaging documentary footage and interviews show gay and lesbian subcultures emerging out of the military and women working together in factories and offices during the Second World War. One group in Los Angeles describes secret meetings in an apartment whose blinds were closed to protect them from the scrutiny of prying neighbors or the police.

An award–winning documentary focusing on homophobia in American life, Robert Epstein's *The Times of Harvey Milk* provides a real-life horror story. The film sympathetically depicts the political rise of gay activist Har-vey Milk as a San Francisco city supervisor, becoming the first openly gay public official in the city. The documentary interweaves footage of the rise of another member of the Board of Supervisors, Dan White, a former policeman and self-proclaimed conservative. White becomes increasingly frustrated as the San Francisco city government becomes more and more liberal, including the election of an African American, a Chinese American, and a self-avowed feminist, all of whom were Milk's allies. The film examines controversy around Proposition 6, a proposed California initiative that would have barred homosexuals from teaching in the public schools. After the proposition is defeated, thanks in large part to the efforts of Milk and his allies, White resigns in anger as city supervisor. White quickly changes his mind, however, and decides after his resignation that he wants to take up his position again. Anticipating that he will have his request denied and seething with rage, White plots to murder both Milk and San Francisco mayor George Moscone. Crawling through a window in City Hall to avoid metal detectors, White shoots and kills Moscone and Milk in cold blood.

During White's trial, the defense mobilizes sympathy for the conservative, allegedly religious, devoted father of two while playing up bigoted attitudes toward Milk. In an incredible verdict, the jury buys the defense's argument that White went temporarily insane due to job pressure and an excessive consumption of Twinkies. As White receives a scandalously light sentence, the film concludes with an angry demonstration. (A graphic title added to a later version of the film notes that Dan White was paroled from prison in January 1985 and committed suicide in October of that year.)

The year's films put on display central features of the regnant conservative ideology, as well as its contestation, and in so doing helped to illuminate important conflicts within U.S. society. They showed U.S. society to be highly divided around issues of gender, race, sexuality, and political ideology—visible conflicts that continue to rage on decades afterward.

NOTES

1. See Orwell's *1984* and the discussion in Kellner "From 1984."

2. In 2004, during the American intervention in Iraq, Peter Hartlaub wrote, "A mere 20 years ago, 'Red Dawn' depicted a nation invaded, overpowered. Only that nation was us." He went on to argue that the Iraqi resistance fighters represented the position of Milius's valorous insurgents in *Red Dawn*, with U.S. troops now the occupiers. Showing that U.S. imperialism is capable of absorbing anything and everything, however, the military dubbed the operation to capture Saddam Hussein "Red Dawn," and the code names given to the two huts at Saddam's hideaway were "Wolverine 1" and "Wolverine 2," referring to the young resistance fighters in the film (see Campbell). When questioned, Milius had no doubt that the references were influenced by his film, claiming that the soldiers who captured Saddam were "Wolverines who have grown up and gone to Iraq."

1985

Movies and Political Landscapes

CHRISTINA BANKS AND MICHAEL BLISS

The world was changing from a landscape still defined primarily by post–World War II political liberalism and economic security to the increasingly conservative and fiscally uncertain terrain that we now inhabit. President Ronald Reagan—former actor and former Democrat now reborn as the popular Republican leader of a new conservatism—began his second term in office, continuing his policies of supply-side economics; his programs favored massive tax cuts, cuts in interest rates, and an attempt to reduce the size of the federal government, as well as large increases in military spending and a confrontational stance toward the Soviet Union. Among the results of these fiscal policies, the United States experienced its highest unemployment rate—over 10 percent—since the Great Depression and became a debtor nation for the first time since 1914, and the federal budget required deficit spending for much of the next two decades.

Mikhail Gorbachev became the leader of the Soviet Union in March, and meetings were held soon after with Reagan to negotiate nuclear arms reductions. Gorbachev's domestic reforms eventually led to the end of the Cold War: *glasnost* (openness) allowed the Soviet people unprecedented freedoms while also acknowledging the crimes of the Stalinist era, and *perestroika* (restructuring) attempted to transform the Soviet economy into a decentralized market economy. However, these policies unintentionally released a mass of discontent that led to the collapse of the Soviet Union six years later. In the meantime, the thawing of the Cold War helped to overshadow the bad news of the period for the president's policies.

The unquiet conflict in the Middle East seemingly spread everywhere in now-familiar violent actions. Islamic fundamentalism, in part adopted by frustrated populations in revolt against various repressive regimes, increasingly directed acts of terrorism at the United States because of its support for unpopular governments and because of America's perceived moral permissiveness. Associated Press reporter Terry Anderson was taken prisoner by the Shiite Hezbollah in Beirut in an attempt to force the United States to remove its forces from Lebanon; one of many Americans being held hostage in that country, he would remain a captive for almost seven years. TWA Flight 847 was hijacked en route from Rome to Athens; thirty-nine passengers and crew were held hostage for seventeen days. One American was killed by two members of Hezbollah; the rest of the hostages were released when Israel agreed to free seven hundred Shiite prisoners. The Italian cruise ship *Achille Lauro,* sailing in Egyptian waters, was hijacked by members of the Palestine Liberation Front demanding that Israel free fifty imprisoned Palestinians. The hijackers killed an elderly Jewish American passenger. After the hijackers accepted a safe conduct in exchange for releasing the ship, the commercial airplane on which they were flying was intercepted by American fighter planes; the hijackers were eventually handed over to the Italian government.

Most of the year's films were blithely incognizant of these events. The majority were pure diversion, comedies such as *Peewee's Big Adventure* (little more than a vehicle to bring Peewee Herman from his children's television show "Peewee's Playhouse" to theaters) and *Back to the Future* (capitalizing on the popularity of Michael J. Fox, then in the cast of the television sitcom "Family Ties").

Various stars were born. The hip film *Desperately Seeking Susan* was notable for the appearance of Madonna, then commencing her campaign to dominate popular culture. The post-apocalyptic *Mad Max Beyond Thunderdome* served primarily to exploit, rather than investigate, Mel Gibson's Road Warrior character. *The Breakfast Club,* one of director John Hughes's innocuous teen films, popularized a group of young actors soon to be known as the Brat Pack, among them Molly Ringwald, Emilio Estevez, and Judd Nelson.

Martin Scorsese's *After Hours* was a superficial psychological romp pretending to be an investigation of a yuppie's *Walpurgisnacht.* The film's striking lack of political awareness or credible social context within which its serio-comic events could be situated made it clear that, like the director's 1983 film *The King of Comedy,* Scorsese had moved far away from the promise of *Mean Streets* (1973) and *Taxi Driver* (1976).

Perhaps the most earnestly serious film of the year was writer/director Paul Schrader's *Mishima.* Beautifully directed, written, and acted, the film was a rarity among the year's offerings. Visually stunning, albeit dramatically flat, the film rendered the psychological and political tapestry of Japanese author Yukio Mishima's life.

But the year's major films could not ignore the harsh realities of international events. The most influential films—*Brazil, The Purple Rose of Cairo, Rambo: First Blood II, Pale Rider,* and *Witness*—represent reactions to this conflicted political landscape. There was a sense in the United States that political events were increasingly out of control. We see a reaction to these situations in director Terry Gilliam's *Brazil* as well as in director George P. Cosmatos's *Rambo* (a sequel to the popular 1982 film *First Blood*). *Brazil* dramatizes a sense of dystopic despair filtered through its central character, a lampooned version of the ultimate petty bureaucrat. Via a testosterone-infused view of taking command of political failures, *Rambo* shows us a comparably cartoon-like character dominating a conceptual political land-scape, the Vietnam War, that had long been thought of as the graveyard of America's political hegemony. As we shall see, the presumably liberal alter-native to *Rambo*, director Clint Eastwood's film *Pale Rider*, offers us the same skewed vision of what is necessary to address inequities, while Woody Allen's *Purple Rose of Cairo* and Australian director Peter Weir's *Witness* sug-gest that despite the desire for a peaceful life, such an alternative may not be feasible for many people.

Interestingly, in all these films the bifurcation of good and evil is repre-sented by a divide between a degenerated landscape and an idealized one. Yet the fantastical escapes from reality dramatized in *Brazil* and *Purple Rose* are not pragmatically different from the overt idealization that makes pos-sible the exaggerated deliverances in *Rambo* and *Pale Rider*, or the desperate escape into simplicity and purity in *Witness*. In each of these scenarios, what directors played out are dramatizations of the American myth of pristine, undeveloped territory. In *Purple Rose*, the impoverished Depression-era streets contrast with apparently carefree Hollywood environments. *Witness*'s dramatization of an urban dweller's escape into the countryside (an action that is also present toward *Brazil*'s end, albeit in the form of a fantasy) allies the film with the American myth of undeveloped territory.

Brazil's and *Purple Rose*'s "green worlds" (symbols of edenic, natural societies) only exist in their central characters' fantasies. The idealized worlds in *Rambo* and *Pale Rider* are less empirical landscapes than hoped-for realities. In *Witness*, the green world is real, but its continued existence is dependent on it remaining distant from the real world. Clearly, the direc-tors' views on the possibility of redemption differ. Gilliam and Allen are skeptical; Cosmatos and Eastwood fantasize about it; Weir is guardedly hopeful.

A Flower in the City

Woody Allen can be viewed as something of an American Chekhov, critiquing social mores and their complacent acceptance by indi-viduals. Most often, Allen comically dissects New York culture, with himself as the primary self-deluded lost soul. In *The Purple Rose of Cairo*, Allen moves his film's action to the hell (at least to New Yorkers) of New Jersey and depicts a quandary in the life of an abused working-class wife. Domestic abuse, which had only recently become an acknowledged social problem, imbues the story with an instant political sensibility. That the film also focuses on the economically disadvantaged raises questions about social inequities in America. A large amount of emotional distance is maintained, however, by remaining inside a comic structure, allowing Allen to treat these subjects for the most part obliquely.

The film is set in the Great Depression, when Americans relied on buoyant film comedies to provide escape from their grim everyday lives. Cecilia (Mia Farrow), a downtrodden New Jersey waitress bullied by both her boss and her lay-about husband, Monk (Danny Aiello), certainly needs the relief that she finds by living vicariously through the films that she frequents at her neighborhood cinema. No genuine escape seems possible for Cecilia, who during a particularly depressing week repeatedly sits through showings of film-within-a-film *The Purple Rose of Cairo* until its heroic main character, having noticed her nearly constant presence in the audience, walks out of the screen and falls in love with her. She thus has the opportunity to incorporate into her life part of an ideal world instead of continuing her passive acceptance of her miserable reality.

The contrast between *The Purple Rose of Cairo*'s real world and its reel world is emblematized in what we are meant to see as the distinction between the color palette of Cecilia's milieu and the striking black-and-white cinematography of the film-within-a-film's universe. Yet this distinction, meant to convey the richness of the celluloid world and the spiritual and emotional poverty of the real world, is compromised by an inherent technological aspect of the medium within which Allen is working. Cecilia's milieu is rendered with muted colors that are meant to reflect the lack of vibrancy in her life. Regrettably, the film-within-a-film's black-and-white cinematography does not have the shimmering quality of a 1930s production because (like the rest of *Purple Rose*) it has been printed on a 1984 color film stock, which compromises its saturation (a 1930s black-and-white film would have been printed onto high-silver-content nitrate stock). The result is that, both from a pictorial and symbolic point of view, the film-within-a-film is deficient as an alternative to the world within which Cecilia lives, an effect that a detail-oriented director such as Allen undoubtedly intended.

The errant film-within-a-film character, explorer Tom Baxter (Jeff Daniels), decides that he wants to be free—something that Cecilia, if she ever thought about it, needs as well. Tom's personality, however, is limited to the qualities provided him by the film-within-a-film's screenwriter; when Cecilia tries to explain the idea of God to Tom, he thinks that the concept of God and a screenwriter are analogous. But if Tom lacks free will, doesn't human Cecilia have genuine choices? It is, however, Cecilia's avoidance of making hard choices in her own life that has led her to immerse herself in movies. Tom is at all times honest and cheerful and faithful in love, unlike a real man and very unlike her husband, and for that reason she is attracted to his two-dimensionality.

As Cecilia and Tom roam the gray neighborhood streets, she tries to explain to him what life in the real world is like: laid-off men (like Monk) hanging about the streets gambling or drinking to escape their dejection; soup kitchens for the hungry; the preciousness of even the worst job. In the real world, there is no freedom without economic freedom. Allen recognizes the drudgery of the modern wage slave in the capitalist wasteland of the 1930s, but he also sees a certain amount of complicity in the workers' passive acceptance of their economic situation.

Tom's leaving the movie-within-a-movie threatens the status quo—revenue from theater admissions will disappear, of course, but the masses will no longer be distracted from their poverty. We are told that movie mogul Raul Hirsch, along with "the police and the FBI," are being mobilized to restore control. "It's a communist plot," someone says upon hearing that Tom Baxters in screenings of the film in other towns are becoming uncooperative. A revolution by the downtrodden looms. Like a Greek chorus, Tom's fellow film character Larry (Van Johnson) warns against inaction: "The fat cats in Hollywood *want* us to sit around and talk." In other words, the social order of rich and poor relies on the continued distraction of the populace. No real escape is allowed, but escapism is encouraged.

Cecilia rejects the impossible "ideal" of life with Tom, and the social order is upheld when she is wooed away by the duplicitous actor portraying Tom, who returns to his movie. "I have to choose the real world," she explains, but she is choosing a fiction, and so she is again betrayed. Paradoxically, Cecilia's "real world" life involves far more illusion—for example, believing that the men in her life are capable of being reliable—than if she took the risks involved in striving for an ideal existence in which she would be impoverished but would at least have her self-respect.

In the end, Cecilia is again immersed in filmic escapism. "Heaven—I'm in Heaven," Fred Astaire sings while he and Ginger dance. Cecilia, misery in her eyes, slowly smiles as she once again loses herself in the darkened theater. It is a horrifying moment when we realize that she has given up the struggle of life and instead chosen oblivion.

The seemingly total distance of Allen's film from the political realm actually gives it a unique perspective. The central character's desire for escape is into a realm which, unlike the retro-future of *Brazil* and the extreme pastoralism of *Witness,* seems both identifiable and accessible. One of *Purple Rose*'s major triumphs is that it places the audience in touch with what is real, even if this reality is one from which an escape is strongly desired. In this sense, *Purple Rose* may be the most socially aware of the five films considered in this essay, paradoxically because it seems to focus almost exclusively on the personal realm.

Huis Clos

T. S. Eliot suggested in his essay "Religion and Literature" that it is perhaps the kind of literature which seems the most inconsequential that has the most effect on readers. Intuitively, Terry Gilliam recognizes the truth in this assertion, using the displacement that the fantastical allows to bypass the audience's critical "screens" in order to communicate his social criticism. (Not surprisingly, Gilliam, who was the lone American in the Monty Python troupe, has chosen to live abroad; apparently, he sees his subject clearest from a distance.) While his symbolism often falls within the Christian realm, Gilliam's outlook is fiercely humanistic. Since irony is often an oblique criticism of the gap between what social/religious behavior should be and what it is, Gilliam uses it within his films' comic formats to decry social and moral problems. Despite the comedy in his films, no other director in the United States has Gilliam's sense of outrage in response to hypocrisy.

In *Brazil,* Gilliam was not merely taking a genre (in this case the dystopia) and playing at updating it, as for example Joel and Ethan Coen are wont to do. Rather, Gilliam seems to be responding to elements of the American scene which he found alarmingly reminiscent of some of the most objectionable excesses of totalitarian states. His criticisms are effective because they attack both societal faults as well as individual moral failures.

Oppositions reminiscent of those in *Purple Rose* are present in *Brazil,* although Gilliam is far more concerned than Allen with ideas of cinematic space. His emphasis is not on overtly stylistic touches such as tracking shots or reductionist symbolism. Instead, Gilliam—like any devoted purist— embeds his meanings in the overall visual fabric of his film's deceptive surfaces. As photographed by Roger Pratt, with production design by Norman Garwood, *Brazil* is a densely packed visual phantasmagoria whose look mirrors its mythical country's convoluted governmental structure.

Terry Gilliam's *Brazil* (Universal Pictures), with Jonathan Pryce (left), offers a darkly comic view of the future as an Orwellian nightmare. Digital frame enlargement.

Indeed, the first thing that one notices about *Brazil* is its rather bleak, 1930s-inspired set decoration (reminiscent of the atavistic set decoration of its dystopian precursor, director Michael Anderson's 1956 film *1984*). *Brazil*'s look suggests that the social failure displayed in the film results from an over-reliance on machines. Perhaps in manic, overcompensatory re-action to social failure, most of *Brazil*'s interior spaces are filled either with obtrusive and invasive ductwork or the manic scurrying of workers who rush around like bees on speed. Yet even in the places in which there is breathing room, there is a sense of desperate, forced leisure.

The only alternative with which the film presents us is fantasies, such as those of the Walter Mitty-ish Sam Lowry (Jonathan Pryce), who works as a functionary each day in the murky halls of the Ministry of Informa-tion, yet whose nightly dreams transform him into a winged angel in shining armor, alternately gliding through the clouds and battling assorted earth-bound demons. Surely, we think, here is a dispirited victim of a totalitarian environment, yearning for freedom like Orwell's Winston Smith in *1984*. Yet it seems that Sam really does fit in rather well at the Ministry of Information. Something of a slacker, Sam only focuses on business when his incompetent superior, Kurtzmann (Ian Holm), needs to be bailed out of some bureaucratic snafu. If this were a film by anyone but Gilliam, the dream plot would be a tale that paralleled Sam's real life. However, Sam's "real life" rescues are hardly as noble as the ones in his dreams.

It is apparent that Sam is fairly adept at operating the technology used at the Ministry for social control, rather than, like Winston Smith, being its passive victim. It is Sam who, to shift responsibility from Kurtzmann and his department, solves the problem by blaming the computer bug that prompted the arrest of innocent citizen Archibald Buttle on another governmental department; it is also Sam who, with nervous yet shameless bonhomie, wheedles Buttle's widow into signing the receipt for the "interrogation" that killed her husband. In his exploitation of the system for his personal comfort, Sam reveals an amorality in consonance with that of his fellows at the Ministry.

Sam's indolence stems from his membership in the social elite and his rebellion against his dominating mother, Ida Lowry (Katherine Helmond), a wealthy and well-connected woman who, like her friends, is embarked on an endless round of self-gratification: shopping, dining in expensive restaurants, patronizing a trendy plastic surgeon. (In fact, she might be considered an "ideal" citizen in this dystopia.) In her presence, Sam acts like a petulant little boy. His avoidance of her is a child's avoidance of authority, not a mature attempt to distance himself from the social corruption that she represents. His rebellion is purely vicarious, either in his dreams or through quietly attaching himself to real, if minor, protesters against the governmental order whom he convinces himself are really members of some terrorist plot.

The raid on the Buttle flat seems now all too familiar and not nearly as funny as it did in the relative quiet of the year in which the film was released. From all directions, black-swathed members of a heavily armed military team break into the Buttle sitting room, disrupting the family's quiet celebration of the Christmas season (which includes a reading of that classic of universal good will, *A Christmas Carol*), holding wife and children at gunpoint while seizing Mr. Buttle, hooding his head and torso in a locking canvas bag, and rushing him away. This raid leads us to understand the immorality of the government of *Brazil*: the peace and unassuming spirituality of the family stands in contrast to the faceless unreason and brutality of the government.

It is not much of a surprise when we are informed that raids such as this are part of the war to stop terrorists. Every so often in *Brazil,* an explosion destroys public spaces, once in a store displaying televisions. Amid the charred ruins, an intact set continues to broadcast, with the Deputy Minister of Information opining: "A ruthless minority of people seems to have forgotten certain good old-fashioned virtues. They just can't stand seeing the other fellow win." Accepting the Minister's explanation, *Brazil*'s citizens are for the most part not opposed to any methods used to control them as long as their culture of consumption is not disrupted. This toleration of totalitarian methods is a measure of the culture's degeneration.

Because the real goal of *Brazil*'s government is to maintain absolute control, any critic of the authoritarian status quo, no matter how insignificant, is automatically branded a terrorist, and an Information Retrieval file is opened to track them. Fugitive Harry Tuttle (Robert De Niro), annoyed at the logy pace of the repairs effected by Central Services, rappels around skyscraper apartment buildings at night, clandestinely fixing wiring- and duct-laden utilities. (Poor Buttle was arrested for Tuttle's crimes against society.) Similarly, when Buttle's neighbor Jill Layton (Kim Greist) takes up the battle to right his wrongful arrest, a classified dossier is opened on her as a terrorist. In a sane or at least democratic world, neither of these people's activities would be considered threatening.

Tuttle bucks social/governmental control via his mastery over mechanical systems. When the air conditioning in Sam's apartment breaks, Tuttle performs a simple fix; even when the Central Services crew, in spite, fills the rooms with a nightmare tangle of ducts, Tuttle can manipulate them and fill the Central Services workers' air suits with human waste. Sam's admiration for Tuttle stems from this ability, which exceeds Sam's own technical mastery. Perhaps Sam even recognizes that Tuttle's method of getting around is analogous to the winged flights of Sam's angel. In real life, though, Tuttle displays a true civic spirit, while Sam uses his skills to keep himself and Kurtzmann comfortable at the expense of innocents like the Buttles.

Similar to Sam's admiration for Tuttle is Sam's attraction to Jill. It may be her independence that paradoxically causes him to imagine that she's the gauze-obscured beauty-in-distress who appears in his avenging-angel dream. Jill is nothing of the kind, of course—she's a butch-haired trucker in baggy jacket and overalls whose vehicle looks like a Humvee on steroids. Sam's dreams quickly evolve into visions of his winged alter ego wielding a blade in her protection, while Sam himself attempts somehow to realize this dream by finding and protecting Jill from Information Retrieval.

In contrast to Sam's fantasizing and delusions, Jill is firmly grounded in reality. While Sam unhesitatingly accepts the government's draconian social control as a necessary part of protecting citizens from terrorists, her view is more mature and skeptical. "How many terrorists have you ever met?" she prods when he parrots the government line. Ironically, his attempts to "save" Jill increase the government's interest in her.

Amid the wreckage of a bombed department store, Sam shows no empathy for the wounded shoppers until Jill forces him to help her tend to them. His immature response to the carnage—initially all he wants to do is castigate her for being a terrorist—illustrates his lack of any real moral grounding. When he at last turns his attention to the wounded, it seems that, instead of him saving her, she may instead be able to save him, from himself and from the social engineers.

When Sam is handed over to his friend Jack (Michael Palin) for "interrogation," we know what will happen, for we have seen jolly Jack at work before: his blood-spattered lab coat, his secretary unconcernedly transcribing an interrogation, including the screams, tell us all that we need to know about him. Through his chipper insistence that his interrogations are normal and inconsequential, Jack demonstrates the banality of evil: in this case, how easily ordinary people can justify their complicity in government-sanctioned horrors.

Although a rather unlikely fantasy sequence leads us to believe that Sam escapes with Jill, in fact, Sam is still strapped in Jack's chair, untouched by the torture implements laid out on a tray at his side and with a vacant, joyful expression on his face. "We've lost him. He's gotten away," Jack mourns. This ending is chillingly ambiguous: yes, Sam has "escaped," mentally at least, and is happy. But he's also lost forever in fantasy or madness—a more extreme retreat than the dysfunctional one to which he has been subject all along.

For the first time in the film, the entire song "Brazil" is sung, the words those of a romantic song about impossible love. (Like the music at the end of *Purple Rose*, the melody here acts as an ironic counterpoint to the action.) An orchestral version of the song is played earlier as part of the sound track, at one point on Sam's car radio. It is the theme song of government control, keeping people lost in complacency, and by the film's end credits, the government is in total control. Or is it the theme of willful self-delusion?

What Gilliam saw in 1984 (when the film was in production) was a lazy trust in government management, a willingness to continue international "business as usual" by dismissing all resistance as terrorism, and a citizenry's self-indulgent grabs for personal enhancement that ignored the world outside of the self. More than twenty years later, these tendencies have only intensified to the point of becoming bloated excesses overshadowing other problems, like a Mr. Creosote that just won't explode. Because his critique was serious, Gilliam could not resolve *Brazil* with a happy ending—by letting Sam and Jill find a bit of lost Paradise, for example. Instead, like Sam, we have spent our subsequent years wrapped in an idle yet deadly dream.

■■■■■■■■■■■■ **The Fourth Seal**

Dreams of a different sort predominate in *Rambo: First Blood II* and *Pale Rider*. In *Rambo*, Medal of Honor winner and Vietnam veteran John Rambo (Sylvester Stallone), whose post-traumatic stress disorder led to havoc in the original *First Blood*, is released from prison to find information about POWs held in Vietnam. The film's plot is predictable (Rambo predominates against bureaucratic corruption and overwhelming military odds to rescue the prisoners) and its acting cannot be measured in terms of verisimilitude. However, the film does accurately pinpoint the symptomatology of a suppurating wound to the country's psyche—grief for the dead, disabled, or emotionally shattered young men and women who fought in Vietnam and a painful awareness that the nation's wealth had been squandered on what proved a futile orgy of destruction. (This lingering national anguish was, at least in part, personified in the psychologically damaged Vietnam veterans described in numerous studies and news reports throughout the 1980s.) What director Cosmatos and actor Stallone seem to have realized is that America needed, somehow, to heal. What the two provided was a vengeance movie, wherein the lost were found—Rambo overcomes his alienating trauma and the missing soldiers are returned home—and in which the country regained its sense of high purpose: through thoroughly and ferociously annihilating the evil communist guerillas and humiliating the corrupt U.S. bureaucrats who were deemed responsible for the whole conflict. Aside from the faultiness of the premise that new violence can undo the injuries of combat and that enemy soldiers are devoid of humanity, there is no denying that the film addressed itself to a powerful anxiety that many Americans felt, and that for lack of any better nostrum, the story of Rambo was popularly embraced as a myth of historical redemption. Yet it should have been clear to viewers that just as the overwhelming military might of the United States was ineffective in preventing the North Vietnamese from winning the war, so too it must have been absurd to believe that one man could right all the wrongs that devolved from the conflict.

The faultiness of this premise seems to have eluded Clint Eastwood, whose film *Pale Rider* reflects the same scenario, albeit with a religious veneer and a more democratic bias. A group of peaceful California gold miners is harassed and attacked by men working for the richest man in the territory, Coy LaHood (Richard Dysart), who wants to run the miners out of the area. The film's dualities are shamelessly exploited. The miners use the traditional panning technique to look for gold. LaHood, who is por-

Clint Eastwood gives the Western an environmental spin in his film *Pale Rider* (Warner Bros.). Jerry Ohlinger's Movie Material Store.

trayed as an avaricious capitalist, despoils the environment by using sluice mining methods. The main character among the miners, Hull Barrett (Michael Moriarty), is in a relationship with a woman, Sarah Wheeler (Carrie Snodgress), whom he treats with great tenderness and respect. LaHood's son John (Christopher Penn) attempts at one point to rape Sarah's young daughter, Megan (Sydney Penny). Into this polarized situation rides the latest of Eastwood's men with no name (unless you take seriously Megan's reading of the Book of Revelation's verses regarding the rider of the pale horse who is named Death). Eastwood's character is a straight shooter referred to as Preacher because at times he wears a pastor's collar. Eventually, Preacher's presence rallies the miners. Presumably at least in part as an agent of God delivering death to the guilty, Preacher dispatches all the killers that have been brought in to eliminate him.

The film, which is beautifully photographed by Bruce Surtees, visually opposes the country and city via their color schemes. The miners' camp and surrounding countryside are lush and green. The forest that intervenes between their camp and the town is old-growth dense. But as soon as one leaves the prairie and enters the town proper, the color scheme changes to the burnt-out straw yellow of the ground and the etiolated colors of weathered buildings. Perhaps nowhere are these distinctions made more apparent than in the scene in which Megan rides into LaHood's sluice mining camp. In a physical reflection of the way in which LaHood (in the words of a Sacramento legislator) is "raping" the land, Megan is physically assaulted by John LaHood. The Manichean opposition that Eastwood sets up between Megan and the behavior of LaHood's men carries over to the contrast between the green of the surrounding forest and the depleted mountainside that is being blasted with high-pressure water. (A literal-minded film scholar could make much of the fact that the near-rape scene is intercut with shots of high-pressure hoses blasting water into what used to be a forest.) The heavy-handedness of what Eastwood takes to be a mythical approach compromises whatever political points he is trying to make.

In its way, *Pale Rider* is as troubling as *Rambo*. In each film, an oppressive situation is relieved through the ministrations of a demigod savior. And while Preacher may seem a bit less fanatical than Rambo, or at least not as clamorous, both serve the same function: to stand as a heroic figure for certain political values. Rambo is a conservative avenger intent on redeeming the United States from its (presumed) shame in Vietnam. Preacher represents a religious redeemer who saves the common people. Yet if we factor out our political predilections, we see that the films are equally objectionable. Not only do both films lack nuances of action and characterization, but, more importantly, they celebrate violence as the answer to political and economic abuses. Indeed, there is no pragmatic difference between the actions of Rambo and Preacher (both of whom seem to feel that they are on divine missions) and those of the terrorist organizations that were perpetrating murder (also in the name of righting wrongs) during the mid-1980s. The supposed solutions offered in *Rambo* and *Pale Rider* are no solutions at all.

East of Eden

Witness offers a more convincing examination of issues related to violence and peace. The film confronts the awful realities with which American politics usually present us by referring to these brutalities indirectly, at the same time offering us a convincing idyllic alternative, thereby providing a delicately balanced portrayal of the two predominant trends in American culture: conflict and peace.

Witness tells a story about the recently widowed Amish woman Rachel Lapp (Kelly McGillis) and her young son, Samuel (Lukas Haas). Rachel and Samuel travel to Philadelphia to visit some relatives. While in a train station bathroom, Samuel sees a murder committed, after which he is questioned by policeman John Book (Harrison Ford). As the sole witness to the crime, Samuel is in danger. He shocks Book by quietly identifying the killer to him at the police station—Detective Lt. James McFee (Danny Glover). Book takes this information to Chief Paul Schaeffer (Josef Sommer), but soon after is shot and wounded by McFee. Clearly the conspiracy goes straight to the top. Now Book, in as much danger as the boy, flees with Rachel and Samuel to the Lapp farm, where he hides until, weeks later, the men arrive there to kill him.

It is clear from the first scenes in Philadelphia that the screenwriters' (William Kelley, Earl W. Wallace, and Pamela Wallace) view of the differences between the country and the city is as exaggerated as their view of good and evil. Although this attitude is tempered a bit (since there are obviously good people in the city, albeit there do not seem to be any bad people in the country), they still remain true to this Manichaean vision. Anyone familiar with Peter Weir's penchant for mythic structures can see how this dichotomizing would have appealed to the director. The Amish, too, easily lend themselves to archetypal characterization, especially since their lifestyle brings with it connotations of simplicity, goodness, and possibility, qualities often associated with Northrop Frye's "green world." Additionally, *Witness*'s Amish invoke the myth of the prairie, a notion familiar to anyone conversant with the ideas in Frederick Jackson Turner's influential essay "The Significance of the Frontier in American History." As Turner noted, "The existence of an area of free land, its continuous recession, and the advance of American settlement westward, explain American development."

In *Witness*, the Amish represent the open, free land, which is most profitable to view as an idea that grows out of the American myth of the West, a myth in opposition to notions of technological progress, much of which is conceived of pejoratively. Indeed, the film encourages viewers to believe that technology is, inherently, a source of moral debasement.

Like Turner, *Witness* at times becomes rhapsodic about the notion of open land, but it does not ignore the dangers of development, especially when notions that grow out of development are metaphorized into the form of power. The implicit analogizing in the film is, roughly, thus: men seek power, power corrupts, corrupt men seek more power. Schaeffer is involved with McFee in selling off a stolen cache of chemicals that are precursors for amphetamine. The linkage here is obvious: power and greed are drugs that create strong dependence. And why amphetamine? Because among the effects of amphetamine on the human body is the creation of an obsessive sense of urgency. One of the street names for amphetamine is "speed." It doesn't take much of a logical leap to see that what amphetamine

Philadelphia cop John Book (Harrison Ford) finds a peaceful refuge among the Amish in
Witness (Peter Weir, Paramount). Digital frame enlargement.

represents in *Witness* is the drug of progress, to which many people in contemporary society are habituated. The slow pace of the Amish lifestyle,
which is associated with morality and the natural world, is therefore con-
trasted with the fast pace of the morally debased modern world. What
Schaeffer is really peddling is contemporary culture and its ethical compromises, all of which are habituating. And what does progress look like in *Witness*? Our only view of a Philadelphia street occurs in the scene in which
Book and his partner, Elden Carter (Brent Jennings), stop outside a bar,
looking for one of the murderers. The scene is garishly lit: the street is dark
and dirty, and we intuit a faint red, virtually satanic, glow. Light from the
street is cast onto Rachel and Samuel, who are in the back seat of Book's
squad car. The city has tainted them. In the film's view, progress represents
corruption.

One could say that the maladaptive behaviors that we see in the film
represent pathological responses to urban life, that the hostility and aggression that are present in *Witness*'s city are responses to the pressures and anxieties that many urban dwellers feel. The more likely explanation, though,
is that the behavior of people such as Schaeffer and McFee is a response not
just to the social environment in which they live, but to the capitalist system that, more than merely reflecting their behavior, actually encourages
it. The self-centered economics of capitalism not only makes opportunistic
behavior possible, it makes such behavior desirable. Opposed to this ethic is
the Amish's privileging of cooperation and sharing. During the film's barn-

raising scene, we are shown how the Amish behave: they work together for the good of the community. Their only pay is their (communal) lunch. If selfish, possessive tendencies do emerge, as exemplified in the behavior of Book's rival for Rachel's affections, Daniel Hochleitner (Alexander Godunov), these attitudes are highlighted as being mean spirited and negative.

Yet just as Book is, in many respects, a member of the Amish community, so too is he reminded of his outsider status. As Book and Hochleitner walk toward the barn-raising site, the following exchange takes place.

> *Hochleitner:* Your [bullet] hole, it's better now?
>
> *Book:* Yeah, it's pretty much healed.
>
> *Hochleitner:* Good, then you can go home.

The use of the word "home" is intended to be ironic here, since Hochleitner knows, as does Book, that Book desires to be wedded to the Amish community (via his yearning for Rachel). Yet Book also knows that, because of the manner in which the city has socialized him, he does not belong among the Amish. The great melancholy of *Witness* derives from Book's inability to comfortably exist in either of the film's worlds. Violence has cast him out of his previous world. Violence precludes him from ever being able to live in an alternative world. Too innocent to enjoy the world of experience, and too experienced to regain his innocence, Book is a city dweller who longs to live in a country that he cannot inhabit. Like America itself, he has been cast out of Eden and is now pitifully, terribly alone.

What we see here are examples of inclusion and exclusion. These harsh, polarized terms, which dictate the film's conceptual landscape, are extensions of ideas concerning the city versus the country that are present in Turner's essay. In *Witness,* the predominant inclusive, protective gesture is domestically associated encirclement, as in the image of Rachel surrounded by Amish women after her husband's funeral. In an iconography that, according to Weir, is derived from the physical placements in Flemish painting, Rachel and the women are at the image's right side. Hochleitner enters from screen left. The way that Weir blocks this scene makes it seem as though Hochleitner is an intrusive, predatory animal entering a protected area. Given what we soon learn via body gestures and language— that Hochleitner is romantically interested in Rachel—this portrayal is not unusual. However, since the film shows us no other man interacting with Rachel after the funeral, there is the suspicion that Daniel's expression of sympathy has a dual purpose: not only to comfort Rachel, but to suggest to her that he is a *male* source of comfort, someone whom, in the future, she might want to consider looking kindly upon as a replacement for her husband.

In a later scene, Weir reprises the encirclement motif, although this time, Book is also involved. Daniel and Rachel are sitting near to each other on the porch's swing. Daniel places his elbow on the swing's back brace, as though he is about to put his arm around Rachel's shoulders. Rachel seems to (mildly) encourage this gesture by demurely bending her head down and shyly smiling. In a reverse angle shot, we see Book at the end of the path to the house. Knowing that she is beginning to care for Book, Rachel stops smiling, in response to which Daniel withdraws his arm. In the same scene, another reverse angle shot visually confirms the motif of encirclement as either protection or threat or exclusion. We see Book framed in the half-circle of Daniel's right arm (Daniel's hand holds a glass of lemonade). In this case, as in the scene with Rachel and the Amish women, encirclement connotes not only protection (Daniel's proprietary interest in Rachel) but also exclusion (Daniel's view of Book as a rival whom he means to keep at a distance from Rachel). Interestingly, during the barn-raising scene, Daniel is also seen holding a glass of lemonade that Rachel has given him. Yet this time, he acts in a friendly manner, sharing the drink with Book. When there is a communal project to be accomplished, then, the Amish tend to act cooperatively. Daniel may still shoot unfriendly glares toward Book when the barn builders take a lunch break, but when the men go back to work, the spirit of cooperation reasserts itself.

Witness raises a significant issue: what is the appropriate response to violence? It would be foolish not to see this question as having a political dimension. Schaeffer, McFee, and their partner, Fergie (Angus MacInnes), intend to sell at a profit the drugs that they have stolen. To whom? Drug dealers, of course. Thus, officers in a government agency plan to sell drugs in order to further their own illegal aims. Their behavior bears a striking resemblance to certain events that occurred in 1984, when a link was discovered between the Nicaraguan contra movement, smuggling and trafficking in cocaine, and the U.S. Department of State. To conclude the link between these actions and certain events in *Witness,* it only remains to note that a great deal of the drugs that were being sold found their way into the United States.

Of course, it might be argued that all this illegal activity on the U.S. government's part was for some greater good. The actions of the stand-ins for the government in *Witness* do not support that viewpoint. Instead, all of the drug trafficking by both the characters in *Witness* and the individuals cited above was in support of greed, greed that is manifested in violence.

We therefore need to inquire into what the film's attitude toward institutionalized violence is, especially the type of violence that is associated with the war-time use of weapons. This issue is addressed in a conversation between Samuel and his grandfather, Eli (Jan Rubes). With Book's gun lying on a table before them, and the ominous sounds of a thunderstorm in the background, Eli asks Samuel, "Would you kill another man?" The following exchange then occurs:

> *Samuel:* I would only kill a bad man.
>
> *Eli:* Only the bad man. I see. Would you know this bad man by sight? You are able to look into their hearts and see this badness?
>
> *Samuel:* I can see what they do. I *have* seen it.
>
> *Eli:* And having seen, you become one of them. Do you understand? What you take into your hands, you take into your heart. Therefore, come out from among them and be ye separate, saith the Lord, and touch not the unclean thing.

Yet the essential point here is not that the gun itself is unclean (a view that was asserted earlier when we saw Rachel pick up Book's gun with her fingertips, keeping it away from her body). The Amish realize that guns are not in themselves objectionable. What is problematic and perverse is what is sometimes done with them.

A comparable kind of perversity is used by Schaeffer when he pressures Carter to reveal Book's whereabouts by appealing to a supposed "code" among the police. Schaeffer says, "We're like the Amish. We're a cult too. Oh, a club, with our own rules. John has broken those rules, as you're breaking them now." Samuel Johnson once said that "patriotism is the last refuge of a scoundrel." Similarly, appealing to group loyalty in order to justify the subversion of that group's ethic is a scandalous act. Thus, Schaeffer deals not with inclusion (as he implies) but exclusion. Despite Schaeffer's assertion, the police are not a club; they are a public service organization. Nor are corrupt policemen such as Schaeffer like the Amish. What bonds the Amish is conformity to a uniform set of moral and religious principles to which they are devoted, whereas Schaeffer only invokes group unity as a way to justify placing himself above the law in order to become wealthy. As Book points out to Schaeffer during a telephone conversation, Schaeffer has betrayed the police force's integrity. He has forgotten "the meaning."

We have previously seen Book use his gun in self-defense, but during his final confrontation with Schaeffer, McFee, and Fergie, he is too far from his gun to retrieve it. Essentially, what defeats the assassins is the natural world. The crushing weight of grain in a silo buries Fergie, thereby allowing Book to get Fergie's gun, which he uses to shoot McFee. Schaefer is defeated by the crushing weight of a nature-oriented community: watching Schaeffer's desperate attempt to either shoot Book or take him away at gunpoint, the Amish stop Schaeffer from acting by witnessing what he is doing. In *Witness,* the community's eyes are always watching.

As is evident in this scene, the passivity of *Witness's* Amish is a form of action. By resisting evil, they set an example for how to respond to evil and violence. However, when people are aware of evil but do nothing, evil prospers. This notion is reminiscent of a famous quotation. In the speech "Thoughts on the Cause of the Present Discontent," which Edmund Burke delivered in Parliament on 23 April 1770, Burke said, "When bad men combine, the good must associate, else they will fall, one by one, an unpitied sacrifice in a contemptible struggle." By "associat[ing]," Burke meant joining a political party. In the context of *Witness,* these parties take the form of the Amish community. Yet it is clear that, as *Witness* demonstrates, Burke's credo can also be misapplied. Schaffer distorts the meaning implicit in Burke's statement when he says to Carter that the police are "like the Amish," just as Reagan distorted Burke's meaning when, after quoting Burke, he called the contras freedom fighters.

As often happens, the best in cinema speaks to the idyllic hopes that so many people harbor: hopes for peace, justice, harmony. The wistful fantasies in *Purple Rose,* the dreams of great achievement in *Brazil,* the barn-raising ceremony in *Witness*—all testify to aspirations that rise above and (at the very least, conceptually) defeat the ethical shortcomings that these same films dramatize. Our wish, as always, is that good will triumph, a wish that finds support in these touchstone films.

1986

Movies and Fissures in Reagan's America

LEGER GRINDON

The New York Mets defeated the Boston Red Sox in the seventh game of the World Series to become champions of baseball; the Nobel Peace Prize went to Elie Wiesel; Larry McMurtry's *Lonesome Dove* captured the Pulitzer Prize for fiction; and popular music took an international turn with the *We Are the World* album and Paul Simon's *Graceland*. But the most memorable events of the year were disasters. On 28 January, the space shuttle *Challenger* exploded shortly after lift-off, killing seven astronauts before a live television audience. In April, at the Chernobyl nuclear power plant near Kiev in the Soviet Union, there was another explosion, but news of the disaster traveled slowly; only days later, after Swedish technicians detected high levels of radiation, did Soviet officials acknowledge the accident. These catastrophes excited public anxiety at our increasing dependence upon, and growing fear of, technology. The taste for nightmare science fiction, already well established with films like *Alien* (1979), *Blade Runner* (1982), and *The Terminator* (1984), received fresh impetus from these spectacular disasters and provided an ominous context for viewing *Aliens* and *The Fly*.

Motion pictures addressed these social tensions and spoke in contending voices to their audience. The box office champ for the year was *Top Gun*, a high-tech extravaganza starring Tom Cruise, in which cocky U.S. Navy fighter pilots triumph over their Soviet enemies. By contrast, *Platoon* portrayed the limited effectiveness of U.S. armed forces during the Vietnam War in spite of their high-powered weapons systems. Together these two films manifested a growing division in America toward the Cold War policies of President Ronald Reagan.

The nation was almost halfway through what would be a twelve-year Republican reign in the persons of Reagan and George Bush, but significant change arose this year nevertheless. Mikhail Gorbachev's consolidation of power as the leader of the Soviet Union helped to ease polarization in the

Cold War. On 1 January the leaders of the superpowers spoke directly via television to each other's people for the first time in years. In the following weeks, Gorbachev announced a three-month extension of a moratorium on nuclear testing and proposed a worldwide ban on nuclear weapons within fifteen years, contingent upon the United States ending development of the Strategic Defense Initiative (SDI), popularly known as the "Star Wars" defense system. Throughout the year the Soviet leader pressed for an international arms control agreement, but the White House was reluctant to give up development of SDI. Still, there was a marked reduction of tensions and a shift in international initiative toward the Soviet calls for arms reduction. The hard-line vigilance of President Reagan was being challenged and a shift was apparent in the public mind. Hollywood fed both appetites, producing what Stephen Prince has called "New Cold War Films," such as *Top Gun* and Clint Eastwood's *Heartbreak Ridge,* but also featuring movies like *Platoon* that raised doubts about America's aggressive foreign policy (Prince 316).

The most overt challenge to Reagan's Cold War policies on the screen was another film written and directed by *Platoon*'s Oliver Stone, *Salvador.* The film portrays the bloody repression by the right-wing government in the small Central American country in 1980–81, including the murder of American churchwomen. The protagonist, a gonzo American journalist (James Woods), condemns the collusion of U.S. officials with the bloody regime, and he barely escapes with his life. In the film the tyrants celebrate the election of Ronald Reagan as a signal that their repressive tactics will continue to enjoy support from Washington, as in fact the administration did support the authoritarian Salvadoran government. Meanwhile, in Nicaragua, the Reagan administration supported the contra rebels against the new Sandinista regime and asked Congress for one hundred million dollars in aid, one more salvo in an ongoing debate about American foreign policy. Though the small audience for an independent film like *Salvador* could not compare with the impact achieved by heavily marketed star vehicles such as *Top Gun,* the erosion in public support for Reagan's aggressive policies in Central America was reflected in the congressional elections in November, in which the Democrats took control of the Senate for the first time since Reagan's inauguration. Late in the year Congress voted to halt funding for the contras, and with a new Democratic majority in the Senate, the administration would become vulnerable to congressional investigations, such as the Iran-contra hearings that were on the horizon.

On a lighter note, sitcoms like "The Cosby Show," "Family Ties," and "Cheers" dominated the television ratings, while film comedies also attracted a wide audience, though clearly they were aimed at the sensibilities of different niche populations. Woody Allen made his most celebrated film of the decade, *Hannah and Her Sisters,* which appealed to Jewish culture and the sophisticated urban audience. Comedies directed at teens, such as *Back to School* and *Ferris Bueller's Day Off,* were among the year's box office leaders. African Americans, among others, flocked to see Eddie Murphy in *The Golden Child,* but more notable was actor-writer-director Spike Lee, who emerged with his first feature, *She's Gotta Have It.* The low budget comedy about three black men vying for the attentions of a vibrant, independent African American woman was a surprise hit. Lee was to develop a distinctive voice portraying the African American community from an uncompromising black perspective, and would help initiate a renaissance in African American film production in the coming years.

Aside from the attention to distinct audience groups, a yuppie angst lurked in the humor of many popular comedies. The year brought to the United States continuing prosperity marked by declining oil prices, low inflation, and soaring stock values. Nonetheless, the high times on Wall Street were marred by scandal and greed. Ivan Boesky was only the most prominent among the investors found guilty of insider trading. He agreed to pay a record fine of $100 million on illicit profits. On 6 November, only eight days before Boesky pleaded guilty, General Motors announced that it would close eleven plants in the United States employing 29,000 people. As a result, the general satisfaction with prosperity included an underside of apprehension. Beneath the laughter and affluence simmered unhappiness and anxiety in comedies such as *Down and Out in Beverly Hills, The Mosquito Coast, Peggy Sue Got Married,* and *Something Wild,* as well as those mentioned earlier. The culture of consumption raised doubts about the values and direction in American life.

That apprehension was vivid in a series of films about small-town America that mixed nostalgia with malaise. In many respects the self-confident optimism, the appeal to old-fashioned values, and the strident anticommunism that marked the Reagan administration evoked the 1950s. A cluster of films, including *Blue Velvet, Stand by Me, Something Wild, Hoosiers,* and *River's Edge,* portrayed small-town life in the 1950s or evoked that period through the habits and fashions of its setting. But in these movies the traditional values touted by Reagan's politics generally appeared to be fundamentally irretrievable or an ideological fabrication. The division between the aspirations and the reality of small-town America spoke for the divided feelings within the culture at large.

While writer-directors Oliver Stone, Woody Allen, and David Lynch were the leading filmmakers of the year, some veteran talents of the previous decade, such as Francis Ford Coppola (*Peggy Sue Got Married*) and Martin Scorsese (*The Color of Money*), retreated from their more distinctive, personal projects to produce mainstream hits. English-language imports, from the Australian smash hit comedy *Crocodile Dundee* to the award-winning British films *A Room with a View, Mona Lisa,* and *My Beautiful Laundrette,* offered strong competition to American films at the box office and for critical accolades. At the same time Hollywood genre pictures, remakes, and series films did lucrative business, with *Karate Kid, Part II, Star Trek IV: The Voyage Home,* and *Aliens* among the top ten box office leaders.

This essay examines four trends in American cinema, each represented by distinguished films of the year: contesting the Cold War (*Platoon*), future torment (*Aliens* and *The Fly*), laughter and anxiety (*Hannah and Her Sisters* and *Ferris Bueller's Day Off*), and the crisis in traditional America (*Blue Velvet*).

Platoon: Contesting the Cold War

A comparison between *Platoon* and *Top Gun* illuminates divisions in American cinema. *Top Gun* was a model Hollywood package, an optimistic summer blockbuster matching a popular star, Tom Cruise, with high technology jet fighter spectacles and a romance—all driven forward with pulsating pop music. Don Simpson and Jerry Bruckheimer (*Flashdance* [1983], *Beverly Hills Cop* [1984]), two of Hollywood's most successful producers, put together the Paramount picture supported by a $15 million budget, an intense marketing campaign, and the cooperation of the American armed forces. Influenced by an earlier hit, *An Officer and a Gentleman* (1982), it was set in the present and dramatized an imaginary triumph of American fighter pilots over Soviet foes. By contrast, *Platoon* was an unusual production, a risky endeavor arising from the margins of the industry. The Vietnam War film was a grim, December release with no romance, a sleeper without star performers. Its modest $6 million budget came from the British Hemdale Film Corporation, after Hollywood studios passed on the project. The film depended upon critical praise and high-profile awards to reach a wide audience. A personal project based on the experience of writer-director Oliver Stone, it was set in the past and dramatized divisions and defeat within the American armed forces. Both movies were big hits. *Top Gun* ended its theatrical U.S. release with a box office return of over $176 million, while *Platoon* earned an impressive $137 million, which ranked them first and third, respectively, among the highest grossing films of those released this year. *Platoon* also sparked a wide public discussion. *Newsweek* called it "one of the rare Hollywood movies that mat-

Sergeants Elias (Willem Dafoe, right) and Barnes (Tom Berenger, left) quarrel over the proper way to wage war in *Platoon* (Oliver Stone, Hemdale Film Corp.). Jerry Ohlinger's Movie Material Store.

ter" (Ansen 57). Looking back from the perspective of the twenty-first century, *Top Gun* appears to be part of a series of jingoistic, Cold War movies associated with the Reagan era, though at the time critics hardly acknowledged its politics and generally dismissed the film as a formulaic diversion. *Platoon,* however, challenged prevailing attitudes and generated serious, political controversy.

The Vietnam War's effect on national unity was a touchstone for these combat films. *Top Gun*'s Maverick is a hotshot but undisciplined pilot in a specialized jet fighter training school, but he is haunted by the death of his father, also a navy pilot, missing under mysterious circumstances during the Vietnam War. Maverick's integration into the navy fighting unit succeeds after he learns that his father's death was honorable, even heroic. The young man's triumph on the fighting front, cooperating with his fellow fliers, comes as a vindication for the earlier tragedy in Vietnam. Banishing the criticism of the Vietnam War and promoting a belligerent nationalism was central to the ideology of this film. *Top Gun* wholeheartedly supported Reagan's mission to strengthen the American military and recommit a unified nation to forcefully promoting our international interests. *Platoon* expressed an alternative perspective.

Platoon portrays the experience of Bravo Company, a unit of American soldiers fighting near the Cambodian border in 1967. The story follows the tour of duty of Chris Taylor (Charlie Sheen), a green infantryman, who finally returns to the States a decorated, wounded, and disillusioned veteran. Many critics observed that *Platoon* did not portray the politics surrounding the Vietnam War, but nonetheless is political. For the men in Bravo Company, the politics of the war becomes meaningless; the soldiers are only concerned with their survival, escaping from the fear, danger, and misery of jungle warfare. Rather than sharing a common cause with the local population, the GIs view the Vietnamese as enemies to be mistrusted, interrogated, terrorized, and killed. Furthermore, the platoon serves as a microcosm of America, and its divisions illustrate tensions within the culture. The soldiers are split in their loyalty between two veteran fighters—the sensitive and decent Sergeant Elias (Willem Dafoe) and the pragmatic but ruthless Sergeant Barnes (Tom Berenger). Elias becomes associated with the counterculture from the 1960s—he smokes dope, listens to Jefferson Airplane and Motown music, dances with his African American buddies, and questions the war effort. Barnes is a career soldier, a hardhat personality who drinks Jack Daniels, plays poker, and instills a harsh, aggressive code into the ignorant recruits. The differences between Elias and Barnes erupt when Elias stops Barnes in the process of killing Vietnamese villagers under interrogation. Threatened by a military inquiry, Barnes kills Elias under the cover of combat. The shooting of Elias marks the death of American ideals in the face of war's savagery. At the climax of the film, Taylor, sympathetic to Elias and at odds with Barnes over his death, shoots Barnes in the aftermath of battle. *Platoon* questions the ethos of a heroic military, characterizes divisive social values, and challenges a ruthless pragmatism that is often disguised behind the slogans of anticommunism. As a result, *Platoon* forcefully contests the politics of *Top Gun, Heartbreak Ridge,* and Ronald Reagan.

Platoon was most widely praised, not for its politics, but for its realistic presentation of the American infantryman in the Vietnam War. Oliver Stone was himself twice wounded and earned a Bronze Star during his fifteen-month tour of duty that ended in November 1968. He subjected his cast to a rigorous two-week boot camp in the jungle under the supervision of Vietnam marine veteran Dale Dye before beginning the seven-week shoot in the Philippines. Stone's dedication of the film to "the men who fought and died in the Vietnam War" inspired his drive for authenticity: "I was under an obligation to show it as it was fighting in the Vietnam War" (qtd. in Ansen 57). The combat episodes include a night jungle patrol, searching an abandoned enemy camp, torching a peasant village, retreating before an advancing Viet Cong force, and finally a chaotic communist assault on the American base camp. In each instance one feels the horror, fear, and confusion of combat as the camera offers the ground-level perspective of soldiers engulfed in war. Many agreed with *Newsweek*'s David Ansen that "*Platoon* captures the crazy-adrenaline-rush chaos of battle better than any movie before" (57).

The attention to the details of jungle warfare and the emotional intensity of battle gave *Platoon* a persuasive power that sparked a widespread public response. David Halberstam, who had covered the war for the *New York Times*, wrote: "*Platoon* is historically and politically accurate. . . . I think the film will become an American classic. Thirty years from now, people will think of the Viet Nam War as *Platoon*" (qtd. in Corliss, "*Platoon*" 57). John Wheeler, chairman of the Vietnam Veterans Memorial Fund, was representative of many Vietnam vets when he declared, "*Platoon* makes us real. . . . It speaks to our generation. Those guys are us" (Corliss 57). In January 1987 *Time* ran a cover story entitled, "*Platoon*: Vietnam, the Way It Really Was on Film." But some, such as conservative John Podhoretz, condemned the film as "one of the most repellent movies ever made in this country" (qtd. in Corliss 56). General William Westmoreland, former commander of American forces in Vietnam, declared, "I haven't seen this movie *Platoon*, but it is full of lies and I don't think anyone should go to see it" (qtd. in Palmer 27). Many found the film divided between the astonishingly realistic depiction of infantry in jungle warfare and a morality play between the saintly Elias and the savage Barnes for the loyalty of Chris Taylor. Indeed, Taylor's voiceover reading of letters to his grandmother was a clumsy, and at times overbearing, means of delivering the message that "we did not fight the enemy. We fought ourselves and the enemy was in us." *Platoon* stirred the debate about the meaning of the Vietnam War and became an important document in the culture's struggle to come to terms with the conflict. The film portrayed the dangers of conducting national policy directed by a ruthless pragmatism shorn of human values.

Future Torment: *Aliens* and *The Fly*

Science fiction and horror films provoke our fears of technology, of the future, and of our inner monsters. Frequently we like to see these fears manifest in fiction so that we can identify and come to terms with the anxieties that have generated them. The *Challenger* and Chernobyl disasters generated plenty of apprehension. The spread of AIDS, its rising death toll, and growing calls for education and treatment made people even more aware of the vulnerability of the body and the dangers of physical desire. These cultural traumas sustained the well-established audience for harrowing visions of monsters and machines, and helped to make *Aliens, The Fly,* and *Star Trek IV: The Voyage Home* among the most popular films of the year. Rather than fostering the belief propagated by the Reagan administration that innovative technology, such as the "Star Wars" defense system, could protect Americans from disaster, these films fed the fear that technology was a false panacea masking deeper troubles.

Though *Aliens* was a sequel to the popular and distinctive *Alien,* writer-director James Cameron (*The Terminator*) wanted his movie to offer a fresh approach while retaining links to its predecessor. Whereas *Alien* brought a haunted house tale to a space ship, Cameron organizes his science fiction like a combat movie, with the tagline of "This time it's war." Here a marine troop investigates an isolated planet when the colonizers disappear. Ripley (Sigourney Weaver), the sole survivor from *Alien,* is intimidated into scouting for the expedition because of suspicions that the monster she encountered may be responsible for the disaster. Once the expedition arrives on the planet, a battle quickly ensues between a herd of ferocious giant insects and the soldiers, whose belligerent posturing and high-powered weapons wilt before the aliens. Ripley finds a sole surviving little girl among the debris of the colony. Maternal instincts arise and transform Ripley into a commanding warrior. Gradually all the soldiers are killed, leaving Ripley to face off against the queen mother of the insects in order to save the child.

The movie exchanges aggression for nurturing as the foundation of maternity, and this alien vision populates the future with Amazons who act remarkably like a bunch of overconfident, belligerent guys. Ripley is matched by, among others, the female body builder Private Vasquez (Jenette Goldstein), the toughest marine in the contingent, and the leader of the monster horde is the mother of them all. This vision of women beating guys at macho virtue is often mistaken for feminist sympathy, but it appears more like an attempt to punish complaining women by making them over as men.

Aliens cultivates cynicism. The military is inept in spite of its overpowering technology, and rather than allowing for the crisis to bond the fighters, as is common in war films, the movie slaughters its characters until only mother and child remain. "The Company," the all-powerful corporate sponsor of the expedition, readily trades human life for profits. This overarching institutional villain, inherited from *Alien,* remains unchallenged. The war movie model refers to Vietnam, and *Aliens* plays both sides of the contro-

Aliens (James Cameron, Twentieth Century Fox), starring Sigourney Weaver, reworks dystopic science fiction into a commentary on the legacy of the Vietnam War and other contemporary ills. Jerry Ohlinger's Movie Material Store.

versy. During the initial foray into the monster's lair, the heavily armed marine troop must put aside its most sophisticated weapons because the monster had built its nest over a nuclear reactor, the power source for the planet. As a result, the troops find themselves handcuffed when the command sends them into battle, resulting in defeat. The situation evokes the conservative criticism that politicians prevented the American armed forces from doing their job by restricting their firepower. From the liberal perspective, the military command in *Aliens* serves the ends of the villainous "Company," and readily sacrifices people for profits. As a result, the fissures marking our cultural memory of Vietnam are incorporated into *Aliens*.

In *Aliens* the future is dark, cold, and dilapidated; machines offer the only comforts, and without them survival is impossible. Apart from the maternal instincts of warrior women, the only note of hope is that the android, a conventional sci-fi figure that typically betrays humankind, sacrifices itself so that mother and child can survive. So machines appear to be an answer in *Aliens* after all. This movie offers no solace or understanding of the challenge posed by technology, or the dehumanizing logic of the marketplace. Instead, the movie assaults the audience and leaves us spent.

While also featuring technology and monsters, *The Fly* is more firmly in the horror tradition. Romance, the erotic, and the body hold the foreground rather than interplanetary combat in the future. Here David Cronenberg, a leading filmmaker in contemporary horror, remakes a low budget success from 1958. Like Cameron, Cronenberg takes a few elements from the original to fashion a work decidedly his own. *The Fly* portrays a melancholy reversal on "Beauty and the Beast" in which longing excites the bestial, and love fails to transform the monster. Instead of the president's smiling face reminding us that it's morning in America, *The Fly* anchors its deep-seated pessimism in the limits of the body.

Seth Brundle (Jeff Goldblum), a lonely inventor, meets Veronica (Geena Davis), a lovely journalist who is researching teleportation. He invites her up to his laboratory to show off his experimental machines, and romance blossoms. The teleportation device Brundle has nearly perfected is an expression of his loneliness, a desire to be transported. The ardent sex between Seth and Ronnie succeeds in sending them on an erotic high that surpasses the trivial capacity of these machines. However, Seth's fragile passion turns jealous when Ronnie visits with her editor and former lover. Morose and drunk, the inventor tries his teleporter, but a fly inadvertently gets in the machine, and the result mixes the genes of the scientist and the insect. In the course of the coming weeks, the man is transformed into a monster, and neither Ronnie's continuing devotion nor his own desperate attempts to undo the experiment can save him. Once technology is set in motion, its power unleashed, humans can do little to stop its destruction.

Cronenberg portrays the pleasure of the lovers' physical communion, and then devotes himself to the dawning realization, gradual change, and the gruesome deterioration of the romance as embodied in Brundle's flesh.

The Fly becomes a gross, detailed exercise in turning a man into a disgusting monster. The horror grows as the viewer returns each time with Ronnie to see her lover's ever more repellent mutation. The struggle to save Seth, and even to embrace his repulsive body, measures the depth of Ronnie's love. Finally, the last remaining vestige of feeling in the former scientist warns her to flee before the monster does her harm. The movie earns its romantic charge from its grotesque means of expressing devotion; its disgusting analogue between romance and the physical becomes the basis for horror.

Though markedly different in tone and intent from *Aliens*, this film presents an even more harrowing vision. Cronenberg is intent on measuring, first, love's fire, and then the ashes—the inevitable misunderstandings, psychic trials, and physical decline that challenge and, in this filmmaker's view, doom romance. Brundle's deterioration has often been compared to disease (AIDS was a frequent reference), but the director sought a more universal expression of the limitations of desire. Cronenberg's dread of the body engages serious emotions and gives his film a repellent power that earned accolades from the connoisseurs of horror. Late in the movie, Ronnie's apprehension increases when she discovers that she is pregnant and wonders whether the conception occurred before Seth's fateful experiment. In a nightmare, she imagines aborting another monster. *The Fly* refuses any prospect that sex and love might prove fruitful. Seth does, however, develop a self-conscious humor as he struggles first to understand what is happening and then struggles to retain his humanity. Our compassion for the man as he turns into a monster gives the film a tragic dimension enriched by Goldblum's winning performance. For Cronenberg, the reasoning of scientists and the craft of the artist attempt to understand, and even circumvent, the sad truths of the flesh, but there is no escaping human destiny because of its anchor in the body. In *The Fly* machines are presented as a pathetic response to loneliness, an expression of the desire to be transported beyond our physical limitations, but the quixotic endeavor only results in a dead end. Contrary to the Reagan administration's belief that innovative technology could propel the American economy and build an impregnable defense shield, *The Fly* portrays machines as an all too human extension of our errant flesh.

Aliens and *The Fly* fashion their grim torment with craft and force. Even though it seems unlikely that either of these films offers relief from the anxiety engendered by our technological culture, they earned critical praise and a wide audience. However, the most commercially successful science fiction film of the year, with a gross box office exceeding $109 million, projects a sunny optimism in a casual production whose conception and execution match the television series upon which it is based. *Star Trek IV: The Voyage Home* sends the members of the Starship *Enterprise* on a mission to save the whales, a quest that succeeds in offending no one. Captain Kirk (William Shatner), Spock (Leonard Nimoy, who also directs the film), and crew must return to 1980s America and transport humpback whales into the future in order to respond to an alien signal and save the planet from destruction. As a result, the film promotes a return to nature rather than a dependence on technology as a means of responding to the challenges of the future. The film presents these familiar space travelers in contemporary San Francisco, where silly jokes and an earnest dedication to good works allow the heroes to realize their mission. The plot eliminates the need for an identifiable villain and barely sustains any dramatic conflict. Nevertheless, the fans of "Star Trek" were satisfied to see their heroes going through their familiar paces. Roger Ebert found the film to be "the most elegant and satisfying 'Star Trek' film so far."

Laughter and Anxiety: *Hannah and Her Sisters* and *Ferris Bueller's Day Off*

Though *Hannah and Her Sisters* and *Ferris Bueller's Day Off* represent opposite ends of the comic spectrum, from the sophisticated to the adolescent, escape drives them both. Lee and Holly, the sisters of the title, and Elliot, Hannah's husband, want to escape from the perfection and self-sufficiency that Hannah represents for them. Hannah conjures up their own inadequacies even as she offers love and support. Similarly, Ferris Bueller wants to escape from school, or more broadly the routine obligations and institutions that suck the pleasures from life. He dismisses what adults tell him he should do or be, indulges in the good times of the metropolis, and evades any rebuke or penalty. However, his desires are enormously innocent and orthodox. Ferris can't imagine values outside of the affluent teen culture he strides atop so effortlessly. Both Ferris Bueller and the characters in *Hannah* end up at home, safely sheltered by the families from whom they fled to begin their adventure. The films circle back to happily embrace what their protagonists sought to escape. Nonetheless, both films express a troubling desire for flight, and a suspicion that dissatisfaction lingers just beneath the surface of their experience, a dissatisfaction that speaks to the fissures in Reagan's America.

Hannah and Her Sisters is an ingratiating and distinctive romantic comedy. Hannah (Mia Farrow) is a successful actress and mother of four who

balances her professional and domestic life with ease. The film begins and
returns to bountiful Thanksgiving celebrations hosted by Hannah for her
extended family and friends in her spacious, comfortable Manhattan apartment. Here we learn that Elliot (Michael Caine), her financial consultant
husband, lusts after her beautiful younger sister Lee (Barbara Hershey),
who lives with a misanthropic painter, Frederick (Max Von Sydow). Holly
(Dianne Wiest), the flighty third sister, lacks confidence and struggles to
sustain a career as an actress. Hannah's elderly parents are former film stars
living in the shadow of their glamour. Woody Allen's film gracefully deploys
a series of related plot lines interweaving five major characters. Elliot
seduces Lee into an illicit affair; Holly is disappointed in her career, her
romance with an architect flounders, and she turns to writing; Mickey
(Allen), Hannah's first husband, undergoes an existential crisis provoked by
a cancer scare; Hannah supports, comforts, and advises them all, and still
finds time for reconciling her quarreling parents and raising her children.

Episodes are bridged by sixteen suggestive intertitles that shift attention
among the mature, sophisticated characters whose self-delusions nonetheless provide for a deft mix of humor and pathos. Perspective changes as a
particular character moves to the foreground for an episode only to recede
in the next. The privileged figure wins our sympathy with voiceover mus-
ings revealing inner feelings, doubts, and desires. The film offers multiple
perspectives on love—conjugal, illicit, sisterly, filial, between friends, of art—
and love in its various stages—initiation, vicissitudes, breakdown, vicarious
experience, and even its lingering memory. Mickey's quest for life's meaning leads him from religion and philosophy to the poets, art, and the Marx
Brothers. In the arts he finds love's centrality, its unpredictability, and the
need to embrace the experience of living in spite of life's uncertainties. The
film closes with a final Thanksgiving: Lee has fallen for and married a literature professor; Elliot realizes that Hannah has always been his kindred
spirit; Mickey and Holly have married and are expecting their first child;
and Hannah, by chance, intuition, and conscious choice, has nurtured the
family that acts as a sustaining circle of human affection. Psychological
insight rather than moral judgment becomes the key to a generous understanding that brings everyone together in comedy's traditional union.

Allen's elegant direction frames his characters in groups or moves with
and around his players, balancing them against each other. Rather than iso-
lating individuals through editing, long takes and master shots shape the
film. The exception is Mickey, whose life crisis is often singled out in montage until at the close he finally joins the rest of the family at the Thanksgiving celebration (Thompson 308–11). The dense sound mix links scenes

and emotions through the Tin Pan Alley musical score, overlapping dialogue, and the interior monologues distributed among the major characters. The style cultivates a harmonious ensemble that enhances our satisfaction in the final union. However, there is a lingering sense that the film's graceful design ties together some flimsy elements.

Yuppie angst arising from the culture of consumption works at the margins of *Hannah and Her Sisters*. Scheming to seduce Lee, Elliot brings Dusty (Daniel Stern), a rock star interested in decorating his Southampton mansion, to Frederick's place to look at paintings. Distracting Frederick with Dusty, Elliot takes the opportunity to make a move on Lee, and his kiss eventually brings her to his bed. Simultaneously, the artist grows impatient, finding that Dusty neither knows nor cares for art; he only wants to complement his home furnishings. The association of Elliot's philandering with Dusty, the pop star with more money than he knows how to spend, extends the culture of consumption to Elliot's desire. Developing the same theme, the married architect David (Sam Waterston) courts both Holly and her friend April (Carrie Fisher), and selfishly undermines their bond with a jealous rivalry. Abundance, leisure, and irresponsibility feed a culture of consumption that finally produces Elliot's indecision and guilt, yuppie angst arising with the prosperity of the Reagan era.

As Pauline Kael wrote, *Hannah and Her Sisters* "is likable, but you wish there were more to like" (*Hooked* 115). In spite of the unbridled enthusiasm of many critics, the film's style floats across the surface without penetrating very deeply. The characters and content are so much more sophisticated than most movies, one wants to embrace it wholeheartedly. However, for all its striving for psychological realism, the final union of the couples is more conventional than convincing. Mickey's exploration of Catholicism displays the vulgar humor of Allen's earlier gags, but the flat jokes (plastic crucified Jesus with rolling eyeballs, white bread and mayonnaise) become an embarrassing response to the pretentious, labored quest. After fourteen films, Allen's neurotic New York Jew has become stale. Mia Farrow's Hannah lacks the commanding presence the other characters attribute to her. After Lee's departure Elliot declares his renewed devotion to his wife, but one wonders. The film unfolds without surprises—the positive ending is too comforting to carry conviction. The anxieties of the characters—Elliot's infidelity, Holly's inadequacy, Lee's need for a man to guide her, Mickey's fears—carry more force than Hannah's serenity and the reassuring view that love's unpredictability will mend every heart.

Ferris Bueller's Day Off is a fantasy of teen omnipotence. Its unpretentious fun targets the youth audience uninterested in the lofty ambition of

Hannah and Her Sisters. Even here, yuppie angst simmers beneath the surface chiefly embodied in the secondary characters, Cameron and Jeanie. Playing hooky from high school on a sunny, spring day sets the challenge for Ferris. Responsible parents, a rival sibling, and the school's Dean Rooney are his nemeses. The teen uses his charm and ingenuity to get what he wants, and he wants so much. He wants a car, but his parents disappoint him with a computer. So he recruits his friend Cameron and convinces him to hijack his father's precious Ferrari for a jaunt into Chicago. Joining up with Ferris's girlfriend, the trio enjoys a posh restaurant lunch, catches a Cubs game, tours the Art Institute, and takes over a parade to celebrate their freedom. Then they manage to beat their parents home so that the escapade remains undetected. Stalking them is Dean Rooney, determined to expose the popular Ferris as a truant, and his envious sister, Jeanie, who resents being condemned to a dreary classroom while her brother frolics. *Ferris Bueller* displays an uncanny feel for the teenage sensibility and continues to realize the fantasies of American adolescents even two decades after its release.

The charm and confidence of Ferris finds its shadow in the adolescent troubles of his friend. Cam is lonely, anxious, and nursing a virus. He knows that Ferris can and will talk him into trouble, and that he will pay the price. Ferris's doting mom and dad find their counterpart in Cam's absent parents. The emblem of Cameron's anguish is his father's sports car—the beloved trophy that receives the attention he craves. Even though the Ferrari serves as his bitter rival, Cam worries that his father will discover his trespass with the car. His concern and caution finally collapse when the car accidentally crashes down an embankment to its death. Facing disaster, Cam recovers his own worth in the car's destruction. He doesn't care and it liberates him. The culture of consumption transforms the Oedipal love object from mother into a marker of conspicuous wealth to be stolen, violated, and destroyed. This epiphany of independence gives Cam his maturity by overcoming the fear of his father in the form of an extravagant car. However, Cam's rivalry with a Ferrari expresses the apprehension simmering beneath American affluence, in which the lure of conspicuous luxuries undermines fundamental human relationships.

The other major expression of social fissure in the film is Jeanie, Ferris's sister. Through much of the picture she tries to expose her brother; finally, when Ferris runs in the back door just ahead of his parents, Jeanie has her chance. Instead, she saves him from Dean Rooney. Jeanie undergoes a transformation earlier that afternoon in the police station where she encounters a delinquent (Charlie Sheen) who asks why she resents her brother. Under questioning, she discovers that she simply envies what Ferris already has—the confidence to indulge his desires and avoid punishment. The recognition draws her into the delinquent's arms for a kiss, more to come later. The voice of the delinquent outsider chides the culture of envy, the resentment of those who measure their unhappiness by the success of others.

Ferris Bueller is a child of affluence whose opportunity for freedom produces nothing more than the rewards promised by middle class success. No sulking rebel harboring an unarticulated malaise, Ferris is a master of self-promotion. He embodies the confidence of a president who wants to set free the entrepreneur from the restrictions of government or, in Ferris's experience, the demands of high school. Ferris Bueller's unimpeded indulgence and ingratiating charm made him the teen idol of a generation. But in the shadows of his triumphs lies the angst of affluence—the neglect fostered by a drive for wealth and the envy harbored by those who see in others what they lack.

Blue Velvet: "It's a Strange World"

From the perspective of two decades later, *Blue Velvet* stands as the cinematic landmark of the year. In two polls of U.S. critics ranking the outstanding films of the decade, *Blue Velvet* placed third and fourth, behind *Raging Bull, E.T.,* and (in one ranking) the German film *Wings of Desire*.[1] In a 2002 survey of fifty UK film critics regarding the top films of the previous twenty-five years, *Blue Velvet* came in fifth.[2] Michael Atkinson has called *Blue Velvet* "the most influential and crucial film of its decade" (11). Upon its release *Blue Velvet* strongly divided critics, though the National Society of Film Critics, the Boston Film Critics, and the Los Angeles Film Critics Association bestowed honors upon the film as well as director David Lynch. The film was produced for a modest $6 million and attracted a limited audience, earning approximately $8.5 million in domestic receipts. Many agreed with J. Hoberman that "there hasn't been an American studio movie so rich, so formally controlled, so imaginatively cast and wonderfully acted, and so charged with its maker's psychosexual energy since *Raging Bull*" ("Return" 56).

The coming-of-age mystery plot is no more original than the Hardy Boys. Jeffrey Beaumont (Kyle MacLachlan) returns from college to Lumberton, his small-town home, when his father is stricken and hospitalized. Shortly after arriving, he comes across a severed human ear in a vacant field. After presenting it to the police department's Detective Williams, Jeffrey cannot shake his curiosity. Encouraged by the detective's attractive

Kyle MacLachlan and Dennis Hopper in *Blue Velvet* (David Lynch, DEG), one of the decade's most distinctive films, which draws a stark picture of evil in small-town America. Jerry Ohlinger's Movie Material Store.

teenage daughter, Sandy (Laura Dern), Jeffrey sneaks into the apartment of suspect Dorothy Vallens (Isabella Rossellini), a singer at the shady Slow Club. There he witnesses her assault and rape by the monstrous Frank Booth (Dennis Hopper), who has blackmailed her into sexual bondage by abducting her husband and child. Later Jeffrey offers to help her as he and Dorothy become lovers by night; meanwhile Jeffrey courts Sandy by day and continues his investigation of Frank. One night Frank and his thugs discover Jeffrey at Dorothy's apartment. Frank takes Jeffrey on a frightening "joyride" that ends with a beating and a warning to stay away from Dorothy. The police, however, with help from evidence gathered by Jeffrey, close in on Frank and his gang. One night Dorothy, naked, battered, and delirious, wanders upon Jeffrey and Sandy out on a date. They take her to the hospital but Sandy learns of Jeffrey's intimacy with the singer and is heartbroken. As the police pursue the villains, Jeffrey goes to Dorothy's apartment and, in a confrontation with Frank, kills him. Afterward, Sandy is reconciled to Jeffrey and they prepare for marriage. Dorothy's husband has been killed, but she is reunited with her young son and peace returns to Lumberton.

On the basis of its plot, the film appears to be an overheated Hollywood mix of crime and romance. So what is extraordinary about *Blue Velvet*? Four

qualities distinguish the film: shocking sexual episodes; startling juxtapositions that leave the viewer off-balance and uncertain; evocative images and
sounds that spark a complex emotional response; and finally a crime plot
that is a pretext for a psychological tale of sexual awakening that withholds
moral judgment. Each of these qualities has multiple dimensions.

The controversy around *Blue Velvet* most obviously arises from its sexual violence, especially violence not only against women but invited by
them. When Dorothy provokes the innocent Jeffrey to "hurt me" as part of
their "lovemaking," she appears to have incorporated Frank's brutality into
her desire. When the reluctant lover accedes to her demand, he too appears
to have taken on an aspect of the villain. Later, he is shaken by the pleasure he takes in violence. Taboo sexuality extends to voyeurism, fetishism,
sado-masochism, and homoerotic violence whose pleasures are heightened
with obscene language, illicit drugs, and ritual sex games. As Pauline Kael
observed, in *Blue Velvet* "sex has the danger and heightened excitement of a
horror picture" (*Hooked* 208).

When an interviewer asked Lynch whether he was worried that the
MPAA would slap his film with an X rating, the director noted that the board
did not "cause me any trouble because all the situations were justified and
wrapped in a context" (Bouzereau 39). For many, however, the justification
for taboo sex only made it more inflammatory. The sex so powerfully portrayed in *Blue Velvet* both attracts and repels the viewer. As Roger Ebert
explained, *Blue Velvet* is "at the center of a national critical firestorm. The
movie is so strong, so shocking and yet so audacious that people walk out
shaking their heads; they don't quite know what to make of it." Clearly the
variety, complexity, and impact of sex in *Blue Velvet* was unprecedented in
a mainstream Hollywood film.

Forbidden sex in *Blue Velvet* takes place not in a sleazy Parisian hotel or
a metropolitan den of iniquity, but in wholesome, small-town America. The
blend of innocence and decadence, naiveté, and kinkiness arises from a
style of startling juxtaposition, akin to surrealism, that pervades *Blue Velvet*.
The film not only pivots between extremes of setting and behavior, but
mixes intense drama and offbeat humor, as when Dorothy greets Jeffrey's
return to her apartment by referring to his earlier hiding place: "I looked for
you in my closet tonight." The art direction slyly blends the fashions, cars,
and songs of the 1950s with subtle allusions to the 1980s, such as Jeffrey's
earring, without clearly indicating its temporal setting. Mainstream entertainment film conventions work with visual and aural symbolism in the art
cinema tradition. These formal devices create a link between appearance
and substance, the social and the psychological, and good and evil that por-

trays bewildering forces hidden in the normal. When Frank hisses at Jeffrey, "You're like me," the audience shares the hero's disturbing epiphany, and the film's style has prepared us for the bond between the gangster and the schoolboy. This complex intermingling confounds Reagan's appeal to stable, clear, and universal values as the bedrock of his conservative creed.

This strategy of startling juxtaposition also cultivates irony, detachment, and ambivalence. Sandy's description of her dream in which robins deliver love to a world enveloped in darkness, told to Jeffrey with a backdrop of a church's stain-glass windows and swelling organ music, usually evokes laughter from the viewer. Or the chubby prostitute dancing slowly on the roof of a car to Roy Orbison's "In Dreams" while Frank pummels a helpless Jeffrey presents an introspective reverie in response to violence that seems as unnerving as the beating itself. The effect leaves the spectator disturbed and confused. As J. Hoberman reported, "One doesn't know what to make of it, which may be as disconcerting for some as it is exciting for others" ("Return" 56). The unusual mixture of elements and shifts in tone, an approach often associated with postmodernism, provokes conflicting emotions that confound understanding. Lesley Stern describes *Blue Velvet* as a "slippery text" that "poses interpretation itself as perverse" (79, 81). Timothy Corrigan lashes out at the film as "illegible" (71). Nevertheless, *Blue Velvet* has inspired a rich critical exchange, especially among feminists, who have lined up among the film's most avid supporters (see Mulvey; Bundtzen; Layton) as well as its most severe detractors (see Jaehne; Shattuc). The film's ambiguity and power invite viewers to come back. Pauline Kael began her review, "'Maybe I'm sick, but I want to see that again'—Overheard after a showing of *Blue Velvet*" (*Hooked* 202). And J. Hoberman assured his readers, "The more you see it, the more you get" ("Return" 56).

Evocative image and sound associations set the emotional tone of *Blue Velvet,* and frequently undermine a conventional response to the story. This poetic quality is central to the style of startling juxtaposition. The songs in the film—"Blue Velvet," "In Dreams," and "Mysteries of Love"—are indicative. Lynch has explained that Bobby Vinton's 1963 recording of "Blue Velvet" was one of the key inspirations for the film (Rodley 134). The pop song evokes the closing of the 1950s, after which the turmoil of the 1960s changed America profoundly. The song becomes a marker for the transformation of American innocence to a desperate, at times beleaguered, sophistication, and for Jeffrey's sexual awakening as well. The teenage melancholy of Bobby Vinton is given an overbearing, self-conscious inflection in Isabella Rossellini's performance of the song. During the credits a blue velvet curtain billows ominously in anticipation of its function as Frank's sexual fetish torn from Dorothy's robe, a death token stuffed into the mouth of Dorothy's mutilated husband, and later used to hang from the barrel of a gun as Frank stalks Jeffrey during the film's climax. The song's lovelorn sorrow becomes invested with erotic perversion, homicidal rage, and social significance. Late in the film, when Sandy and Jeffrey embrace dancing at a teen party to "Mysteries of Love," the tune shadows the young couple with the sadistic trysts at Dorothy's apartment and the irrational force that sex can unleash. In a similar chain of associations, the battle of the Darwinian bugs underneath the Beaumonts' lawn, the insects crawling over the severed ear, Jeffrey's disguise as an exterminator, and the bug in the robin's mouth at the close all reverberate with the primal drives that need to be held in check for the wholesome Lumberton values to prevail over Frank's seething underworld. I can only suggest a glimpse into the network of allusions, many of them arising from popular culture or psychosexual archetypes, that create a dreamlike, charged, erotic atmosphere. They weave into *Blue Velvet* an astonishing range of associations that enrich and transform the simple plot.

Critics often invoke Alfred Hitchcock in discussing *Blue Velvet*. The connection is appropriate because Hitchcock generally used a fantastic crime or espionage plot, but the powerful meaning of his films arose from the psychosexual dynamics of the romance. As in Hitchcock, the crime plot of *Blue Velvet* becomes a means to explore psychology and sexuality. Here lies the film's immediacy for its audience. The mystery pertains not simply to the crime plot, but more importantly to the irrational and often inexplicable power of sexuality. Many commentators have understood the film as a Freudian parable in which Jeffrey witnesses the primal scene between Dorothy and Frank and undergoes an Oedipal struggle with the villainous father in order to save the mother, only to eventually transfer his affections to a woman of his own age (Bundtzen; Layton; Mulvey). Though the conventional plot establishes a moral framework around crime and punishment, the psychological drama reserves judgment of the taboo sexual practices, and this detachment contributed to the controversy surrounding the film. The ambivalence, uncertainty, and moral detachment challenged the small-town ethos celebrated by Reagan's politics as the foundation of American values.

Blue Velvet's closing episode cultivates ambiguity, ending the film on a perplexing note. After Jeffrey shoots Frank and embraces Sandy, an ellipsis follows, bridged by "Mysteries of Love" on the sound track. A slow-motion reverse zoom retreats from a close-up of Jeffrey's ear as he rests on a chaise in his sunny yard. The young man looks up to see a robin on a tree branch. Sandy calls him in to lunch and, as he moves to the house, he greets first Detective Williams and his father, now fully recovered, and then, once in the house, his mother and Mrs. Williams. In the kitchen Sandy marvels at a robin sitting on the windowsill with a large bug in its mouth. "Maybe the robins are here," Jeffrey says, looking affectionately at Sandy. Aunt Barbara shudders with "I could never eat a bug" and then takes a bite of food herself. Sandy replies with a smile, "It's a strange world, isn't it?" A close-up of the robin makes it obvious that the bird is fake, a mechanical prop. Then the scene fades to Dorothy on a park bench accepting the embrace of her young son, running to her arms in slow motion with the propeller cap that Jeffrey found in Dorothy's apartment. As they hug, Rossellini's rendition of "Blue Velvet" replaces "Mysteries of Love" on the sound track, and the mother's joyous face changes to a melancholy reverie at the words, "I can still see blue velvet through my tears."

The question arises, how has his experience in the underworld changed Jeffrey? The wholesome family setting indicates a return to simplistic social relations that cannot acknowledge the irrational, powerful sexual forces shaping human experience. The mechanical robin suggests that the coming of love, the realization of Sandy's dream, is false—an ideological fabrication much like Reagan's political platitudes about "Morning in America." The insect in the robin's beak suggests that instincts such as eating must be satisfied. The combination of the joyous embrace of mother and child with a melancholy acknowledgment of the sexuality necessary to realize such purity carries the film's paradox. However, the violent primal drives appear to be genuine, powerful, and basic to experience, whereas the forces of good, though intertwined, function largely as a discipline holding bestial behavior in check. This view privileges the power of evil and renders good as naive or fundamentally repressive rather than offering a more nuanced, optimistic sense of human prospects and social possibilities. David Lynch's explanation of the film's ending carries with it a sense of resignation: "That's the subject of *Blue Velvet*. You apprehend things, and when you try to see what it's all about, you have to live with it" (139).

Though often described as unique, *Blue Velvet* was the most conspicuous representative of a broader trend in Hollywood cinema this year. *Stand by Me, Hoosiers, River's Edge,* and *Something Wild* also mixed nostalgia for small-town values and the 1950s with malaise. Though *Blue Velvet*'s primary address is psychological, it joins with these other films in questioning the simple-minded optimism that disguised Reagan's politics. John Powers and Fredric Jameson saw in this trend a "New American Gothic," an expression of the disturbing underbelly of social fissures and malcontents. Though these films fail to offer alternative values, they testify to a division within the United States, and a willingness to confront the darker side of human experience necessary in unmasking the social fantasia that often characterized American popular culture in the 1980s.

Hollywood movies were charting the fissures in Ronald Reagan's America. The contrast between *Top Gun* and *Platoon* brought to light the continuing national division over the legacy of the Vietnam War. The success of *Platoon* contested the aggressive international policies pursued by the president backed by the rhetoric of anticommunism. The nightmare vision of the future portrayed in *Aliens* and *The Fly* challenged an optimism based on technological progress promoted by Reagan and forcefully expressed in his Strategic Defense Initiative. Though comedies such as *Hannah and Her Sisters* and *Ferris Bueller's Day Off* found humor in the leisure activities of our affluent society, beneath the laughter lurked a disquieting sense that wealth, self-indulgence, and the culture of consumption were eroding the family bonds that sustained our most meaningful relationships. While the Reagan ideology had looked back to the 1950s and small-town life as expressions of the stable verities of our culture, their screen treatment in films such as *Blue Velvet* and *Something Wild* presented a disturbing vision of passion, confusion, and violence erupting to shatter a thin veneer of complacency. Beneath the desire for a more tranquil union simmered divisive tensions. The best work of our nation's filmmakers vividly expressed the contentious moods animating American society.

NOTES

1. In an *American Film* poll of fifty-four critics, the top ten domestic movies of the 1980s were *Raging Bull, E.T., Blue Velvet, Hannah and Her Sisters, Atlantic City, Raiders of the Lost Ark, Platoon, Once Upon a Time in America, Prizzi's Honor,* and *The King of Comedy* (with *The Fly* placing fourteenth) (McGilligan and Rowland 23–29). The top films of the decade in a poll of twenty-three critics in *Premiere* magazine were *Raging Bull, Wings of Desire, E.T., Blue Velvet,* and (tied) *Hannah and Her Sisters* and *Platoon* (Hearty 106–07).

2. The top films in *Sight and Sound*'s survey were *Apocalypse Now, Raging Bull, Fanny and Alexander, Goodfellas, Blue Velvet, Do the Right Thing, Blade Runner, Chungking Express, Distant Voices, Still Lives,* and (tied) *Once Upon a Time in America* and *A One and a Two (Yi-Yi)* (James 20–23).

1987

Movies and the Closing of the Reagan Era

JACK BOOZER

The most significant films of the year provide an interesting if sometimes veiled commentary on the national scene, whether through plot, characterization, theme, tone, and/or atmosphere. Their meanings are often embedded in and seem to grow out of their historical settings and some of the concerns that prevailed then. As the two-term Reagan presidency (1981–89) drew to a close, its record of performance and impact was already widely apparent and can serve as the touchstone for most of the discussion of this year in film. I have identified five key issues that were strongly reflected on the screen, not only in the arenas directly associated with Reagan's presidency, but also in the stressed cultural fabric of the American family.

The first issue was the ongoing struggle of the Cold War and the international Cold War profiteering that it encouraged. Reagan's obsession with this struggle, particularly as it was unfolding across hot spots in the Persian Gulf and Central America, led his administration into secret deals and eventually into what became known as the Iran-Contra scandal. This scandal was echoed in an important Hollywood film, and not in a way that has been previously recognized. The second issue was directly related to Reagan's trickle-down economic policies and attitudes, which did not address growing problems in the business finance sector. This becomes apparent in two national financial scandals that blew up at this time: one concerning the savings and loan (S&L) industry, which seems curiously reflected in a small David Mamet film, and the other pertaining to the junk bond market and the high-roller world of corporate raiders and deal makers, insightfully reflected in a memorable Oliver Stone picture. A third issue concerned Reagan's desire to get the nation out of its lasting depression over the Vietnam War, which by late in the decade Hollywood again looked upon as an open wound to be treated rather than simply covered over. The fourth issue is actually a trend and has some connection with the fact that Reagan was a media-trained and unusually image-conscious president. This added to the increased national awareness of the influence of television in politics and news, and the deterioration of national television media as a reliable source of news and information, much less a locale for professional journalism. The fifth and final issue is also a trend and concerns the growing stress on the American family and its proper child-rearing functions.

There were two films this year that received notable attention but which are not considered here: the top box office entry, *Beverly Hills Cop II*, an unconvincing sequel to the street-smart attitude and unexpected comic turns of the original, and the award-winning epic *The Last Emperor*. Many believe this exotically beautiful but culturally rather obscure Italian-British-Chinese production by the Italian director Bernardo Bertolucci may have stood out due to an absence of any really big films of similar scope from Hollywood.

Ronald Reagan's waning presidency increasingly reflected problems in some of his policies, particularly where accounting methods and separation of government and business were concerned. He had devoted himself to a reallocation of the federal budget, including a large reduction in the tax rate that was most favorable to the rich, and pushed the government away from discretionary domestic spending toward increased spending on defense and interest payments (by necessity, due to the ballooning deficit). At the same time Reagan also exercised a desire for deregulation and privatization across the government and business economic fronts. Even the Iran-Contra scandal had a significant association with over-enthusiastic entrepreneurial business methods in covert government dealings. Government oversight of business was severely downplayed in this administration in favor of deregulation and a no-holds-barred form of capitalism.

International Cold War Profiteering

As the brutal war between Iraq and Iran continued to accompany Reagan's years in office, the official government policy was one of neutrality, while in fact there was considerable jockeying for influence behind the scenes between the United States and the Soviet Union. The public became aware in late 1986 that Reagan's cabinet-level National Security Council (NSC) had secretly sold missiles to Iran and used the profits to support a right-wing insurgency against the legally elected Sandinista government of Nicaragua. Reagan claimed that the Iran missile deal was intended to free seven American hostages taken in Lebanon, although this was never proven (the final hostage was not released until 1991), and in any case the scheme violated Reagan's own public statements that his administration would never negotiate with terrorists. The resulting scandal became a constitutional issue because Congress had neither approved nor been informed of the actions of the NSC and the CIA in this regard. Reagan was soon compelled to set up a bipartisan commission in December 1986 to investigate the matter. Two months later, the commission, chaired by former Republican senator John Tower, delivered a stinging rebuke to the president for failing to control his security staff.

Though the Tower Commission officially castigated the president and his administration, the prison sentences that were eventually given to the leaders of the NSC staff would be voided on appeal because of the commission's earlier interrogation. This included sentences for Reagan's national security advisor, John Poindexter, and his deputy, Oliver North. North became known for his extensive shredding of documents to maintain the secrecy of U.S. arms sales to Iran and clandestine activities in Central America, which included aid to Honduras in return for assistance with the contras. The Iran-Iraq War had been going on since 1980 at great cost to human life, and the NSC made the secret missile deal with Iran in 1986 to impact the balance of the warring factions there. Supplying Iran's war effort and using the subsequent income to support the contras obviously contradicted official U.S. policy and was in defiance of international law.

The covert trading in government property and diversion of cash for a secret war effort also prompted the creation of a private, profit-making business within the NSC called simply "The Enterprise" (Hershberg). The Enterprise operated parasitically within the taxpayer-supported U.S. government structure, and it added a new dimension to the sense of "privatization" of government functions. By November, Congress's final report on the Iran-Contra affair cited not only Reagan's ultimate responsibility for his aides' misdeeds, but noted further that his administration had exhibited secrecy, dishonesty, and disregard for the law. While the wrongdoings of President Richard Nixon in the Watergate scandal in the 1970s were thoroughly documented in television hearings as well as in books and films that followed the investigation of that scandal, no feature-length fiction film based directly on Iran-Contra has ever been produced.

Hollywood did, however, release a science fiction film that has strong parallels with that scandal, both in its focus on secret internal government/corporate crimes, and in the failed effort to cover them up. In essence, *Robo-Cop* is a near-future satire based on the dual premise of a corporate conglomerate that has taken over and thus privatized a city police department, and which quickly develops robots as super-enforcers to help the police

Political satire disguised as science fiction: *RoboCop* (Paul Verhoeven, Orion Pictures), featuring Nancy Allen and Peter Weller, finds the United States heading for economic collapse and an anti-democratic ruling elite. Jerry Ohlinger's Movie Material Store.

fight crime. The filmmakers—including screenwriters Edward Neumeier and Michael Miner and director Paul Verhoeven—push their plot of runaway privatization to a madhouse extreme. While the huge Omni Consumer Products (OCP) company tries to run Detroit's police force under a private contract, larger problems quickly emerge at the corporate executive level. Similarly, following President Reagan's Cold War decision to turn specific difficulties in the Persian Gulf and in Nicaragua over to his NSC operatives, their plan for funding the contra army, too, spun out of control through their development of a private, for-profit company, which was also used for money-diverting activities. Reagan's covert operatives showed a desperate zeal in their efforts to please him, much as the OCP corporation's vice presidents compete aggressively to please their chief executive.

Both the tactics that Reagan's operatives believed were required in Central America and that OCP determines are necessary in downtown Detroit involve military force. OCP executives working through their subsidiary, Security Concepts, Inc., compete to develop the ideal robot as a militant enforcer, much as the NSC worked with the CIA to build up and transport a contra fighting force. That covert army support operation, however, had problems in addition to the illegal sale of missiles to Iran. The Enterprise was shipping weapons and cheap supplies to the contras with jacked up prices charged to the government. Some of the CIA planes carrying supplies to the contras from the United States were also, according to the CIA's inspector general, working with suspected drug traffickers ("Reagan Legacy" 3).

The same kind of problem arises inside OCP when it becomes obvious that the vice president in charge of crime fighting, Dick Jones (Ronny Cox), is not only building a police robot but is in business with the key underground cocaine making and distribution business in Detroit run by Clarence Boddicker (Kurtwood Smith). Jones also supplies this criminal with the latest military weapons. When Clarence asks about this access to weapons, Jones replies, "We [OCP] practically are the military!" These armaments are meant to protect Clarence's hold on his drug operations against increased police pressure, which Jones and his company are charged to develop. This double dealing by Jones, again much like the operation of The Enterprise, does not end here. There is a third stage to Jones's plans that relate to his corporate position. OCP has undertaken the police contract in the first place because it happened to have a major financial investment in the development of a massive downtown living and business complex in Detroit called Delta City, which would benefit from aggressive police security measures. Jones, operating under the auspices of his legitimate conglomerate, expects the future inhabitants of this downtown complex to create a further market for drugs and other vices, which would in turn require further police efforts on the part of his company. The absurd, circular pattern of corporate crime fighting and profiteering within OCP mimic the NSC/Enterprise operation of secret military armaments and drug sales.

Thus the facts of the Iran-Contra scandal and the fiction of *RoboCop* both involve the creation of a private armed force, an illegal trade in weapons, a convenient venture with the illegal drug market, and an effort to hide and deny all this within the corporation/ government and the public forum. After the Iran-Contra scandal broke, in fact, U.S. secret operatives continued to play both ends against the middle in the Iran-Iraq War (which helped to set the stage for the first President Bush's justification for invading Iraq). The irony of this kind of covert foreign policy is highlighted in *RoboCop* not only by Jones's outrageous intrigues, but by the TV sequences scattered throughout the film involving ludicrous news broadcasts and an advertisement for the board game called "Nuke 'em." This game offers hypothetical nuclear attack as an exciting solution to its version of international problems. The inclusion of such scenes clearly implicates certain government attitudes and policy. Dick Jones is presented as a powerful rogue within OCP (his inside corporate competition isn't much better), even as John Poindexter and Oliver North become operatives of Reagan's wink-and-nod preferences in the loosely run administration.

RoboCop may not have been intended as a literal satire on Iran-Contra, although the parallels are striking. The mythic force of this tightly paced dystopian vision derives from its quiet personal moments as well as from its violent action and hard-edged themes. At the center of all this is the regular police officer Murphy (Peter Weller), whose martyr-like death and resurrection as RoboCop lends a significant character study to an otherwise full-bore and politically conscious action film. Murphy is a street cop transferred to a police district so demoralized that it is ready to go on strike, owing in part to the way it is run by OCP. When Murphy tries to stop drug distributors led by Clarence without the help of police backup, they torture and kill him, and his bloody carcass is taken to OCP's developmental labs for transformation into a mostly mechanized reincarnation as a cyborg. His steel-encased brain operates a metallic body by electrical impulse, including two large, fully automatic machine pistols he draws and fires like a western gunslinger.

Now a version of the new cyberpunk hero, Murphy/RoboCop becomes a powerful police enforcer who is still plagued by a nightmare of his past death. "He" gradually retraces his human fate all the way back through his murder by the ruthless Clarence to Clarence's boss, Dick Jones. However, the cyborg is limited by a fail-safe device that prevents him from the capture or arrest of company executives like Jones. Thus weakened, he barely escapes the attack of Jones's own fully robotic killing machine, Ed 209. Failing this, Jones proceeds to loose the police force against RoboCop, leading to the cyborg's rescue by his old police partner, Lewis (Nancy Allen). RoboCop then locates his former house and sees a video of his former wife and son, which refocuses his revenge on the homicidal Clarence, who finally confesses his business association with Jones.

RoboCop is able to provide evidence to the full OCP board and CEO, since his camera "eyes" also double as a video memory system. This releases "him" to fire on the gun-wielding Jones. The concluding implication is that over-friendly business and government alliances are constantly ripe for abuse, and thus require constant vigilance and regulations to prevent their spiraling out of control, as did the NSC leadership with its Iran-Contra affair. Reagan's well-known emphasis on business deregulation, privatization, union-busting, and extensive military buildup appears to have met its dark cinematic double in this science-fiction fantasy film.

████████████ National Government-Encouraged Financial Speculation

The two other major scandals surrounding the Reagan presidency were financial ones. The first problem really began in 1980 and continued to worsen throughout the decade. The savings and loan system was originally created to promote housing and home ownership, but when it ran into problems during the high inflation years of the early 1980s, the federal government began deregulating it and giving it increased government-backed insurance coverage, more lenient accounting standards, and an expansion of the types of banking activities it could undertake. By 1986 the Government Accounting Office estimated that the loss to government S&L insurance funds had reached $20 billion. If the government had acted on this at that time, the red ink might have been stopped. Instead of controlling the problem, however, Congress passed a bill in August 1987 (the Competitive Equality Banking Act) that authorized a $10.8 billion recapitalization of the Federal Savings and Loan Insurance Commission, including forbearance measures designed to postpone or prevent S&L closures (see www.fdic.gov).

On the economic side, Reagan's policies have been most frequently faulted for increasing the national debt, which in many ways was symbolized by his failure to control the growing S&L problem. As one nonpartisan economist noted: "Reagan eased or eliminated price controls on oil and natural gas, cable TV, long-distance telephone service. . . . Banks were allowed to invest in a somewhat broader set of assets, and the scope of the anti-trust laws was reduced. . . . The failure to address the savings and loan problem early led to an additional debt of about $125 billion" (Niskanen). Corruption in the S&Ls was widespread and continued to grow, and certain "bank" owners such as Charles Keating of Lincoln S&L later went to prison despite pumping large sums into lobbying efforts to influence government officials. Keating, who was called "the godfather of the S&L scandal," was personally responsible for losses of over $2 billion, and he was one of the few who were eventually prosecuted. It wasn't until 1990 that the S&L losses across the country were finally brought to a halt. The final cost to U.S. taxpayers for the S&L looting was estimated at $500 billion, and, with the ultimate bailout costs for the S&L system that dragged on for seven years, around $1.4 trillion, probably the largest theft in human history.

The manner in which the institutionalized greed and eventual collapse of the S&Ls unfolded historically has some compelling associations with the seduction and victimization of the main character in writer/director David

Mamet's *House of Games*. Just as the S&Ls were founded under President Jimmy Carter with the good intention to help low mortgage housing starts across the country, the film's protagonist, Dr. Margaret Ford (Lindsay Crouse), begins as a devoted professional psychiatrist and writer. And just as the S&Ls received the official benefit of government insurance backing, Ford makes a legitimate $85,000 royalty on the sale of her book, *Driven*. Ford's proclivity for clinical observation of "driven" types, however, leads to a fascination with and increased time spent around a group of shysters, who seem to have perfected methods for conning individuals and systems alike. She realizes that those who get conned for bad and sometimes illegal investments do not like to advertise their gullibility or law breaking, and therefore do not tend to go public with complaints and charges. Hence, she cannot resist the temptation to join them in a group effort to make a large but apparently low-risk profit.

Similarly, the S&L system operators, once it was up and running with government backing, also showed an apparently irresistible tendency to increase its profits by expanding its "services." S&L owners lobbied Congress to elevate the size of their loans and the extent of their service options, and certain members of Congress from both parties, who also benefited from financial contributions for this effort, rushed to support their cause. The increased lack of restraints in how the S&Ls were allowed to make money was also a good fit with the enthusiastic pursuit of deregulation under Reagan. The S&Ls proceeded knowingly to make questionable real estate loans with very low demands for collateral, and usually when the loans fell through, they collected more government insurance money on the loss than the properties were initially worth. In the process, they also bilked honest S&L borrowers, who had no way to recover their personal losses from certain S&L transactions. A book about the scandal, *Inside Job* (Pizzo et al.), revealed that criminal activity took place at every single S&L that the authors investigated.

In the film, Ford, too, becomes more and more like the character studies of compulsive, power- and money-motivated individuals in her book. The film follows this sophisticated woman's point of view as her involvement with the con artists' scams and with their group leader Mike (Joe Mantegna) increases. The narrative's emphasis on the level of deception by an entire group of shysters organized around an approach ripe for exploitation seems particularly close to the way the S&L investment and loan schemes worked in practice. The film unfolds initially as a testimony to the intrigue of entrapping others through the appearance of sympathy and trust—the calculated misrepresentation of intent. Since Ford is in no real need of financial returns, her romp with the group of grifters is initially an attraction to their thrill of identifying and exploiting a mark's weakness. This approach, notably, is the exact opposite of what Ford once sought to do in her patient therapy, where neurotic vulnerability became a challenge for curative procedure. It is finally in the carefully coordinated big con that Ford unknowingly finds herself over her head. As she takes up her unfamiliar role as a big con participant, the viewer shares in her limited perspective and increasing anxiety about what is going on. At one point, her cohorts suddenly need to use a suitcase full of all of her $85,000 in order to pull off the particular scam that they appear to be operating on someone else. She is stunned when she is suddenly alone without her money or her shyster buddies. Ford finds herself—like the film viewer who has all along been limited to her point of view—the object of the con (and the film narrative).

The shift in her position from big con accomplice to unknowing victim reflects what happened to many S&L investors whose money was put to speculative use, as well as to taxpayers when the government insurance was used up and the S&Ls began to go bankrupt one after the other. In one case, a man named James Fail invested one thousand dollars of his own money to buy fifteen failed S&Ls, for which the government then reimbursed him $1.85 billion in federal subsidies. The huge losses that followed S&L closures have been best represented in the public mind, however, by the biggest S&L figure of all, the aforementioned Charles Keating, whose family-run "banking" operation eventually landed him in jail. *House of Games* takes a slightly different tack here, as Ford's bitter outrage about her huge financial loss results in a violent attack on her unrepentant lover and former con artist colleague, Mike, whom she tracks down at an airport before he can escape, and then pumps him full of bullets with her handgun. Here and throughout the film, Mamet's extremely unemotional and flat style of dialogue and lighting become conscious as they work along with the plot against the emotional engagement of the viewer, who can find no character or clear moral position with whom or with which to sympathize. This may be compared with the S&L scandal as a whole. The president and Congress appeared as foolhardy and irresponsible as the S&L operators who raked in increasing profits with every lobbyist-advocated expansion of government largesse. Obviously, no political or business figure wanted to be associated with the S&L scandal once its misguided and criminal aspects became clear.

Following Margaret Ford's homicidal attack on Mike, she has a final lunch meeting in an upscale restaurant with her older psychiatric mentor, who encourages her to forgive herself for whatever she feels guilty about. The con game for Ford, then, as she proceeds at that moment to steal an expensive cigarette lighter from another woman's nearby purse, will continue. Hence, the film suggests that the professional world is now also implicated in the creeping expansion of exploitative "games." Mamet's film is thoroughly pessimistic in its rendition of the powerful psychological appeal of an institutionalized form of economic arrogance and fraud. In Ford's final self-denial of guilt for murder, Mamet suggests a yet more violent form of self-interest that is being encouraged in the American psyche. Being "driven" to personal "success" can sanction a highly destructive ethical and social disregard. *House of Games* is ultimately a metaphor for the demise of all professionalism and fair play. Its tracing of the way even well-to-do citizens can be mentally and financially destroyed by highly organized forms of corruption and greed is a bitter pill, especially if that organizational structure takes on the systemic forms of government-sanctioned financial operations propped up by taxpayers' money.

If these high-handed transfers of S&L debt to taxpayers were not already enough, there was at the same time a third and closely related scandal under Reagan's watch that related to even more audacious big business attitudes and speculative behavior. Michael Milken—who made $550 million this year at the investment firm Drexel Burnham Lambert—was already a leader in a major financial movement into junk bonds and their frequent use in aggressive corporate buyouts. Called "the junk bond king" for his overuse of these high-risk bonds, Milken was eventually sent to prison for violations of federal securities and racketeering laws, which was central to the broader junk bond scandal that added to the debt and dislocation of the American economy. The federal deficit by the end of 1986 had reached $220.7 billion, and the national debt by the end of Reagan's second term would reach over $2.5 trillion, or almost 55 percent of the GNP.

The junk bond scandals of speculative financing that were so rampant in the Reagan years seem closely associated with director Oliver Stone's landmark film, *Wall Street,* which he co-wrote with Stanley Weiser. The film's concern with greed and the abuse of the speculative marketplace also appears prescient given the stock market crash in October, as well as the junk bond scandals that finally fell under the national spotlight by 1989. Honest American taxpayers and investors were fleeced by these events, which is very much the theme and emotional impact of both *Wall Street* and of *House of Games.* Unlike Mamet's small and subtle film, however, *Wall Street* found a wide, appreciative audience, with particular acclaim for Michael Douglas's potent performance as the corporate raider Gordon Gekko.

Michael Douglas as Gordon Gekko, who personifies the "greed is good" capitalism of the decade's soaring stock market, in *Wall Street* (Oliver Stone, Twentieth Century Fox). Digital frame enlargement. Jerry Ohlinger's Movie Material Store.

In some ways the tone in *Wall Street* seems to be as much about out-of-control monetary speculation connected with the savings and loan scandal as it is about the character and plot particulars that connect Gekko to the junk bond scandal. It is true that Gekko's "greed is good" speech in the film is an echo of speculator Ivan Boesky's graduation address at Berkeley in 1986, where he said, "Greed is healthy. I believe that you can be greedy and still feel good about yourself." Boesky, in fact, soon repaid $100 million to settle insider trading charges against him, and he also helped to finger Milken for criminal acts (Stewart 335–37). This latter event seems to be echoed in the *Wall Street* scene where Bud Fox (Charlie Sheen) collects evidence for the SEC case against Gekko.

Significantly, though, Stone's film offers a story that is larger than the Gordon Gekko–Ivan Boesky–Michael Milken similarities. It is a narrative of two father figures who offer two very different approaches to career life and consumer lifestyle for the youthful main character, Bud. His commercial urban milieu has already taught him to be awed by public financial power figures such as Gekko, rather than by less visible but no less dedicated salaried workers like his father, Carl (Martin Sheen), who is a union rep for an airline maintenance division. The allure of Gekko's personal empowerment myth derives from his rapacious approach to the stock market and corporate property transactions (arbitrage), which captivates Bud for its sheer audacity and profitability. Bud's worshipful tutelage also suggests, by association, the seduction of American youth generally by monetary values (Boozer, *Career* 2–4). Bud's hostile attitude of fiscal empowerment under Gekko's wings also has the additional effect of distancing him from his family and community. His work for Gekko, as he soon learns, is also tied to this corporate raider's methods, including stock manipulation, insider trading, and the dissolution of companies. Clearly, Gekko's warlike profiteering presents one of the worst faces of capitalism. It is in this mythic guise that his "self-justifying social Darwinism enshrines profit as the supreme god, and its acquisition as his religious practice" (Boozer, "*Wall Street*" 96). Charles Keating, as he made off with the life savings of elderly Americans, would certainly have identified with Gekko.

Wall Street effectively dramatizes the tantalizing pull of big money and power for Bud, who quickly finds himself enjoying its many benefits. If Bud has to cut a few corners to fulfill his over–the-top yuppie dream, so what? His materialist fixation is noted repeatedly, as when he initially borrows money from his dad for expensive suits and an apartment, or splurges on a city penthouse as soon as money begins to roll in from Gekko's "leveraged" corporate buyout operations. *Wall Street* is thus recognized by many as the quintessential film of the greed decade, particularly in the way it signifies the dangers of speculative laissez-faire capitalism. More than any other film of the 1980s, it marks an active challenge to an era of grossly avaricious values that were going out of vogue, if not out of practice, toward the decade's end.

Oliver Stone may be rightfully challenged for being Frank Capra-esque in his moralistic treatment of the problems of capitalism. *Wall Street*'s rather didactic approach, however, now appears justified historically by the sheer scale and number of Enron-like corporate scandals in the new millennium. And as noted, this film was timely given the huge stock market crash a few months later on "Black Monday," 19 October, which suddenly dampened the chauvinistic appeal of the age's flamboyant high rollers. The crash sent the Dow Jones tumbling 508.32 points to close at 1,738.40, a record-breaking percentage loss nearly double that of the crash of 1929. Although no depression followed this crash, its effect on the spendthrift 1980s was unmistakable. *Wall Street* and the attendant stock market plunge punctuated the end of an era. The strength of Stone's film, finally, lies in the way he coalesces the psychological with the circumstantial reality of his characters, much as he did in *Platoon* the previous December, or as he would in *Born on the Fourth of July* two years later. All three of these films share a basic attention to the dilemma of a smart young person who is brought up to believe in a certain mainstream American ideology, only to learn something radically different through the process of painful personal experience.

After Bud turns over evidence to the FBI before he rides with his parents to court, where he will likely receive a prison sentence, the potential for positive reform appears evident. Stone's film offers hope in a nevertheless easily maligned system of increasingly loose market regulation and SEC oversight. In such a government atmosphere, there is also little encouragement of alternative ways for ethical profit-making and service to the community. In this sense, Bud's vulnerability to Gekko's message remains particularly troubling. From the perspective of U.S. business culture and its success myth, there simply was no more important film as the Reagan era wound down.

Another Vietnam War Film Cycle

One dark legacy of the nation that had still not been put to rest by this time was the Vietnam War, which is evident in Stanley Kubrick's *Full Metal Jacket* and in the other notable combat film of the year, John Irvin's *Hamburger Hill*. There were also two non-combat war film releases, Barry Levinson's *Good Morning, Vietnam* and Francis Ford Coppola's *Gardens of Stone*, which are not discussed here. These four films are all critical of the U.S. military presence in Vietnam, and hence constitute a basic thematic resurgence of the initial war film cycle that took place ten years earlier. They also reject the historically revisionist Vietnam War films from 1980 to 1986, which rely on macho, muscular super-hero stars, such as Sylvester Stallone and Chuck Norris, playing characters who blame the "overcautious" and politicized military system back home for losing the war rather than the war policy itself.

This is far from the case in the ensemble combat films *Full Metal Jacket* and *Hamburger Hill*. The focal mission of each platoon or regiment is accomplished by the end, but only at a cost so great as to negate sense and meaning in the effort. American field officers as well as regular ground troops or pilots are sometimes shown to be their own worst enemies under the stresses of this particular war. The lack of clear battle lines in the usually random, spatially chaotic enemy engagements presented on screen brings the very notion of individual and group integrity and positioning into question. The potential 360-degree attack zone that often surrounds the visually impaired battle patrols on the ground introduces a new dimension of physical and mental breakdown. Booby trap wires may be at their feet, or Claymore mines may be hung in the trees for detonation by ground fire.

In the first half of *Full Metal Jacket*, marine recruits ("pukes") are trained relentlessly day and night by their Parris Island drill instructor, Sgt. Hartman

(R. Lee Emery). He demands that they be tough and hard, like the bullet heads referred to in the title. They are taught literally to embrace their weapons like lovers as they become hollowed out into killing machines for the corps. There is no privacy, escape, or useful rationale for these men once they are in the wartime military. If they can't fit the killer's mold, as the recruit nicknamed Gomer Pyle (Vince D'Onofrio) cannot, only the violence of his gun ironically becomes a way out when he reaches the breaking point. Notably sitting atop a john in the bunkhouse latrine in his underwear with live ammunition for his M-14, Pyle first shoots Sgt. Hartman, who once again has been screaming in his face, then turns the gun on himself and splatters his already useless brain in a bloody mess across the white tiles. This metaphorical punctuation mark on the film's first half suggests that the casualties of war not only end up at home but begin at home through the process of military brainwashing, or by extension to the nation, through a single-minded policy reliance on military solutions.

The death of Sgt. Hartman and Pyle also occur right in front of Pyle's fellow recruit who was assigned to help him, Private Joker (Matthew Modine). When the film's second half opens in Vietnam, Joker has become a war correspondent with the military newspaper *Stars and Stripes*. His superior officer informs him that "this is not a particularly popular war in case you don't know," and that the newspaper publishes only two kinds of war news: stories of conversion of the Vietnamese enemy to the cause, or stories of exaggerated enemy "kills" that suggest combat victories. The military doesn't tolerate mental ambiguity or analysis; hence Joker wants to be closer to the real action. When he gets his wished-for transfer to a combat platoon, he writes "Born to kill" on his helmet and carries a peace button on his jacket. This prompts a senior officer standing in front of a mass grave of lime-covered corpses to dress him down for confusion about the cause. "Don't you love your country? . . . Then how about getting with the program? Why don't you jump on the team and come in for the big win?" Later, when Joker's unit is interviewed by a camera crew in the field, the soldier called Animal Mother (Adam Baldwin) responds to the notion of losing comrades for freedom by saying, "Died for freedom? Think we waste gooks for freedom? This is a slaughterhouse." Another soldier comments at one point on the Vietnamese people: "We're supposed to be helping them and all they do is shit on us."

While earlier commentaries on this film tended toward humanitarian conclusions regarding the platoon's coming-of-age redemption in war despite a troubled U.S. policy, more recent criticism has focused on the importance of a brutalized language and on self-negating contradictions among the characters in the film. These have been viewed as a key to its nihilism. The idea is that Kubrick's movie, based loosely on Gustav Hasford's novel *The Short-Timers,* sees this war as a fruitless disaster, a self-contradictory "mission impossible" that was all wrapped up in often random, desperate incidents void of an overarching story line with any meaning. Part of the problem for American troops in the real war was distinguishing the Viet Cong (V.C.) from friendly Vietnamese, since "friendlies" by day could become "enemies" by night. A related example in the film is the helicopter door gunner who fires indiscriminately down upon Vietnamese farmers and their families. His rationale (addressed to Joker) is simply this: "Anyone who runs is V.C. Anyone who stands still is well-disciplined V.C." There is no victory in this devastating war, only the glimmer of survival. The platoon's extended confrontation with the sniper in the burning remains of the city of Hue builds to the film's climax as three marines are shot down one by one. After the young female sniper is finally wounded and rendered harmless on the ground, Joker is left to finish the job with a shot to her head. There is relief but no sense of victory in this long sequence. Also, when what remains of the unit marches deliberately out of Hue, the singing of "The Mickey Mouse Club" theme song is entirely ironic. Vietnam is no Disneyland, and any real victory celebration is impossible. There is only a desperate camaraderie in arms and a longing for release from the battlefield and the military. This is the import of the closing shot as night falls and Joker's final voiceover is heard, as if he has all along been reading from his war journals. He is thankful to be a survivor and going home. But can he, like America, really say goodbye to the war and the memories of death all around him, including the one recently at his feet who will live on in his dreams, however deserving of her last bullet?

The greatest irony in the narrative is gained not only through the constant presence of self-contradictory images within scenes as well as scene juxtapositions, but through the soldiers' different responses to the news crews in the field. Joker was a cynical war correspondent in the beginning before he becomes an active combatant. Joker chooses the true reality of a warrior over the intentional misinformation of military news, but what he finds in battle is an even more invasive contravention of meaning. He explains sarcastically but flatly to his belligerent comrade Animal Mother: "I wanted to visit Vietnam, the crown jewel of Southeast Asia. I wanted to meet people of an exotic and interesting culture and kill them. I want to be the first person on my block to score a confirmed kill!" The platitudes of American promotional language are quickly inverted here. There are no principles; the battlefield is only about killing those on the other side and staying alive. The same conclusion can be drawn from the less sophisticated but thoroughly combat-driven *Hamburger Hill*. This film is a discourse on the meaning of futility based on a real ten-day campaign in the war, in which two-thirds of an American regiment were destroyed taking a hill that was simply abandoned a few weeks later. When a platoon sergeant is interviewed in the field about the squad's failure to take the hill, he replies to the camera crew, "You really like this shit don't you? It's your job, the story. You're waiting here like a fucking vulture, waiting for someone to die so you can take pictures. I've got more respect for the little bastards up there. At least they take a side. You just take pictures."

Both films certify that Vietnam combat doesn't make one a better person or necessarily get one closer to ideological insight about the war. The only problems that can get resolved in the heat of battle are the clashes of rank, race, and personality among the fighting men. Their personal frustrations can be directed against the threats to life and limb posed by the Viet Cong or North Vietnamese army regulars, who hold the facetiously nicknamed "Hamburger Hill" in Irvin's film. The fighting unit has to be cohesive in mutual trust and support in order to be effective at all, whatever the larger policy issues surrounding the desired goals and outcomes of the military's role. And this is exactly what does not happen, as a call for aerial help from the ground troops struggling up the hill brings in friendly helicopter gunships that rake and kill the U.S. forces by mistake. Moving by implication from the individual soldier's extreme frustration in the field to the military's goals, it is apparent that military hardness—the full metal jacket approach to foreign policy in Vietnam—created built-in failure from the outset. The military effort could not and did not win the hearts and minds of the Vietnamese people in great numbers because there was no local government ideology that the people sufficiently trusted or believed in as their own. Imported democracy through attempts at military-enforced stability did not work.

In Kubrick's film, Joker's evasive explanation to the colonel who questions him about the inscription on his helmet and his peace button implies much the same thing: "I think I was trying to suggest something about the duality of man, sir." Again, the first half of *Full Metal Jacket* concerning the military brainwashing process of combat training already provides a powerful dramatic trope for the limitations of a monolithic, one-sided military that is expected to solve larger cultural problems of nation-states that it is in no way equipped to solve. The limitation of military solutions seems to be Joker's particular lesson, which was also meant almost fifteen years after the end of hostilities for a nation that in Kubrick's view had still not learned it.

Television Infotainment

If these two combat films also gave some attention to news gathering out in the field, there are two motion pictures that view TV production and infotainment from behind the scenes. This is the subject of the dramedy *Broadcast News* and of the futuristic dystopian *The Running Man*. James L. Brooks wrote and directed the former, which provides a thoughtful look at the recent changes in the world of broadcast news and news personnel. Aaron Altman (Albert Brooks) is the well-informed and thoroughly knowledgeable newsman who nevertheless does not fit the mold of the attractive TV news anchor. His look and manner are too ethnic, and he is too nervous under the glow of studio lights. In contrast is the empty-headed but charmingly smooth Tom Grunick (William Hurt), who also photographs very nicely and therefore will soon command the salary and public influence of the anchor position. The third lead in the film is the tightly wound news producer Jane Craig (Holly Hunter), who admires and depends on the intellectual Aaron's talents, but doesn't respond to his personal emotional appeals. She thus becomes the unintentional center of a troubled love triangle. She falls for Tom until she catches him faking tears in an interview reaction shot. This incident doesn't stop Tom's promotion to a major international news desk, however, while acute people like Aaron get demoted. The theme of the demise of hard TV news in favor of fluff feature material is obvious in an era that favored high style and flash over substance and hard work. It is also apropos for an era that featured a former movie and TV star who became president partly on the basis of an ability to project a positive, avuncular image on the ubiquitous tube.

The Running Man pushes all these concerns with television substance and legitimacy in *Broadcast News* several steps further. Set in a totalitarian society of the future, it poses an eponymous TV reality show structured around a warrior game format. The host of the show, appropriately named Damon Killian (Richard Dawson), is driven by audience ratings and constantly seeks the biggest and toughest gladiator types to fight in actual life-or-death battles. The participants in this violent show are criminals who can win their freedom should they survive all the other muscle-and-weapons men whom Damon throws at them while on the air. Ben Richards (Arnold Schwarzenegger) is a policeman who is imprisoned for refusing to kill starving citizens, and because of his spirited resistance, he gets the nod as the invincible new guest to be challenged on the show. The bulk of the movie is a demonstration of combat techniques, as Ben faces one strong man after the other in his "run" to freedom. Directed by Paul Michael Glaser, this film as well as *Broadcast News* articulates a present and future for commercial television that was already in motion. In August of this year, the Federal Communications Commission rescinded the Fairness Doctrine, which had long insisted that television and radio stations present controversial issues in a fair and balanced way. While the regulation had proved often difficult to enact in programming and unwieldy to enforce, it nevertheless aided journalistic impartiality in the face of growing commercial pressures for constant entertainment at all costs and at all times. While television was quickly becoming the primary news and entertainment source for most U.S. citizens, these two films nevertheless articulate how this medium was simultaneously functioning at a low common denominator for reliable news and information, much less for progressive entertainment. Spectacle and melodrama was sucking in audiences and sponsors for this entirely commercially defined medium.[1]

The Struggling "Family" and "Adoptive" Parenting

Among the five top grossing films of the year were two that focus on the stressed family and "adoptive" parenting: *Fatal Attraction* and *Three Men and a Baby*. There were also two other important films that fit this category—*Raising Arizona* and *Baby Boom*—which make it the largest of this chapter's five issues or trends in terms of the numbers of singularly focused films. While I discuss only the first film at some length, all four taken together attest to the rapidly changing status of the American family, which was no longer the assumed two-parent-and-children nuclear norm with the mother at home for the rearing of children. Notably, all four films emphasize some form of adaptive or adoptive parenting.

The one dramatic representative in this issues category, *Fatal Attraction*, situates the seemingly perfect middle-class family in a zone of threats, possible disintegration, and finally homicide in self-defense. Most critics attribute *Fatal Attraction*'s amazing financial success to its ending, which was revised after test audiences complained. They felt that the original ending with the suicide of the threatening outsider woman, Alex Forrest (Glenn Close), was insufficient justice for her assault on the institution of the family. The single book editor Alex doesn't simply have a one-night stand with the married lawyer Dan Gallagher (Michael Douglas), but harasses him and

Fatal Attraction (Adrian Lyne, Paramount) depicts the middle-class family under siege, as Alex (Glenn Close, left) invades the domestic sphere of Dan (Michael Douglas) and Beth (Anne Archer). Jerry Ohlinger's Movie Material Store.

his wife to the point of momentarily stealing their child. Her escalating psychosis quickly exceeds the issue of Dan's sleeping with her, and the audience takes the side of Dan and his family. The sexually forward Alex thus takes on the violent mantle of the 1980s femme fatale (Boozer "Lethal"). The revised ending elevates Alex's acts of intimidation to the point of an attempted murder of Dan's wife, Beth (Anne Archer), whose family role Alex wants for herself. The film ultimately shifts from thriller to horror text as the knife-wielding Alex is drowned in the tub by Dan, rises once more from her apparent death, and is finally shot conclusively by Beth. The tension built in the film is pure potboiler, but the specific paranoia-invoking guilt felt by the protagonist Dan, and the highly vulnerable state of his family unit, has also suggested to some critics yet larger and more systemic threats to family security. The new epidemic of AIDS was finally publicly recognized by Reagan this year, and the stock market crash further challenged middle-class family stability and confidence despite material appearances of affluence.

The three comedies in this category that pertain specifically to adoptive parenting deserve at least a brief summary. *Three Men and a Baby* and its sister film, *Baby Boom,* both speak of the problems of alternate parenting. *Three Men and a Baby* goes only so far as to suggest that men as well as women can be good single parents, and that it is good for them. *Baby Boom* pushes the notion that single working adoptive moms can be either entrepreneurial or corporate careerists and still win great wealth and happiness as "moms," and with the perfect new man. The Coen brothers' satire on parenthood, *Raising Arizona,* demonstrates virtually everything a couple should not do to become responsible adoptive parents, beginning with the kidnapping of a baby from a set of quintuplets (isn't the wealthy quintuplet family already more than big enough?). When the couple needs diapers for their new acquisition, they rob a store. The fact that the couple consists of a man who is an ex-con (Nicolas Cage) and a woman who worked for the police (Holly Hunter) suggests a further contradiction in this satirical comment on America's obsession with the perfect family and children. At one level, the solution to family and career stress in America for the sake of comedy is apparently the softening of single men and the superwoman-toughening and marriage of single women. But the deeper issue in the child-and-family-stability obsession in these three comedies points to a great insecurity in the generational cycle and anxiety around the continued ability to parent effectively under the increasing expectations and pressures of contemporary life. Even the dramatic thriller *Fatal Attraction* reaches its initial crisis point when Alex temporarily kidnaps the married couple's young son. This act, more than the killing of the child's pet rabbit or the boiling of Dan's car with acid, sets up the final confrontation with Alex, who will obviously do anything to assume the maternal role now desperately defended by Beth. In all four films, the viability and perseverance of the family through child nurture seems to hang in the balance as a last outpost of meaning and value in a decade of self-interest and greed.

It is difficult to draw conclusive observations from one year of Hollywood film, but clearly an era largely characterized by eight years of an increasingly profligate presidency that favored the wealthy was coming to an end. This age of rapacious high rollers, government deregulation, runaway covert activities, bloated military spending, and a leisure world with cocaine as the glamorous drug of choice was well represented and critiqued in these films. So too were the concerns about the growing dependence on commercial television for one's view of the world, and the increasing vulnerability of the nuclear family to all of these and other challenges. The overwhelming thematic and/or tonal commonality across these film texts suggests a growing disenchantment with political presumptuousness and the highbrow, and thus the beginning of a significant break from this dominant attitude of the decade. There was a growing recognition of the real price to be levied for unabated materialism, arrogance, and a "privatized" disregard for the common good. The long era of "avarice as state religion" (Barol et al. 42) had become weighed down with economic and social debt by the end of the year, and most of the Hollywood films cited here seemed to be sounding some version of a wake-up call.

NOTE

1. As an aside, the final scene in *The Witches of Eastwick*, a film about a devil's (Jack Nicholson) seduction of three women in a small New England town, ends with his toddler children glued to a wall of TV monitors watching their daddy's programming. This satire on the nature of seductive forces in America, whether mediated or not, could also well fit "The Struggling 'Family' and 'Adoptive' Parenting" category in this chapter.

1988

Movies and Images of Reality

DERON OVERPECK

This was the year in which things were not as they seemed. As the Reagan administration wound to a close in this, its last full year in office, a dialogue began that examined how well the retiring president had delivered on his promise of restoring America to its traditional values of godliness and family and thus to its former greatness. For eight years, Reagan had used his ease with the media to promulgate his message. More than any president before him, Reagan understood the importance of image to the presidency. His public appearances were coordinated for maximum televisual impact (Weiler and Pearce 36–38). Reagan's communicative strategy was "light on substance but quick on slogans (for example, 'Are you better off today than you were four years ago?' . . .). Reagan knew that the public neither understands the intricacies of issues nor focuses much attention on their resolution. What matters is the short, memorable response that electrifies the viewing audience" (Dunn and Woodard 117). The electrifying image Reagan presented was of a dedicated patriarch come to restore America to greatness. He frequently appeared in a cowboy hat, jeans, and denim shirt, a rugged everyman with the moral certitude to guide the nation back to strength and security. But Reagan and his wife also struck the contradictory image of the unapologetic rich who did not understand the meaning of thrift. Their taste for expensive goods justified the decade's renowned conspicuous consumption and, according to their critics, condoned the culture's increasingly callous attitude toward the poor and needy (see Carter 35–38, 58–60; Erie and Rein; Imig 74–78; Michener).

By the end of Reagan's second term, the results of this contradiction were apparent. Reagan positioned himself as fiscally responsible but had put the federal government over two trillion dollars in debt. The economy had improved but the wealthiest one percent of the nation received most of the benefits, while more families lived below the poverty line than before Reagan took office. With the convictions of Ivan Boesky and Michael Milken for securities fraud and the stock market crash of 1987, materialism seemed to slip from fashion: the Reagans, who had once appeared as symbols of the joys of profligacy, now were becoming whipping posts for its failures. At the beginning of the new year the cover of *Newsweek* prematurely announced, "The Eighties Are Over," and with it the decade's single-minded pursuit of lucre; the authors of the accompanying article seemed mildly perplexed that the First Family's materialist indulgences had managed to comfort the nation for most of the decade (Barol et al.). And the president's image as a man who knew the difference between right and wrong also faltered. Throughout its two terms in office, the Reagan administration was racked by various scandals, including the ongoing Iran-Contra affair. Further, the president's conservative Christian supporters were disappointed to learn that, despite Reagan's religious rhetoric, he and especially the first lady relied on astrology when making key decisions.

Nevertheless, Reagan ended his second term with the highest approval ratings of any president since Eisenhower, and some commentators have glossed this to mean that he enjoyed public support for the entirety of his presidency (Berman 3–7; Kengor 369–70; Goode). But this elides the difference between public approval of Reagan as a person and public approval of his policies. Voters liked the image he projected but were not as fond of the real effects of his policies (Davies 215–16; Schneider, "Political" 62). Indeed, his job performance ratings swung wildly throughout his presidency (*Public Opinion* 40), and in January, for the first time during his tenure, polls indicated that the American public felt pessimistic about the future of the country (Roberts 1; Barol 45; Schneider, "Political" 97–98). Even his admirers admitted that the president's image had been as much a hindrance as a benefit to the nation. Columnist George Will wrote that the always-smiling Reagan seemed addicted to "the narcotic of cheerfulness" that clouded his ability to face the fiscal realities of supply-side economics (16). Donald Regan, who served in the administration as secretary of treasury and later as White House chief of staff, described Reagan as "a master of illusion and deception" (qtd. in "Goodbye" 23).

In this chapter, I read the year's films as attempts to deal with the contradictions between an image of or expectation about the way something should be and the divergent reality of how it actually is—a reflection, I argue, of the contradictions between President Reagan's homespun discourse of common-sense values and the actual results of his political and economic programs. Families became suspicious, as an astronomer and his daughter discover when his loving new bride arrives from another planet in *My Stepmother Is an Alien*. Families, in particular, appeared to be hiding something: *Running on Empty* presents a seemingly normal, community-oriented family that is actually on the run from federal agents because the parents were radical activists during the 1960s. In *Little Nikita* a CIA agent must protect the son of Russian "sleeper" agents posing as a Southern California family from a rogue assassin. An undercover federal officer becomes part of a racist family when she infiltrates a white supremacist organization in the seemingly placid American Midwest in *Betrayed*. In *Married to the Mob,* Angela would like to leave her husband, Frank, but is bound by a particular kind of family values—those of the Mafia. When the local boss kills Frank and then tries to seduce her, she moves to the city and falls in love with a man who, unbeknownst to her, is an undercover federal agent pursuing her because of her mob ties. But perhaps the most telling image/reality split occurs in *Moon over Parador,* in which a struggling actor finds himself in charge of a small Caribbean country when he is hired to impersonate its deceased dictator.

At the movie theater, capitalists became something to overcome, or at least to educate. In *They Live,* a homeless construction worker learns that America's capitalists are really aliens exploiting America like a Third World country. Omnipresent advertisements are actually subliminal orders to obey, buy, marry, and reproduce. Films like *The Milagro Beanfield War* and *Miles from Home* resumed the mini-cycle of films, including *Country* and *The River* (both 1984), in which rural heroes struggle against monied interests threatening the family farm; *Miles from Home* includes the radical touch that the endangered farm was once blessed as the world's best by Nikita Khruschev. In *Bull Durham,* small-town values and the fundamentals of America's pastime unite to teach a materialistic young pitcher and a liberated woman the enduring truths of baseball and monogamy. Tom Cruise, who had developed his career by portraying toothsome exemplars of the rejuvenated American can-do spirit in films like *Risky Business* (1982) and *Top Gun* (1986), maintains his confidence in *Cocktail* but his yuppie character needs a new environment to thrive. He eschews the corporate world and takes his MBA to Jamaica to become the world's best bartender, an occupation in which the chances of going to jail are greatly reduced. On the other hand, in *Rainman* he learns that family trumps money. As Charlie Babbitt, an overly leveraged car importer, he kidnaps his autistic brother, Raymond (Dustin Hoffman), in order to get half of an inheritance. As they cross the country, Charlie continues to spend money he doesn't really have and uses Raymond in schemes to win more. By the end of the film, Charlie recognizes that his human connection with his brother is more important than any financial gain, returns Raymond to his doctors, and drops his claim to the inheritance. *Beetlejuice* also features yuppies learning life lessons. When a materialistic couple buys a house in a bucolic Connecticut community, the two married ghosts who still live there go to extremes to defend their home from tacky modern art, and the community from predatory real estate practices. Preferring tasteful floral print wallpaper and model making, the spectral pair even inspires the yuppies' morbid daughter to attend the local Catholic school and get better grades. *Bull Durham, Rain Man,* and *Beetlejuice* touch on the theme that the traditional values Reagan promoted had no place in the America his policies fomented: the American pastime remains trapped in a small North Carolina town; Raymond must return to the secluded mental hospital; and the conservative ghosts are trapped in their small-town home by edict of a heavily bureaucratic afterlife.

The Reagan administration invoked a happier America that had existed before the unhappy social unrest of the 1960s, but several films from this year problematize that idyllic image. *Who Framed Roger Rabbit* is a Reagan-era version of *Chinatown* (1974): Beneath its flashy state-of-the-art animation and Looney Tunes–inspired slapstick hides a history of Los Angeles as a self-centered city built on the suppression of a segregated labor force. *Tucker: The Man and His Dream* dramatizes the defeat of an American visionary by the sclerotic but politically well connected automobile industry after World War II. A soft visual scheme imbues the film with an oneiric atmosphere, but for the titular hero, the American Dream is a waking nightmare in which his can-do spirit and determination are not enough, and the marketplace does not unerringly deliver the best product. *Everybody's All-American* portrays the Eisenhower era as a time of personal unhappiness, in which a star running back and his beauty-queen wife struggle to maintain their fraying relationship as his professional success threatens their marriage. *Running on Empty* can also be read as a critique of conservative social rhetoric, as it casts its radicals-on-the-run story as a nuclear-family drama. Rather than threats to the traditional family structure, the Popes are a tightly knit unit hounded by the federal government, but suffer their greatest trauma when the eldest son desires to escape his roots and study music at Juilliard.

Reagan's Cold Warrior image shifted as he softened his "Evil Empire" rhetoric in light of the social and economic changes initiated by Mikhail Gorbachev in the Soviet Union. The thawing American-Soviet relations also caused problems for Cold War–inspired action films, which could no longer rely on the clichés of insidious communism for villainy. One approach to accommodating the new political reality was to use the buddy film to explore the burgeoning American-Russian friendship. *Red Heat* condenses the history of the two countries' relationship. A Russian police officer

The box office fate of *Rambo III* (Peter MacDonald, Carolco Pictures) suggested that Cold War tensions were easing in the latter part of the decade. Jerry Ohlinger's Movie Material Store.

travels to Chicago to capture a Muscovite criminal; there, he and his temporary American "partner" must overcome their ideological differences to work together for the benefit of both countries. Other filmmakers simply chose to ignore the passing of the Red menace. In *Rambo III*, for example, Sylvester Stallone continues his struggle against the Soviet army, this time helping the mujahideen rout the Russians in Afghanistan. In *Braddock: Missing in Action III*, Chuck Norris finds another reason to win the Vietnam War single-handedly. Both *Rambo III* and *Braddock* lost money at the domestic box office, while *Red Heat* was a modest success, perhaps indicating that America was prepared to view its erstwhile enemy as a future friend. Other genres were affected as well. Anticipating George H.W. Bush's "kinder, gentler nation," the producers of *The Dead Pool* went the path set by *Red Heat*, transforming Harry Callahan from the racist scourge of liberalism in *Dirty Harry* (1971) to a wizened loner detective who bends rules but takes little pleasure in tormenting his foes. And, as no new nemeses immediately replaced the retreating Russians, the original faceless serial killer was revived in *Halloween 4: The Return of Michael Myers*. The blank expression of his mask allows him to stand for most any villain, and the new target of his killing spree—his prepubescent niece—underscores the insecurity with which families were viewed at the end of the Reagan era.

The analyses of six films here further illustrates the tensions between image and reality circulating at the end of the decade. Some feature characters who are not as they appear: a thirty-year-old man is actually a thirteen-year-old boy, and an ambitious secretary poses as her boss to further her career. Others focus on characters struggling with the contradictions between the traditional social values the Reagan Revolution purportedly restored and the cultural reality created by his policies: white males struggle with the challenges to family and social privilege represented by women and nonwhites, and rock 'n' roll stars recognize that business acumen is a more desirable trait than rebellion or hedonism. All the films encapsulate a certain ambivalence about the changes they reflect, be it immigration, changing gender roles, or the reality behind rock star clichés. Taken together, the films demonstrate a culture struggling to come to grips with the gap between the images of a nation returning to its traditions and the more venal society that developed during the decade. How—whether—that gap can be bridged remains an open question, as innocent or independent protagonists find themselves marginalized or forced to accommodate to new social realities at odds with traditional family values.

Corporate Values

The film that best encapsulates this ambivalence is *Big*. Twelve-year-old Josh (David Moscow), frustrated that he isn't growing up faster, makes a wish on Zoltar, an enchanted fairground amusement, that he might grow up overnight. The next morning, his wish comes true: he's now a twelve-year-old boy in the body of a thirty-year-old man (Tom Hanks). With the help of his best friend, Billy (Jared Rushton), also twelve but a little wiser in the ways of the world, Josh moves to New York and gets a job working at the MacMillan toy company. He impresses the company's owner with his natural understanding of what pre-teens want in their toys. Soon he is promoted to vice president, draws the romantic attentions of a female co-worker, Susan (Elizabeth Perkins), and moves into a loft apartment full of pinball games, trampolines, and other diversions.

Josh's journey from innocent pre-pubescent boy to innocent, successful adult represents a fantasy that one can grow up and have it all yet remain untouched by adult concerns like ethics or economic planning. It is, in a nutshell, the American Dream with arrested development as the key to economic prosperity. The suburban town in which Josh lives is a Rockwellian vision of shady trees and modest brick houses, stay-at-home moms and children playing on perfectly manicured lawns. Josh and Billy are in

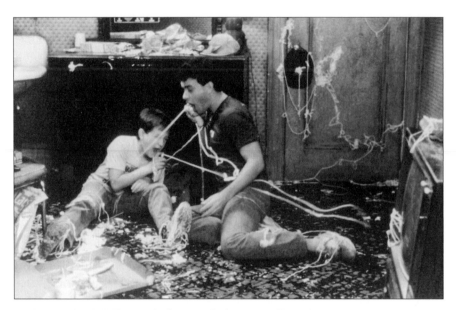

Big (Penny Marshall, Twentieth Century Fox), starring Tom Hanks as a thirteen-year-old boy in the body of a thirty-year-old man, exemplifies the tension between image and reality. Jerry Ohlinger's Movie Material Store.

the "Leave It to Beaver" mold of wholesome media youth: they trade base-ball cards, wear letter jackets, are awkward around girls, and have a special song they sing to one another to demonstrate the depth of their friendship. Only Billy recognizes Josh after he becomes "big," when Josh sings this song to him. In contrast to this idyllic suburban world, New York—the world of adults—is a maze of danger, a concrete jungle into which the adult Josh is exiled from the suburban garden of his innocent pubescence. The first city denizens Josh encounters include a homeless person muttering violent threats and prostitutes offering their services. Josh rents a room in a flophouse and cries himself to sleep as gunshots ring out in the streets and a man carries on an angry conversation in Spanish in the hallway. The city also prevents him from regaining his youthful body when the Bureau of Consumer Affairs takes a month to process his request for a list of all the fairs that had recently operated in the area, slowing Josh's drive to find the Zoltar machine in order to reverse his original wish.

Josh maintains his innocence, though, and that allows him to survive in the scary adult world. Billy visits him frequently, and they spend Josh's first paycheck on pizza and silly string. His success at the MacMillan toy company relies entirely on his youthful energy and common sense approach to product development. Josh first encounters Mr. MacMillan (Robert Loggia), the company's owner, when he knocks him over in the hallway while rushing to make copies. MacMillan appreciates Josh's "hustle" and recognizes in Josh the attitude he wishes his executives would have, the kind that recognizes that "if a kid likes a toy, it sells." When Josh decides to escape from the pressures of adult life by playing with the other children in the FAO Schwarz toy store, MacMillan is there as well. But rather than wonder why an apparently grown man is playing Lazertag with prepubescents, MacMillan tells Josh that he visits FAO Schwarz every week to watch children play. MacMillan and Josh tour the store together, and their conversation reveals not only that MacMillan and Josh share similar attitudes toward toys, but also that Josh is ignorant of the basics of corporate practice:

> *MacMillan* (gesturing to the playing children): You can't see this on a marketing report.
>
> *Josh*: What's a marketing report?
>
> *MacMillan* (impressed): Exactly.

MacMillan mistakes Josh's confusion for a more instinctive approach to the toy business. Their bond is further cemented when they play "Heart and Soul" together on a giant keyboard on the store's floor, in the film's most famous scene. The unaffected insight that Josh brings to the toy business is thus linked to the past; he shares a spiritual bond with an older generation that, though jaded, recognizes truth and honesty when it sees it.

Josh's promotion to Vice President in Charge of Product Development initiates the film's critique of 1980s capitalism. Most of Josh's day is spent sitting in his large office playing with toys. His chief competitors at the company, Susan and Paul (John Heard), rely on market-share projections and make no consideration as to whether a toy is actually enjoyable. Josh speaks in commonsense terms; Susan and particularly Paul know only the corporate logic that reduces everything to numbers derived from impersonal market research. Josh's approach succeeds. After guilelessly pointing out that Paul's new toy isn't any fun, he gains more responsibility in the corporation. The same traits that serve him well in the boardroom also serve him well in the bedroom. Susan falls in love with him, responding to his honesty and innocence; she overlooks that he still sleeps in a bunk bed. After a date on Josh's thirteenth birthday, they make love, and adult life begins to corrupt Josh. He trades in his blue jeans and T-shirts for smart business suits and works with Susan on formal business proposals. He loses touch with the playful vigor and insight that marked his youth, and begins to become an adult in mind as well as body.

Though Josh is just as successful at MacMillan as an adult, Billy protests the change by reminding him of the importance of their friendship. After spending the day watching children play in his old neighborhood, Josh finds the Zoltar machine and returns to his true physical age. Susan tries to stop him but is unsuccessful; her last image of Josh is of a thirteen-year-old boy stumbling home in an adult's clothes. It is also an appropriate image for the film's dichotomy and the paradox of the Reagan years: the ill fit between traditional social values and corporate culture. Josh could survive—thrive, even—in corporate America, but only at the cost of his innocence, ironically the value that brought him success in the first place. Josh rejects this loss, but at the same time, the image of teen Josh in an adult's suit is ambiguous: is it too big for him, or is he not big enough for it? Josh asks Susan to wish for Zoltar to make her physically thirteen as well, but she refuses—she remembers all too well the pain of learning about how the world works. Innocence, then, is proper only to childhood; to recapture it is presented as regression. The business world might benefit from having the untroubled common sense Josh represents, but not so much that turning back the clock would be wise. Susan leaves Josh to grow up in isolated suburbia—and lose his innocence over time, just as she did.

Susan's role in *Big* demonstrates the inconsistent images of women during the 1980s. She is knowledgeable and active, yet unhappy until she finds the right man. Conservative social rhetoric claimed that women should stay at home to fulfill their "natural" roles as caregivers, while Elizabeth Dole, Jeane Kirkpatrick, and Sandra Day O'Connor were prominent examples of women who pursued active careers outside the home. A welter of press articles presented a return to motherhood as the option more women were taking. Actually, women were moving into the workforce in greater numbers, and earning less pay (Faludi 80–95, 397–98). At first blush, *Working Girl* appears to be an uplifting story of a woman succeeding in the corporate world. Tess McGill (Melanie Griffith) is a secretary with dreams of becoming a stock broker. The opening shot of the film is an aerial view of the Statue of Liberty, which Tess passes on the Staten Island ferry on her way to work, an inspirational image of a determined woman shepherded into Manhattan by the feminine symbol of American acceptance and freedom. The lyrics of Carly Simon's theme song, "Let the Rivers Run," present Manhattan as the "New Jerusalem" waiting to be settled by energetic young workers flocking to its streets each day. Tess is an immigrant of sorts—from Staten Island—and she struggles to assimilate into Wall Street culture. Her big hair and cheap clothing set her apart from the sleekly tressed and dressed yuppies promoted over her. Her male co-workers do not respect her; they send her on "job interviews" with cocaine-snorting executives who expect sex. At home, she has no support from her philandering boyfriend, Mick (Alec Baldwin), or from her female friends who think she should be happy with a secretarial job and marriage to Mick.

When Tess gets a job working for a female executive, Katharine Parker (Sigourney Weaver), she believes that she has finally found the mentor who will listen to her ideas and help her develop a career. Katharine's statuesque bearing and calm demeanor set an image not unlike that of the Statue of Liberty that guided Tess to Manhattan in the opening scene. Unfortunately, in reality Katharine is duplicitous. She steals Tess's idea about radio's potential as an investment for companies that are looking to diversify, presenting it as her own stroke of genius. When Katharine is bedridden in Switzerland following a skiing accident, Tess becomes duplicitous herself, assuming Katharine's identity to pursue her radio station plan. She even manages to unwittingly seduce Katharine's boyfriend, Jack Trainer (Harrison Ford). Together, they crash a wedding to interest a wealthy CEO, Oren Trask (Philip Bosco), in Tess's idea. Although Katharine makes a last-minute attempt to push Tess out of the deal, she cannot replicate Tess's grasp of the details of the merger. Tess is rewarded for her hard work with a junior executive position in Trask's company.

The female characters in the film illustrate the contradictory expectations of women during the 1980s. The extent to which Tess and Katharine display femininity determines the outcome of their battle. Katharine is a quintessential yuppie: ambitious, corporate-minded, materialistic. To Tess, she is a sensible but supportive female executive, interested in helping Tess grow into a career on Wall Street. However, Katharine is as belittling as any man. Before stealing Tess's ideas, she has her perform demeaning tasks, including serving food at a reception and helping Katharine try on ski boots. Her femininity is also an image: she looks like a woman but behaves like a man, not only in her dealings with Tess but also in romance. To her, marriage is a business transaction; she coolly tells Tess that she has made clear to her boyfriend that she would be "receptive to an offer" and that she has cleared her schedule for the month of June. For the majority of the film, Katharine is presented as an unerotic object. Only when she is laid up in the hospital with a broken leg does she become feminine. Leg injuries in men have traditionally been a sign of emasculation (Lehman 59–62), and *Working Girl* extends that trope: with her leg broken, Katharine loses her mannishness, lounges in lingerie, and parties with her male nurses. When she returns to New York and hobbles on crutches to a meeting to reveal Tess's true identity, she resumes her masculine behavior. That she needs crutches to walk, however, foreshadows her eventual downfall. Tess soon persuades Trask and Jack to back her in the deal, and she gloatingly tells Katharine to "get [her] bony ass out of here." Katharine's comeuppance draws attention to her lack of femininity. By comparison, Tess's strength is her ability to retain her femininity in the corporate world—in the film's most famous line, she boasts of having "a mind for business and a bod for sin." While other yuppies scour the business pages for leads on how to get ahead, Tess finds insight in gossip columns. Jack first notices her at a business reception; Tess has dressed provocatively and proceeds to get drunk enough to pass out. And Tess is still drawn to family traditions though she would have to give up her dream to pursue them; even after she learns of Mick's infidelity, she considers marrying him.

The film seems to end happily: Tess has a career, and she and Jack live together. Despite her rise to the top, she hasn't lost her working class roots: Jack gives her a functional metal lunch box, and Tess tells her new secretary that she will be treated as an equal. The secretary is impressed by her generosity, and the scene establishes that Tess intends to be the kind of supportive boss that she had always hoped to find. But despite this seemingly upbeat resolution, a certain cynicism permeates the film. The female protagonist has won, but displays weakness at crucial moments. She makes her first important business contact by behaving in a manner that would in other contexts be considered slutty. She also requires a man—named Trainer—to shepherd her through the negotiating process with Trask and to give authority to her ideas. Like Josh in *Big*, Tess, the film's voice of common sense and honesty, ends up in an ambiguous position. The final shot of Tess calling a friend to tell her she has her own office inverts the opening image of Tess being guided to Manhattan by the Statue of Liberty. This time, the aerial shot pulls backward until Tess is lost in a sea of windows in an ocean of office buildings. Simon's theme song returns as well, but its jubilance is now an ironic counterpoint to Tess's new anonymity. Tess has succeeded in her goal, but at the cost of her individuality—she's just another junior executive in a city teeming with them.

Aliens Within

Big suggests that in the confrontation between tradition and progress, tradition will lose out, while *Working Girl* presents at least the possibility that a woman could succeed in the corporate world and maintain a loving, committed relationship. *Die Hard* denies the first premise but offers an uncertain response to the second as it reasserts the right of white men to protect their families. The film's representational politics are so conservative that they hearken back to World War II: even the primary villains are Germans and Japanese. The film also adds the threat of feminism. New York police officer John McClane (Bruce Willis) travels to Los Angeles for Christmas to save his marriage to his upwardly mobile wife, Holly (Bonnie Bedelia), now an executive with the Nakatomi Corporation. Holly took their children with her when she moved west, separating a devoted father from the children who adore him.

Though the enemies might be of a previous generation, their methods and motivations are different. Just as the Japanese attack on Pearl Harbor initiated the U.S. entry into World War II, so McClane encounters them first. His arrival at the Nakatomi Tower emphasizes the power that the nation's former enemy now has within our borders: the building is a steel and glass behemoth gleaming in the setting California sun. During the 1980s, Japan and other Pacific Rim countries had made dramatic gains in global economic power, problematizing Reagan's claim to have rebuilt America's preeminent economic strength. As American automotive companies such as General Motors closed domestic production plants, their Japanese counterparts opened new ones in Indiana, Ohio, and other states. Some economists predicted that the 1990s would begin "the Pacific Century" in which the United States would be reduced to a second-tier economy— large and not without resources, but still not a major player in world markets (Powell; Schlossstein 23–24, 422–38). Other economists noted that much of the American economic recovery was fueled by foreign investment (Tolchin and Tolchin).

The Japanese played a troubling role for Americans this year: maker of reliable cars and audio equipment, but also a once-vanquished enemy risen again to dominate the American economy. But if the Japanese were to be our new conquerors, in *Die Hard* they seem far more benevolent than the fascistic warriors of the 1930s and 1940s. Instead of being inscrutable and severe, Holly's Japanese boss, Mr. Takagi, is friendly to McClane, showing him around the office and complimenting Holly. But he also jokes that the success of Japanese companies in the United States is nothing but militarist expansion in another arena: "Pearl Harbor didn't work out, so we got you with tape decks." Takagi's national heritage is revealed later in the film. He was born in Japan, but moved with his family to California at age five; during World War II, they were detained at an internment camp. Thus, Takagi is a long-term resident of the United States and an example of the self-made individual who pulled himself up by his own bootstraps. But he also is an executive in a Japanese conglomerate that he freely, if sardonically, admits

Die Hard (John McTiernan, Twentieth Century Fox) launched the film career of Bruce Willis and spawned two sequels. Jerry Ohlinger's Movie Material Store.

is invading America. More than forty years later, he has in effect become that which the internment camps were unjustly created to contain: a Japanese sleeper agent, working to undermine American hegemony from within. He proudly represents an entity that through its power in the American economy directly threatens McClane's control of his family. When McClane angrily challenges his wife about her decision to return to her maiden name, she explains that she had to do it because the Japanese treat married women differently. Although she too would like their family to reunite, Holly makes clear she intends to keep her job. Through her desire for her own career, Holly becomes identified with the changes to American business culture and family structure that stood in opposition to the values espoused by Reagan.

When the Nakatomi Christmas party is interrupted by terrorists, the Germans become the prime enemy in the film. The leader, Hans Gruber (Alan Rickman), escorts Takagi away from the party, and their brief conversation reveals that far from being idealistic revolutionaries, Gruber and his band are cultured, proper, and entirely venal. Gruber compliments Takagi on the tailoring of his suit, then flaunts his own classical education in London. Before killing Takagi, he reveals that he has no political motivations but instead wishes to steal $640 million from the Nakatomi vault. When he does demand the release of various political prisoners after the police have been alerted, he reveals in an aside to a henchman that he read about them in *Time* magazine. One commentator has argued that *Die Hard* "reduces the concept of freedom-fighter (or even terrorist) to a greedy hypocrite, in effect denying the validity of any non-U.S. crusader" (Yacowar 2). Perhaps; but in his zeal for financial gain and appreciation for the finer things in life, Gruber also represents the kind of villain then dominating headlines, the corporate arbitrageur. Denying Gruber the courage of any conviction other than the pecuniary establishes him not only as a foreign raider, but also as the symbol of profligacy that had nearly sunk the economy the year before. He is a terrorist of another sort, only dimly cognizant of moribund European radical cells like the Baader-Meinhof Group; rather, he is at home in the late 1980s corporate world—he reads *Forbes*—and is more familiar to an audience used to avaricious capitalists who take the money and run.

The film's presentation of race is at once comfortable and discomforting; nonwhites are presented as inactive unless called upon to act by whites. McClane manages to make contact with Powell (Reginald VelJohnson), an African American police officer outside the building, and their interactions provide an extra human element to what is otherwise two hours of exploding guns and shattering glass. A member of the police force and thus easily identified as American, Powell is what Fred Pfeil has described as the kind of cinematic Black man "who hardly threaten[s] white audiences at all" because he exists to define the excessive virility of the white male (12–13). Pudgy and reluctant to use his own gun, Powell gives McClane the emotional ground he needs to rescue his wife and her co-workers from the terrorists, who are also white. Only at the film's conclusion, when called upon to save McClane and Holly from the last gunman, does Powell demonstrate the ability to act heroically. And while the villains of the film had at first appeared to be the Japanese, as signified by the Nakatomi building towering over Los Angeles, this danger is almost immediately downplayed through Takagi's friendliness and then eliminated when the terrorists easily take control of the building and kill him. Thus by reestablishing the dominance of whites as both heroes and villains, the film denies the nonwhite power initially presented as a threat to McClane's family. In fact, by shooting Takagi, Gruber inadvertently promotes Holly within Nakatomi, placing control of the Japanese company's American offices into the hands of a white woman.

Several commentators have argued that Holly is marginalized in the film, effectively the damsel McClane fights the villains to rescue (Jeffords 60–61; Pfeil 17–18; Yacowar 3–4). At the end of the film, when McClane and Powell finally meet, she introduces herself as Holly McClane. The threat to her family from the Japanese eliminated—thanks to the threat to her husband from the Germans—Holly has no need for her maiden name and can proudly claim her husband's as her own again. Holly clearly still loves McClane at the beginning of the film and openly hopes for reconciliation. But her behavior during the terrorist siege suggests she has a strength that neither Pfeil nor Yacowar acknowledge, and introduces an ambiguous tone to the film's reassertion of traditional male privilege. At several points during the hostage crisis she speaks up for the needs of her co-workers, and manages to conceal information from Gruber that could jeopardize McClane's ability to move throughout the building. Given the fact that she is a hostage, she is as active as she can be. Although she ends the film back in McClane's protective embrace, nothing that happens suggests that she has any intention of giving up her job. Her office features prominently placed photos of her family, including McClane; she can balance both work and life as wife and mother. The image of the reunited couple is not a secure guarantee that male privilege has been completely restored.

Los Angeles also serves as the setting for another film about a police officer struggling to accept the changes brought about by the arrival of outsiders. *Alien Nation* presents the foreigners streaming into American society as actually alien: 250,000 extraterrestrials stranded in Los Angeles when their spaceship crashes in the Mojave desert. Dubbed Newcomers, the aliens are quickly assimilated into Angeleno society by the federal government, though only after civil libertarians go to court to win their release from quarantine camps. In a canny (or perhaps cynical) moment, the film includes a clip of Ronald Reagan calling upon citizens to rise to the challenge of accepting the Newcomers, suggesting that only his fellow Americans could have the insight and strength to do so. The aliens are humanoid; their bulk and mottled bald heads are the main features that set them apart physically from humans. Bred to be slaves, they can breathe fumes that would be lethal to humans, so they become the primary laborers in petroleum factories. Other Newcomers display a flair for business and become shop owners, capitalists, and civic leaders. As symbols of the immigrant and nonwhite masses streaming into the United States, the Newcomers collapse multiple racial tropes into one overdetermined Other: they have the willingness to work any job no matter what, stereotypical of Mexican immigrants; they open up convenience stores on virtually every street corner and excel in school, stereotypical of Asians; and they form street gangs and are oversexed and prone to substance abuse, stereotypical of African Americans. By embodying all the perceptions (good and bad) of the various ethnicities living in the United States, they speak for them all. The message the Newcomers carry for Americans is one of both unconditional gratitude for promising such a rich bounty of freedom and opportunity, and bewilderment that the image of this free land is so rarely matched in reality.

Nonetheless, only white men have any voice regarding the presence of the Newcomers. One unhappy white male citizen complains that he fears competing against ten-year-old aliens in the classroom and in the job market, because he will have no chance against their intelligence and motivation. Los Angeles law enforcement officers are particularly inclined to intolerance, including homicide detective Matt Sykes (James Caan), the film's white male hero. Sykes and the other police officers are not racist—Sykes's partner, Tuggle (Roger Alan Browne), is African American, and the more virulently anti-Newcomer detectives are of Polish and Mexican descent. Sykes and his partner are close friends; Tuggle plans to attend the wedding of Sykes's daughter, Kristin. The vulnerable Sykes is a far cry from the lone male hero in *Die Hard*. Divorced from his wife and barely able to make ends meet on his detective's salary, he is too ashamed of his situation to attend Kristin's wedding himself, despite her pleas.

This sensitivity explains why, despite his oft-stated mistrust of "slags" (slang for Newcomers), Sykes quickly cooperates with one, Sam Francisco (Mandy Patinkin), after Newcomer gang members murder Tuggle. Sam is promoted from patrolman to detective through an affirmative action program, and Sykes volunteers to be his partner because he believes Sam will help him track down the murderers. Although Sykes tells Sam on their first day as partners that he hates all Newcomers, Sykes quickly grows to trust Sam and treat him as an equal. Sykes brings Sam to his house and they bond by getting drunk (for Sam, spoiled milk hits the spot) and exchanging family photographs. Sam even reveals his own respect for tradition when he tells Sykes that he worries his "progressive" wife wants to divorce him, although Newcomers mate for life. On their second day together, Sam and Sykes work closely together, and Sykes angrily defends Sam to the more hateful detectives. When Tuggle's murder is connected to the trade of a narcotic to which the Newcomers become heavily addicted, Sam must trust Sykes not to condemn all Newcomers because of their weakness for the drug. Sam even risks his life by plunging his arm into the ocean (salt water is like hydrochloric acid to Newcomers) to rescue the drowning Sykes. The following weekend, Sykes brings Sam and his wife to Kristin's wedding. As in *Die Hard,* the white family is reunited, but unlike in that film, Sykes does not need to vanquish the foreigners around him to achieve the reunion—he must embrace them. *Alien Nation* is about the acceptance of the Other as a means for peace within American culture. Through the rejection of racism (or here, speciesism), the white hero expiates his guilt and learns to live up to his own image.

The centrality of white attitudes toward race also illuminates both *Mississippi Burning* and the critical response to it. Reagan's social rhetoric had encouraged contradictory images of African Americans. Blacks who adopted conservative social values were promoted, as demonstrated by the success of television's "The Cosby Show," a situation comedy about a stable, upper middle class Black family that apparently never experienced anything remotely approaching racism. But negative images of Blacks circulated widely as well, particularly of irredeemable, violent gang members in South Central Los Angeles. The decade had also seen an increase in violence against nonwhites, both in the cities and in rural areas, where separatist hate groups gained a foothold (Gup 25; Leo 57). Race played an important role in this year's presidential campaign, particularly in Republican candidate George H.W. Bush's use of ads featuring Willie Horton against his Democratic opponent, Michael Dukakis. While Dukakis was governor of Massachusetts, Horton, serving a life sentence for first-degree murder, had been released on a weekend furlough. Horton illegally traveled to Maryland, where he held a white couple hostage and raped the woman. In political ads run by the Bush campaign, Horton became the symbol of liberals' supposedly soft stance on crime—he was made famous as "the Black Rapist who haunts the cellar of the public imagination" (Wills, *Under* 74). *Mississippi Burning* can be understood as an attempt to negotiate these conflicted images of middle class acceptance versus political demonization.

Based on actual murders that occurred in Mississippi in 1964, the film focuses on two white FBI agents as they lead a federal investigation into the disappearance of three civil rights activists. The agent in charge, Ward (Willem Dafoe), embodies the "best and brightest" stereotype of the Kennedy administration: he is a liberal who believes in the necessity of federal intervention in state affairs when human rights are threatened. His deputy, Anderson (Gene Hackman), is older and a former rural Mississippi sheriff. Somewhat wary of returning to the South to interfere in racial relations, he takes a different approach to solving the activists' disappearance. While Ward and the other agents set themselves apart from the white residents of the small Mississippi town from which the activists disappeared, Anderson relies on both his comfort with southern life to build connections with the wives of the chief suspects and his familiarity with backwoods justice to intimidate Klan sympathizers and ultimately solve the mystery.

Mississippi Burning presents the pursuit of the murderers—indeed, the civil rights movement itself—as the efforts of whites. In the opening scene, as the three young civil rights workers are chased by racists as they drive along a Mississippi back road, the two white workers are in the front seat while the Black worker rides in back. In the real incident, according to witnesses, the Black man, James Chaney, drove the car (Toplin 34–35). Later, when the white FBI agents walk in solidarity with quiet African Americans during a civil rights march, they are framed in a way that places them at the center of the demonstration, and marginalizes the Black marchers. At another point, after a church has been firebombed, African American town members react almost angrily to the FBI's presence, believing that the white power structure would not attack them if northern whites would mind their own business. As the white agents plead for information, the African Americans dissipate into the countryside, too fearful and angry to assist the white federal agents struggling to protect them. This portrayal of the town's African Americans brought the loudest criticism. "African American people are transformed from historical agents into props," complained Sundiata K. Cha-Jua (126). African Americans risked life and liberty during the 1960s to protect and express their rights as American citizens. In response to their efforts, racist southerners bombed churches and homes, and murdered both African Americans and northern whites whom they saw as interlopers with no respect for southern traditions of racial segregation. In *Mississippi Burning*, African Americans are almost uniformly frightened subalterns, only reluctantly providing the white FBI agents with assistance.

Such a curious—indeed, offensive—presentation of the events of 1964 becomes more understandable, if not necessarily desirable, when the film is understood not as a dramatic portrayal of the civil rights movement but of the lingering cultural confusion white Americans carried into the 1980s. Some critics of the film understood this: "*Mississippi Burning* . . . purports to chronicle an episode in the Black struggle for human rights, but becomes instead fanfare for white liberals who struggled mightily on behalf of the disenfranchised" (Staples 13). But the filmmakers never claimed that the film was about the Black civil rights movement. At the time of the film's release, director Alan Parker frankly said, "Our film is not about the civil rights movement. It's about why there was a need for a civil rights movement" (qtd. in Corliss, "Fire" 58). *Mississippi Burning* presents racism as a white problem, to be solved by whites; it effectively turns the fight against white privilege into a reassertion of white privilege. Beyond mute victims of southern racism, Africans Americans play almost no role in the civil rights struggle. The exception is when Anderson arranges for an African American FBI agent to pose as an angry southerner who threatens the town's mayor with castration to persuade him to reveal what he knows about the murders. In reality the FBI did not have any Black agents in 1964 (Toplin 30–31). The fictional FBI uses exactly that which white southerners fear: the threat of racial violence directed at them. Of course, because he is actually a federal agent, his threat is a bluff and no voice of African American rage actually speaks. The Black agent doubly underscores the year's image/reality split: in the diegetic reality, he appears first as an enraged, violent southern Black when he is really a law-abiding federal agent; in actual reality, he is a fictional federal agent in a film set in a period when the FBI employed no African American agents.

The role of African Americans in this film, then, is of a kind with the role of Willie Horton in this year's presidential campaign: as signifiers of white guilt, both as victims of white racism and as a barely controllable threat to white males. African Americans clearly suffer at the hands of the monstrous whites of Mississippi, the guilt of the Klan members and at least the complicity of the white police force is never in doubt, and the African Americans hover at the margins of the film as the objects of that racism and rarely the subjects of action taken against it. At the same time, the one active African American relies on the tropes of Black rapacity that southerners for generations had presented as evidence of the dire need to control their uncivilizable African American population. That he is actually, if mythically, a federal agent only underscores his similarity to Horton: both are tools in a federal campaign to persuade fearful whites to do as told—divulge information about the murders, don't vote for the liberal Democrat. Each instance carries with it the ability or promise that the existing power structure—the fictional FBI, the incumbent Republican Party—can control the rampaging threat presented by African Americans, either through their inscription into the federal law enforcement system or through their continued incarceration in state or federal prisons. Whereas guilt is expiated through accepting the Other in *Alien Nation,* it is here expiated by accepting the utility of racist stereotypes in the fight against racism. Their deployment by whites is necessary so whites can win a skirmish in the civil rights struggle that is, by rights, their struggle, as southern whites were the problem. Once the crime can be solved—the bodies found, the Klan members tried—then white guilt is over and African Americans are freed to join in the American dream. The system of representation itself remains, to be used again as necessary in political campaigns or feature films.

■■■■■■■■■ ■ **"Hard Bloody Work"**

Rock 'n' roll has long occupied an ambivalent place in American culture. As both a means of rebellion and a mass-produced commodity, it can serve as a safe medium for the flaunting of certain social mores. In her first documentary, *The Decline of Western Civilization* (1981), Penelope Spheeris examined one of the less safe areas of rock 'n' roll, the Los Angeles punk rock scene. That genre was defiantly and sometimes violently opposed to mainstream rock 'n' roll, which it saw as hopelessly decadent. Although some bands addressed social problems in their songs, the genre overall was marked by nihilism, as evidenced by the brutal, despondent lyrics, the crashing of bodies on the dance floor, and the embrace of heroin and other hard drugs by the musicians. During the Reagan years, however, the punk scene was replaced by another rock genre, a subgenre of heavy metal sometimes derisively known as "hair metal," and characterized by pop-inspired song structures and melodies, fast but fluid guitar playing, and glamorously dressed musicians. Spheeris returned to Los Angeles in 1987–88 to document this music scene for *The Decline of Western Civilization II: The Metal Years.* Mixing interviews with veteran heavy metal acts, including Aerosmith and Ozzy Osbourne, Los Angeles metal bands that have already experienced success, and unheralded bands struggling to make their music heard amidst the din, Spheeris reveals an entirely different attitude toward rock 'n' roll as a career and a musical form. *Decline II* presents the L.A. metal scene as one marked by the contradictions between the glamorous image of the rock star and a reality struggling to cope with internal changes. Money—or the lack thereof—is the main issue for many bands, female musicians compete for attention with male musicians who dress like women, and the deleterious effects of the rock 'n' roll lifestyle are addressed.

That money is a frequent topic of conversation demonstrates the culture-wide effect of the Reagan Revolution. Many of the fledgling rock 'n' rollers express a cavalier attitude toward money, casually mentioning that to pursue their dreams of stardom they have put themselves deeply in debt (the musical equivalent of deficit financing), or put almost all the money they make back into promoting their bands. All the struggling bands follow a do-it-yourself ethos (the musical equivalent of pulling yourself up by your bootstraps), printing their own advertisements and walking around Hollywood and the Sunset Strip handing out flyers. Their rock 'n' roll rebellion does not extend much further than an aversion to work. "I can't stand to work," one hopeful singer tells the director. When she asks him what his last job was, he informs her, "I've never had a job." However, interviews with veteran musicians implode the mythic image of musicians who rock 'n' roll all night and party every day. In a situation that would later become familiar on the MTV reality show "The Osbournes," Ozzy Osbourne prepares breakfast while discussing his career. Echoing the feelings of many of the young hopefuls, the domesticated and somewhat addled singer says the outlaw image of rock 'n' roll attracted him as a young man unwilling to hold down a traditional job. Once his band, Black Sabbath, became famous, they learned that while they had been bedding groupies and getting stoned, their manager had been embezzling money from them. The demands of constant touring, money management, and drug addiction quickly stripped the veneer of rebellion from rock 'n' roll for Osbourne: "It's hard bloody work! You've got to be a businessman!"—a lesson not lost on at least some of the new generation of heavy metal stars. The members of Poison, which had already sold three million copies of its debut album, assert that their love for rock 'n' roll motivates them, not the chance to make riches. But when Spheeris asks bassist Bobby Dall if this would be true "even if that meant not having the money," he smilingly tells her, "I've already got the money." Dall's Cheshire cat grin implies he knows well that his financial stability gives him the means to pretend that financial stability no longer matters. Unlike the punk bands from the first documentary, who accepted a hand-to-mouth lifestyle, several of the musicians in *Decline II* display an awareness of financial planning that would better fit a yuppie than a headbanger. Despite his insistence that he is in a band because he loves rock 'n' roll, the guitarist for Seduce sees himself somewhere else in ten years: "Retired. Living someplace nice. My stocks working for me. My investments, bonds, securities, shit like that. I'm responsible. I've got long hair, but fuck, I'm a businessman, you know?"

The film also explores the status of women and gender in heavy metal. Most of the heavy metal bands are male and they make no secret of their use of female fans to pay for meals and advertising expenses. However, as in other fields, during the 1980s, more women moved into hard rock performance. The female musicians interviewed by Spheeris all assert their equal rock 'n' roll chops. And, unlike the men, many of the women hold regular jobs. Several also admit to a romantic weakness for male musicians who treat them as little more than automatic teller machines. Spheeris does not include any interview footage of male musicians discussing the entry of women into this traditionally testosterone-infused arena. Perhaps this is because the Los Angeles metal scene was also known for the gender-blurring attitude many male performers took to personal appearance: they wore makeup, elaborately teased their hair, and dressed in flowing shirts that in other circumstances would mark them as effeminate. Even nationally prominent bands such as Poison and Mötley Crüe became famous wearing as much hair spray and lipstick as homecoming queens. One guitarist calmly remarks that wearing make-up is "just a way of life," but not everyone appreciated the men's ambiguous appearance. One made-up musician mentions that his mother believes that he is going through a "phase" that he will grow out of. Although one film critic argued that such face painting was "strictly heterosexual" (Moore 37), several males complain that other men mistake them for women. The female musicians in the film do not appreciate men appropriating their look; one complains that "it's a real turn-off to me if a guy's lipstick is redder than mine." Even as the women encroach into the traditional male rock world, they disdain a similar encroachment of men into a traditionally female mode of appearance. The Los Angeles heavy metal scene was just as susceptible to ambivalent or even negative reactions to shifting gender roles as the year's Republican National Convention.

Decline II makes clear the extent to which the Reagan Revolution had trickled down through American culture; even many rock 'n' rollers recognized that, despite the hedonistic image, being a rock star is hard work and requires a certain business acumen. None of the bands who had not yet become famous ever did, perhaps because so many of them seemed disinclined to work at it or anything else. But the film also emphasizes that several of the shifts that occurred in general society also occurred in this subculture, and with similarly uncertain results. All the films in this chapter display a similar ambivalence about what they document, be it the incompatibility of traditional values with corporate culture, or the distrust of the foreign elements behind the American economy. Given that one of Reagan's selling points was his ability to see the world in terms of clear right and wrong, perhaps the cultural ambivalence about the rightness or wrongness of the changes that occurred under his administration is a fittingly ironic testament to his legacy.

1989

Movies and the American Dream

JENNIFER HOLT

By the end of the decade, mainstream American cinema was redefining the upper limits of profitability for the global entertainment industry. Hollywood was realizing record levels of financial success and business was growing in all directions as the blockbuster phenomenon reached staggering heights by the last summer of the eighties. Yet, even as the big budget events continued to define the quality and character of American film, the spectrum of production was expanding far beyond the usual dramas, action-adventure spectacles, and traditional genre-oriented blockbuster fare. Instead, a new independent cinema was born—one that was immensely lucrative and attractive to filmgoers, critics, and industry executives alike. This year's newly commercial "indie revolution" began redesigning much of conventional wisdom about how to find success in the film business and what that success might look like once up on the big screen.

Many films of this year, whether they were big budget spectaculars or small, interpersonal dramas, were notable for the way that they began to question the American institutions or various dimensions of the American Dream that had been celebrated throughout the decade, mythologized by politics, and embraced by the dominant culture and social discourse. While Hollywood films are by nature quite conservative and often worked to re-affirm much of the ideology that had been prevalent throughout the Reagan era, there were indeed many prominent films of this year that were quite productively and articulately questioning mainstream values and core beliefs. Healthy images of family, community, a multicultural society, a strong national identity, the belief in capitalism, individualism, and free-dom—all crucial to the construction of the American collective conscious-ness and the vision of the American Dream that thrived throughout the 1980s—were embattled on the screen throughout the year in productions big and small. Even the television premieres of "The Simpsons" and "Sein-feld" contributed to the overall send-up of traditional American values and images of family. Ironically, as the business of entertainment was realizing unprecedented financial windfalls and the lifestyles of its biggest players offered proof that this elusive American Dream can indeed come true, Hollywood's product was actively interrogating the essential elements and building blocks of that dream as it was circulating throughout the culture at large.

In January, America inaugurated President George H.W. Bush, who vowed to continue the conservative agenda of the departing president, Ronald Reagan, while also promising a "kinder, gentler America." That America was quite hard to find on film in the year that followed; the urban jungles, war zones, interpersonal crises, and treacherous landscapes of all varieties far outnumbered the mythical cornfields in Iowa where dreams did come true. In fact, based on what was available at the multiplex, it appeared that America—in its present, past, and hope for the future—was full of intense chaos, confusion, and cultural struggle. The retreat to fantasy worlds became quite prevalent as the country's reality proved to be less appealing as a backdrop for entertainment.

The reality in this year's films was driven by a nation going through fundamental change. In fact, the entire world was experiencing dramatic geopolitical and economic changes that had implications that reverberated far beyond national borders. Previously unthinkable transformation took over Eastern Europe and the Soviet Union, ending the Cold War after forty bitter, long years. The last Soviet tanks pulled out of Afghanistan, and the Eastern Bloc and its communist empire came apart amid the fall of the Berlin Wall. Chinese students tried desperately to bring democracy to their country in June, staging a pro-democracy demonstration in Tiananmen Square, but the world watched in horror as it turned bloody on live television when government troops violently crushed the rally and killed hundreds of innocent young people. International politics were anything but business as usual for President Bush as he took office, and the uncertainty in the new world order filtered down into American culture.

However, the national crisis as it symbolically played out on celluloid was great for business. This was the best year Hollywood had ever seen in terms of box office returns. The industry was already coming off an all-time high from 1988 and had been on an upswing for the latter half of the decade. Nevertheless, this year, and particularly this summer, would send the decade out with an unforgettable bang that would resonate into the next millennium. With over $5 billion at the box office from 446 films released, Hollywood was undergoing a period of considerable growth in terms of size and scope of productions as well as the massive profits realized by the studios and major distributors. Ticket sales were the highest they had been in five years and the industry actually seemed to be surviving the threat from home video, in fact, finding a way to use it to advantage.[1]

As far as size went, everything was bigger this year and bigger was definitely better than it had ever been—especially once summer began. The summer will forever be known as one of the best seasons Hollywood has ever had, thanks to *Batman, Lethal Weapon 2, Indiana Jones and the Last Crusade,* and *Ghostbusters II*—a film that made over $100 million at the box office but was still widely considered to be a major disappointment, providing one indication of just how high the stakes had soared this summer. It was a blockbuster summer to end all others, actually deserving the hyperbole in the trade papers that were furiously heralding new industry benchmarks at every turn: June was the biggest month the industry had ever seen, and the release date of *Indiana Jones* was the best day ever—until *Batman* came out one month later. *Ghostbusters II* raked in the biggest three-day total ever—until *Batman* also broke that record the following week. All in all, the summer box office reached a record of over $2 billion.

Release patterns were taking on epic proportions as well, with more than twice the number of films opening on at least 2,000 screens than in any previous year in Hollywood history. *Indiana Jones* came out on 2,300 screens Memorial Day weekend, and *Star Trek V, Ghostbusters II,* and *Batman* were each on over 2,000 screens in their initial debut during the month of June. The trend continued with massive wide releases for *Lethal Weapon 2* (2,100 screens) and *License to Kill* (1,500 screens) in July, and even the fifth installment of the slasher *A Nightmare on Elm Street* came out on 2,000 screens during August. Of course, this added to the increasing costs of distribution at a time that films were also on average about 30 percent more expensive to make than they were one year earlier, a trend that would continue spiraling upward in the future. As the risk increased, though, so did the rewards. The industry benchmark for true blockbuster status was now well established at $100 million: there were nine films that achieved that distinction this year (five were summer releases!), more than double the four "blockbusters" in 1988.

Even independent films got bigger, creating an uproar of their own. This year provided the breakthrough for many films outside the major Hollywood studios' production and distribution network, and independent cinema went through a fiscal renaissance of sorts. As a result, the independent filmmaker finally found a measure of success to carve out a new space in cinema this year, right alongside the major studio releases. With the release of Steven Soderbergh's *sex, lies, and videotape,* public and industry perceptions of what constituted an independent film were redefined. Previously, the label suggested a renegade, low budget picture exemplified by the raw experimentalism of John Cassavetes, the fantastic trash of early John Waters, or the bleak irony of Jim Jarmusch—all of which traditionally embraced an aesthetic and profit margin that was incompatible with Hollywood cinema. However, with the tremendous success of Soderbergh's debut, an independent film suddenly became something that was profitable, viable, and appealing to studios, critics, *and* audiences. As a result, this year brought a renewed swell of American independent filmmaking into the fold of the Hollywood machinery, spawning a movement that would eventually bring forth Quentin Tarantino, the commercialization of the Sundance Film Festival, and, more immediately, a distinct shift in industrial practices.

The other big story was about the dramatic shifts taking place in corporate ownership of the film industry. Hollywood began to embrace "synergy" as a structural principle by the end of the 1980s and was focused on formulating tightly integrated media conglomerates that could combine their holdings and exploit them fully with each project for more profitably packaged entertainment. Thus by this year many small or mid-level entertainment companies such as Lorimar, Cannon, De Laurentiis, Vestron, and others had gone bankrupt, been reorganized, or were swallowed up by bigger fish in Hollywood. The march toward consolidation had begun.

In March, the majors took the plunge: Columbia merged with Tri-Star (originally a joint venture of Columbia, CBS, and HBO that began in 1983) to become Columbia Pictures Entertainment amid rumors of a planned takeover by the Sony Corporation. The deal would indeed take place by the end of the year when Sony bought Columbia from Coca-Cola, paying approximately $4.7 billion after all was said and done. They also spent an estimated one billion dollars acquiring the services of Peter Guber and John Peters from Warner Bros., which remains one of the most overly expensive, overly mythologized, and ill-advised deals in industry history. Of course, this was not the Japanese company's first foray into the U.S. entertainment industry; it had bought CBS Records for about $2 billion in late 1987, acquiring in the process such lucrative artists as Michael Jackson and Bruce Springsteen.

Sony's merger of hardware and entertainment software signaled the changing of the guard in the entertainment business and prepared the industry for what came next: Time's $14 billion takeover of Warner Communications. This deal produced the world's biggest media conglomerate, bringing together holdings in film, broadcast, cable, publishing, music, video, retail, and other ancillary markets. TimeWarner created a new paradigm of the media corporation that would become the model by which all others would emulate within the next decade, as a host of mergers drastically changed the ownership structure and industry practices of the largest players in global media entertainment.

In an attempt to manage the increased risk inherent in this marketplace, studios and new conglomerates were relying quite heavily on sequels, which were part of an unmistakable trend. However, it was a strategy that did not always pay off; while sequels certainly drove the summer box office, they were also some of the season's biggest disappointments. As Hollywood was heading toward a $2 billion summer, several sequels dropped off sharply to cool things down. *Ghostbusters II* was considered to be overrun by *Batman*, since the film's $40 million take during opening week fell 53 percent once *Batman* opened. *Karate Kid III* was an unqualified flop, *Star Trek V: The Final Frontier* had a very disappointing opening, as did the sixteenth James Bond film, with Timothy Dalton in his one and only turn as 007, *License to Kill*. Nevertheless, sequels continued to appear. Some (*Indiana Jones, Lethal Weapon 2*, and *Back to the Future Part II*) did better than others (*Toxic Avenger Part II*, *Police Academy 6: City Under Siege*), but the steady stream continued throughout the year with films such as *Friday the 13th Part VII*, *A Nightmare on Elm Street 5*, and *National Lampoon's Christmas Vacation*.

Aside from the reliance on risk-reduction, increasing concentration of the industry, and growing presence of independent films, there were other indications of cinema's future in the landscape of releases this year. In a surprisingly low-tech year, James Cameron made *The Abyss,* which provided a glimpse into what the future held for computer-generated images on film. The gorgeous, metaphysical presence of special effects and computer animation used in this film would be enhanced and propelled into new realms of creative expression in the decade that followed, thanks largely to efforts by key players in this film, Cameron and the George Lucas-owned special effects house, Industrial Light and Magic. Many composite shots used in *Indiana Jones and the Last Crusade* represented even more breakthroughs by ILM on the evolving path of digital special effects and the use of technology to create cinematic fantasy. Disney also made advances with computer animation, using new technology that they developed with Pixar for the final sequence in *The Little Mermaid*.

Fantasy—whether in the form of special effects or escapist themes—provided Hollywood a common refuge from the harsh reality accompanying the decade's end. Indeed, most of the $100 million films were action-oriented, spectacle-laden dramas that relied on fantasy and leaps of faith to sustain narrative coherence. *Batman, Indiana Jones, Honey, I Shrunk the Kids, Look Who's Talking, Back to the Future Part II,* and *Ghostbusters II* all provided some measure of relief from the hard edges of reality and the difficult project of reconciling America's identity at this point in history, within and beyond its own borders. The other option was to manifest some of these crises directly on screen, using the hard edges of unflinching reality as narrative building blocks. This year saw Hollywood using both approaches to examine the spectrum of the American Dream and how illusory it had become. As a result, the images on screen resonated with the insecurity facing our nation as a whole, representing much of this anxiety as an American Dream in crisis.

Batman, Do the Right Thing, and the Dark Side of the Dream

Tim Burton's gothic version of the comic book hero and Dark Knight is a perfectly packaged combination of nearly every significant trend in American cinema this year, both on- and offscreen. Its relevance to discussions of political economy, synergy, and renewed vertical integration in the entertainment industry, as well as the overall thematic resonance it had to the American Dream in crisis that was being played out in multiple reels throughout the year, makes it the key film in this year's cinematic landscape. By offering all these issues up for industrial and cultural debate in such grandiose and spectacular fashion, it was impossible to escape the Batmania in America and its implications for screen culture at the end of the decade.

Of course, the film and its domestic gross of over $250 million were Warner's biggest this year by far. The studio also had a huge summer hit with *Lethal Weapon 2,* and with these Warner Bros. raked in almost 25 percent of the $2 billion summer box office returns. Nothing, however, had the impact of *Batman.* Its success, including an unprecedented $40 million opening weekend, "broke every record in the books," according to *Variety*: the single-day record, the two-day record, the three-day record, the record for a Friday, Saturday, or Sunday: the film's economic impact was nothing short of extraordinary (McBride 1).

At the time, Warner Communications, Inc., owned Warner Bros. studios, its television production and distribution entities, America's most successful record company (with the Warner Bros., Atlantic, Elektra/Asylum/Nonesuch, and Geffen Records labels), the third largest cable system in the nation with significant interests in The Movie Channel, as well as MTV and

Michael Keaton as *Batman* (Tim Burton, Warner Bros.). The film was a blockbuster hit that, paradoxically, offered a dark, anarchic vision of society. Jerry Ohlinger's Movie Material Store.

Nickelodeon, which were distributed by Warner Cable. The *Batman* project was a virtual shrine to the WCI holdings and the art of synergy, promoting everything from a DC Comics character to one of their best-selling recording artists with the film itself, plus novelizations, sound tracks, merchandise, and a seemingly endless stream of interactions with the character, regardless of its narrative relevance or artistic merit.[2]

Time's holdings included a publishing empire (including *Time, Life, Fortune,* and *Sports Illustrated*), American Television and Communications (the second largest cable company in the United States), HBO, Cinemax, and 14 percent of Turner Broadcasting. Soon after the release of *Batman,* these companies and all their media properties would officially merge and begin operations under the roof of the world's largest media conglomerate. Time-Warner would begin to rewrite the way Hollywood did business and *Batman* would provide the new paradigm of a developing conglomerate aesthetic, one in which a film's narrative would be designed to capitalize on all potential revenue streams and corporate holdings.[3]

The merger was not without its complications. Talks and negotiations had been ongoing for two years, and in June, just two and a half weeks before *Batman*'s release, Paramount launched a hostile takeover bid for

Time, Inc., and the "showbiz showdown" was on. The entire episode was reminiscent of the "greenmail" strategy that was a more common tactic throughout the earlier part of the decade—basically a form of extortion that symbolized to many the ruthless nature and lack of morality that characterized many hostile corporate takeovers in the 1980s. In the end, Time and WCI remained committed to their original deal and, with some help from the courts, shut Paramount down. They even had George Lucas and Steven Spielberg on their side: Lucas stated his support for Warner and Time in the *Wall Street Journal* and Spielberg was frequently spotted walking around town in a WB baseball cap.

Ironically, despite the unpleasantness, Paramount and Warner were actually in business together, partners in Cinamerica Theaters, comprising 500 domestic screens that the two companies jointly owned. Warner Bros. also won complete relief from its consent decree that remained from the 1948 *Paramount* case; the antitrust implications were thrown out because of changes in the industry, but Warner was still required to keep its Cineamerica interests separate from its other holdings. Nevertheless, even the Department of Justice and the courts charged with policing the industry had practically thrown in the towel by this year. The *Paramount* decree was largely an empty threat,[4] and it was becoming more apparent, especially with this year's Time-Warner merger, that all regulatory bets were off. Vertical integration would once again be the wave of the future and become an accepted reality of the marketplace.

The expanding profits, concentration of ownership, and new profit potential embodied by the new global media conglomerate of TimeWarner provided a true spectacle of the American Dream and its fundamental values of private ownership and wealth. However, that was all offscreen drama taking place behind the scenes of *Batman*. Once the film made it into the theaters, director Tim Burton presented audiences with a very dark and dystopic vision of America and one of its heroic cultural icons that clashed with the triumph of pure capitalism and free enterprise that was simultaneously on parade in the Time-Warner deal.

In Burton's film, Gotham City was a hell on earth—a carnivalesque pit of corruption and a wasteland of decay. There is lawlessness, chaos, random violence, and darkness everywhere. It is the urban jungle with a German Expressionist aesthetic and a Gothic flair. Within the first fifteen minutes of the film, we are presented with crooked politicians, graft, bribes, scandal, extortion, backstabbing, cheating, lying, set-ups, betrayal, and murder. The city has become a hideous perversion of promise, a paradise lost. New York City as a terror-filled urban jungle was also a running theme this year in the lackluster *Ghostbusters II,* in which the heroes have to save Manhattan from being sucked down to the tenth level of Hell. Saving New York from itself was an interesting thread to follow this year, especially in light of the fact that this city more than any other represents the promise of the American Dream for all, but at the end of the decade, Hollywood seemed to be focused on the city's dark side.

Batman himself (Michael Keaton) is a hero in conflict, much like the dream of a safe and secure society that he is trying to preserve and uphold. Bruce Wayne is also lost, a tortured soul. Like the city around him, he is full of darkness and pain that stems from watching his parents murdered as a child in Gotham, which we see as a flashback in one of the film's early scenes. He is rich, isolated, and mysterious, but still very much of a regular guy who prefers hamburgers in the kitchen to a formal meal in his dining room. His wealth and many possessions have not brought him happiness, however. He appears to have the trappings of the American Dream, but we see Bruce Wayne leading a very lonely and rather depressing life when he is not out fighting crime as Batman. His secret forces him to remain imprisoned in Wayne Manor and prevents him from finding any true intimacy or honest relationships. He is as haunted as his surroundings.

The Joker (Jack Nicholson) helps to further undo the idea of the American Dream in Gotham City by turning the tables on its primary mouthpiece: television. Gotham watches in horror as the Joker spreads his terror in heavily advertised consumer products that are poisoned. Cosmetics, food, and alcohol sold on television become Gotham's shopping nightmare, which the news people warn the public about as they decompose, grow ill, and die on the air from the tainted products. The Joker continues to undermine our myths about the benevolence of capitalism and freedom in a market economy with his horrifying spectacle of evil greed, as he winds his way through Gotham City throwing money all over the streets in the parade just before the final showdown with Batman.

Despite the film's darkness, anarchic society, and psychologically tortured superhero, *Batman* was immensely popular with the general moviegoing audience. On opening weekend, the lines for the film typically went around the theater and, in many cases, entire city blocks. This level of anticipation and excitement had not been generated by a Hollywood release since perhaps the *Star Wars* series, leading to the film's astounding $40 million opening weekend. The darkness and seemingly empty stylistic exercise (many critics complained that the film was sorely lacking in substance) did not deter moviegoers, and *Batman,* along with TimeWarner's boardroom drama behind it, would become the definitive cinematic event of the year.

It would also stand as one of the most ironic indictments of the American Dream on screen, as it was spawned by the largest media corporation that rested its fortunes on packaging and selling this dream to the entire globe.

A much more serious look at the nightmare that had become New York was found in Spike Lee's *Do the Right Thing*. However, this vision of the city and its attendant social and moral decay was not part of any comic book fantasy or imaginary space of triumphant production design. This place was in fact very real and present, and if there was any doubt about its immediate relevance for the audience, the film opens with Public Enemy exclaiming "1989!" as their song "Fight the Power" sets the tone for the film and expresses the frustration and rage fueling the conflicts to follow. The song, with its call to action and unapologetic attack on venerated American icons in the name of class warfare and racial equality ("Elvis was a hero to most / But he never meant shit to me, you see / Straight up racist that sucker was simple and plain / Motherfuck him and John Wayne") immediately established the film's hostile position vis-à-vis dominant culture and would be a recurring motif throughout the film.

With his third release, Spike Lee brought the ugly reality of racism to multiplexes everywhere in blazing color. His story about an explosive day in the Brooklyn neighborhood of Bedford-Stuyvesant, where tensions over race, identity, and ethnicity had reached a boiling point, did not pull any punches. Instead, the film aggressively challenges the audience, presenting bigotry of all kinds, deeply ingrained prejudice, and an implication that we are all to blame for this American nightmare of intolerance that divides this country and continues to tear our social fabric apart. This film has a desperation about it, a sense of urgency that is continually underscored by Public Enemy's insistent and unsettling chorus, questioning who has access to the American Dream and whether or not its promise can survive our present struggles.

Do the Right Thing, released at the end of June, was also part of the blockbuster summer; while the returns were a long way from *Batman* territory, the film wound up doing quite well for a $6 million production that opened on just over 350 screens. It made over $26 million in its initial release but, perhaps more significantly, served as a catalyst for cultural debate about the state of race relations in America at a critical moment for the country. *Newsweek* ran separate pro and con reviews about it over the Fourth of July holiday; the *Village Voice* published eight articles about the film in its 20 June issue, accusing Lee of being an "Afro-fascist" in one (Crouch 73); and many other media outlets engaged in heated discussion about whether the film would incite violence. Lee strongly rejected those who

Spike Lee (left, with Danny Aiello) was at the forefront of an emerging generation of black filmmakers, and *Do the Right Thing* (Universal Pictures) made an enormous impact on the culture, sparking national discussions about race relations. Jerry Ohlinger's Movie Material Store.

asserted it would and in the end was proven right: there were no outbreaks of violence around any screenings.

Because of its uncompromising and extremely risky approach to such a controversial subject, its sensibility was much more akin to that of an independent film than a major studio release. Nevertheless, the film was financed and distributed by Universal, and its success would bring Lee into the ranks of contemporary auteur filmmakers as one of the most significant African American directors in Hollywood, giving him the cachet and access to financing that he would use to further his career.

Every scene in this film is rife with conflict. There is animosity and hostility within and between every racial and ethnic group in the neighborhood around Sal's Famous Pizzeria. Italian Americans, African Americans, Korean Americans, Chicanos, and Latinos—everyone is at war within and between their own groups. There is even hostility evident in the film's style. The canted frames, exaggerated angles, and direct address employed by Lee literally confront the audience with a display of hatred and social prejudice that had never before been depicted with such venom in mainstream cinema. One interlude had a member of each group spewing racial epithets and slurs directly at the camera, taking turns hurling insults beyond the fourth wall until Senor Love Daddy (Samuel L. Jackson), the film's conscience, cuts in and demands that we all "Cool that shit out!" This scene functions as one of the most powerful in the film and a dramatic implication of the audience, reminding us that everyone plays a role in this cultural crisis.

Do the Right Thing does not provide any easy answers to the questions and issues it raises about our country and its character. There is a unique ambiguity and depth to Lee's portrayal of race and identity as it relates to the American Dream and the struggle for assimilation and communal integration. What is at stake here is the very notion of identity in a multicultural America. How can we understand who we are in relation to those around us and negotiate difference without erecting social walls and cultural barriers? How can we retain our identity without alienating others? Is it possible for all these different cultures to learn to get along? The one answer the film does provide is in relation to that question (three years before Rodney King asked it in the wake of riots in Los Angeles): undoubtedly, if we do not learn to get along, we will destroy ourselves and our society with it.

Sal (Danny Aeillo) proudly displays only Italian Americans on the wall of his pizzeria and refuses to acknowledge the black customers' demand that he put up pictures of African Americans as well. The three old African American men who drink beer on the corner bench all day curse the Korean across the street for having a thriving business "less than a year off the boat!" and resent the presence of his market in their neighborhood, yet they freely admit that no black entrepreneurs have tried to do the same. Nobody is beyond reproach: Radio Raheem (Bill Nunn) preaches peace and love but treats anyone outside his group with hatred and disrespect; Sal is exceedingly proud of his establishment and hospitable to most customers, but when pushed he exhibits some of the ugly racist bias that he has been reprimanding his son for displaying; Buggin' Out (Giancarlo Esposito) tries to organize a boycott against Sal's but winds up alienating his own community with such aggressive hostility and antagonism that he cannot even rally his own friends to support his cause. All these characters, embodying very problematic and complex political aspects of race relations in America at the end of the decade, function as part of Lee's refusal to deal with this issue in any reductive or easily digestible manner.

In the climactic melee at Sal's, the police choke Radio Raheem to death, which triggers a series of events that end with an angry neighborhood mob burning down the pizzeria. The names of African Americans who had been killed in real life by police in similarly dubious circumstances, such as Eleanor Bumpurs and Michael Stewart, are invoked as the crowd realizes that Radio Raheem has died at the hands of the NYPD. It is then Mookie, the character closest to Sal and played by Lee himself, who throws the garbage can through the window that sparks the looting and the torching of Sal's American Dream. The destruction of property and loss of a family business is one more community casualty of the hatred fueled by racism and intolerance.

Lee's unwillingness to provide the audience with a neatly wrapped package is well illustrated by the film's ending: after a quote by Martin Luther King Jr. advocating peace and nonviolence and another quote by Malcolm X supporting violence as "intelligence" in situations of self-defense, we see a picture of the two men with their arms around each other. This image of two leaders who embodied drastically different approaches in their struggles for civil rights ends the film on an exceptionally sad note; both died for their causes at the hands of murderers who were driven by the same bigotry that destroyed Bed-Stuy in *Do the Right Thing* and continues to be one of this country's greatest struggles. That one image forces us to ask ourselves: What have we done to honor the battles these men waged to make the American Dream a reality for everyone?

Alternative Visions and Independent Dreams

Steven Soderbergh's *sex, lies, and videotape* also confronted its audience with a less than perfect image of morality and character in this country, all while ushering in the renaissance of independent cinema at the end of the decade and creating more space and interest in Hollywood for filmmaking that went beyond traditional boundaries. Instead of tackling racism, Soderbergh looked at family relationships and the institution of marriage. His film delivered its cultural critique in a much more subtle and insidious manner than *Do the Right Thing*. *Sex, lies, and videotape* smoldered as a quiet, scathing look at deceit, betrayal, and emotional frigidity as four people are crushed under the weight of social pressures and act on the compulsion to either blindly accept or boldly reject all that is conventional and expected.

After Soderbergh's film premiered at the U.S. Film Festival (which would later become Sundance), Harvey Weinstein won a bidding war to secure the film's distribution rights for Miramax. Weinstein then maneuvered the film into the main competition at the Cannes Film Festival; remarkably, it went on to win Cannes's most prestigious award, the Palme d'Or, beating out stiff competition that included *Do the Right Thing*. Soderbergh, who at twenty-six was now the youngest director ever to win the festival's top honor, instantly found himself being celebrated as Hollywood's new golden boy.

The film grossed $24.7 million in its initial domestic release, more than twenty times its $1.2 million budget. After taking its international revenue into account, which brings its total to well over $100 million, *sex, lies, and videotape* qualifies as one of the most profitable films of the decade, with a better rate of return than even the year's most successful big budget blockbusters. It was also the biggest hit by far for Miramax, which was now celebrating its ten-year anniversary.

Soderbergh's commercial triumph served to open the door for other independent filmmakers as well; once the profits from this film registered on industry radar, all of Hollywood began turning to the U.S. Film Festival for a piece of the independent pie. The prestige and participation in the festival grew dramatically, and after *sex, lies, and videotape* its primary focus shifted from art to the art of the deal, dramatically raising the stakes along with the opportunities for those in attendance. The growing recognition and importance of Sundance that is often directly linked to the role played by *sex, lies, and videotape* also conferred the concept of independent film with extraordinary marketing cachet that would resonate for years and complicate any future definition of independent film.

Soderbergh and his film arrived at an opportune moment in the marketplace; with the explosion of home video taking place throughout the decade, there was an increased demand for product beyond the output of the major studios. Moreover, video distributors had begun to finance lower budget films in exchange for video rights, creating new sources of accessible production funding. In fact, RCA/Columbia Home Video and Virgin Visions video backed *sex, lies, and videotape* in precisely this manner. Finally, as the legion of independent distributors grew, with Miramax playing the most significant role, independently produced films were at last able to secure a

Steven Soderbergh's *sex, lies, and videotape* (with Andie MacDowell and James Spader) demonstrated that even indie films could be hits for studios like Miramax. Jerry Ohlinger's Movie Material Store.

pipeline to the theaters more easily than ever before. All these factors coalesced with the film itself to create a very significant moment for the advancement of independent film in Hollywood.

Sex, lies, and videotape is a dialogue-heavy film with no special effects, action, or big stars. Yet the film's stylish package of understated sensuality and searingly perceptive commentary on intimacy and relationships resonated with audiences and received excellent reviews. Without a single stable relationship or healthy dynamic to be found, the film dismantled many of the conservative myths of marriage and family promoted in American culture. All the dysfunction at work in *sex, lies, and videotape* offers a very bleak statement about the reality or even possibility of a lifelong partnership and happy family in the videotape era.

The characters in the film are eerily detached, alienated, and almost unable to fit in with the world around them. Graham (James Spader) serves as the poster child for disaffection. He is impotent and has a "personal project" of videotaping women discussing their sexual experiences, but he remains unable to forge a true connection with anyone in his life. He utilizes the video camera to distance himself from and provide an alternative to the reality and experience of intimacy. He comes into town and awakens

Ann (Andie MacDowell) to the fact that she is in a miserable marriage, and then acts as a catalyst to its demise. This is complicated by the fact that Ann's husband, John (Peter Gallagher), was Graham's best friend in college. John is not around much, however, because he is busy having an affair with Ann's sister.

Ann is strangely disconnected from her true feelings. As the film begins Graham is riding into town and Ann is in her therapist's office, where she is obsessing over garbage. She has little ability to face her life honestly and says that being happy "isn't all that great . . . the last time I was happy I got so fat, I must have put on twenty-five pounds. I thought John was going to have a stroke." Happiness and marriage are mutually exclusive terrain in this film. Security and safety in relationships are shown to be nothing more than myth. When Graham asks her why she likes being married, Ann offers that she likes owning her own house ("it's a nice house") and really likes the fact that her husband just made junior partner at his firm. She enjoys the security of marriage, she says—the irony being that this conversation follows a scene in which her husband and sister are making love and mocking her.

Ultimately, it takes Graham's videotapes to release the hidden truths about everyone's feelings. His video camera liberates Ann from her sexual repression, reveals many secrets of her marriage to John, and ultimately frees Graham from his own inability to be intimate. The camera is the only thing in plain sight throughout this film. Everything else is buried deep in the perfect facade, concealing unhappiness and deceit beneath a beautifully manicured lawn and pleasant exchanges. The setting of New Orleans is quite appropriate, since something wild and untamed is always lurking in the Big Easy. In this case, it is the stranger riding in from out of town coming to wake everybody up to their own misery.

There were certainly many other visions of marriage and family put forth this year, most of which were much less threatening to social stability than *sex, lies, and videotape*. Films like *The Little Mermaid* and *When Harry Met Sally* managed to recuperate some of the idyllic dreams surrounding the notion of family and relationships in American culture. Disney's animated fantasy about a mermaid who falls in love with a prince on land is quite traditional in its attitude toward marriage and typically heavy-handed in reinforcing gender stereotypes about a women's place in society. While it does celebrate individualism and the mermaid Ariel's adventurous spirit, her role and her character are truly contained within a patriarchal social order.

The risks Ariel takes are limited to those in pursuit of her prince and marriage. She makes sacrifices for love when she gives her voice away for

Prince Eric and also sacrifices her family in order to have her man. She even gets schooled in how to be attractive to him so he will kiss her. It is all worth it to her, as she says, so that she doesn't have to go home without him and "be miserable for the rest of [her] life." She resorts to disguises and trickery to win what is presented as rightfully belonging to her, and finally—after being saved from the evil sea witch by her prince—Ariel gets her father's blessing and has her spectacular royal white wedding. In this case, the dream did indeed become reality for the heroine in one of the year's most popular films.

When Harry Met Sally takes a more circuitous route to the same end: giving women what they really want, which according to this film is a conventional, stable marriage. The many vignettes of old, happy couples recounting their courtships and early romance interspersed throughout the film offer sweet, tender evidence that the possibility exists. As Harry (Billy Crystal) and Sally (Meg Ryan) take their relationship from acquaintance to annoyance to friendship and finally to marriage, actually proving Harry's rule that "men and women can't be friends because sex always gets in the way," we are given a love that will supposedly last as long as that of the elderly couples. The promise of happily ever after, just like the fairy tale above, sustains this film and appealed to an enormous audience; *When Harry Met Sally* came quite close to the magic $100 million mark, remarkable for a romantic comedy.

Still, there was a wide assortment of other films such as *The 'Burbs, Parents, Parenthood, Steel Magnolias, Honey, I Shrunk the Kids,* and even *Driving Miss Daisy* and *Back to the Future Part II* that offered various takes on the notion of home and family that were neither as attuned to prevalent cultural mythology as *The Little Mermaid* nor as neatly packaged as *When Harry Met Sally*. These films offered a variety of unique and eccentric family situations that brought new slants on the suburban ideal and conventional family, dismantling all illusions of perfection and often mocking those tropes in comic horror. In some cases, the suburbs even became hellish landscapes of terror, with the "Cleavers as cannibals" in *Parents* offering the most extreme example of the American Dream turned nightmare.

One of the year's more interesting alternative family units was found in Gus Van Sant's independent film *Drugstore Cowboy*. This was quite a risky project. Drug abuse had become a widespread social problem in America and did not discriminate by race or class anymore, especially with the prevalence of cocaine use among white, upper-middle-class professionals. The project was rejected by scores of potential backers but was ultimately given life by Avenue Pictures on a $4.5 million budget (Gold 17). After post-production, the subject matter alone could easily have earned an X rating from the MPAA, given that Van Sant's treatment of drug use was far beyond what was culturally acceptable in the age of Nancy Reagan's ubiquitous "Just Say No" anti-drug campaign; indeed, President Bush appointed the nation's first "drug czar" just a month before the film's release.

The film offers a first-hand look at the lifestyle of drug addicts and their exploits in the early 1970s as they steal drugs from pharmacies in the Pacific Northwest. In this case the addicts form a unique type of family and are portrayed as a rather lovable brand of junkies, somehow endearing despite their self-destructive and criminal behaviors. They look out for one another and maintain their relationships as they chase their next high. The film even allows for the possibility of redemption for the film's main character, Bob Hughes (Matt Dillon). Though an addict, Bob has a measure of personal strength and character that shines through as he takes care of his "family" as best he can. *Drugstore Cowboy* was unusual for the manner in which it examined the psychological, economic, and social factors that create addicts without passing judgment on the people themselves, and for the family it developed far outside the boundaries of the American Dream.

Michael Moore's *Roger & Me,* a personal documentary about the devastating effects that resulted from the closing of the General Motors plant in Flint, Michigan, is also worth noting in this discussion of independent American visions. While the film details the story of a large corporation that wound up destroying the American Dreams of families in an entire community, it was also distributed by TimeWarner, now the largest entertainment company in the world.[5] It was a prime example of the way in which major entertainment corporations were achieving the American Dream of wealth and riches while they produced and/or distributed films that explored the darker, more problematic sides of that dream as it existed in American culture. That contradiction and the one Moore poses between the America of Reagan and Bush and the lack of corporate responsibility to the citizens and communities they serve presents one of the year's most comprehensive and pointed attacks on the facade of the American Dream.

Fighting for the Dream— Reality, Fantasy, and Iowa

The American Dream has served as motivation in times of war, and the values of freedom, nationalism, and patriotism are often paraded right alongside the flag as a reminder of what the fight is for. However, in the case of Vietnam, many of those ideals and their relationship to the war in Southeast Asia were hotly debated in America during a time of tremendous social struggle and civil unrest. Oliver Stone brought that conversation back to the screen in one of Hollywood's most powerful antiwar war films, *Born on the Fourth of July*. After *Platoon* (1986), his examination of soldiers in combat, Stone used *Born on the Fourth of July* to expose the American nightmare of coming home for veterans, many of whom were severely injured and forgotten about in the deplorable squalor of VA hospitals, or treated with disrespect and hostility by a country at war with itself over America's role in this conflict. The film was a dramatic slice of realism, using Vietnam veteran Ron Kovic's autobiography to reexamine the values behind this war and the devastating impact it had on those who fought there. At an early stage the film was slated to begin production starring Al Pacino, but the financing fell through and more than a decade passed before the finished product reached the screen. Tom Cruise eventually took the role of Kovic in what was an extremely risky career move for a leading man with all-American good looks and boyish charm, but his star appeal wound up giving the story previously unthinkable exposure.

Stone opens the film as a celebration of small-town American life. Ron Kovic shares his birthday with that of the United States and is staunchly patriotic. The opening parade in Massapequa, Long Island, where everyone is waving the flag and talk is of God and Mickey Mantle, presents both a community and the film's hero as part of a nostalgic dream in which life is uncomplicated, the future is bright, and the foundation of American values is based on an unquestioning loyalty to one's country, devotion to family and community, and religious faith. These values are all severely tested, even undermined, by Kovic's experience in Vietnam, but more so by his homecoming. After being paralyzed in combat, Kovic and his fellow veterans return to America only to endure appalling conditions at veterans hospitals and what has been called the "second war": the one waged with hostility or, worse, mass social indifference toward veterans and the physical, emotional, and spiritual traumas that they suffered. It is a further cruel irony that war, which appeals to a specific social construction of masculinity in recruiting and sustaining men as fighting soldiers, returns them home in a wheelchair, impotent and emasculated.

For many Vietnam veterans like Kovic who saw themselves as guardians and ambassadors of the American Dream, the reality of fighting that war and returning home certainly destroyed those earlier notions. And as the flag loses its color and brilliance throughout the film, the clarity of the values behind it also fades. "Who is going to love me?" Kovic cries when assessing his life as a paraplegic in a wheelchair. Sadly, his own country had largely abandoned him, and his terrible loneliness pointed to the most unflattering portrait of America's character and a shockingly dismal view of the way we treat our heroes.

The wartime drama of *Glory* and *Casualties of War* also viewed the mythology of the American Dream with a critical eye and presented various viewpoints about whether these values could survive armed conflict intact or not. *Glory* was the most optimistic, with its depiction of the first all-black regiment to fight for the North during the Civil War. The 54th Regiment of Massachusetts treated its soldiers with dignity while the soldiers themselves found courage and self-respect in spite of their struggles to be accepted in their own country. They fought to make America "a whole country . . . for all who live here, so all men can speak." Ultimately the regiment was slaughtered to the last man in a battle that turned the tide of the war, but they died (some of them while holding the American flag) for an idealism and honor that they maintained until the end. Brian DePalma's *Casualties of War,* however, was much less forgiving in its depiction of a platoon that gang-rapes and murders a Vietnamese woman. The American soldiers are depicted as more brutal than any enemy combatant, and the horrifying realism of the film and its overtly political statement about the war was a frontal assault on American gingoism.

Of course, no discussion of heroism or this year's cinematic landscape would be complete without the inclusion of the third installment in one of the most successful film franchises of all time: *Indiana Jones and the Last Crusade*. Steven Spielberg's fantasy goes a long way toward redeeming national character and integrity with the heroic appeal of the legendary Indiana Jones (Harrison Ford). This film catapults the audience back to the realm of nostalgia that had been fueled by the discourse of the Reagan presidency, giving viewers a black and white world of good and evil set in a mythical past that puts America squarely back on the side of the good guys with nothing left to chance. When the enemies are Nazi spies who are an army of darkness trying to steal the Holy Grail, there is not much room for gray areas. (Jones even runs into Hitler at one point at a Nazi rally in Berlin!) Providing the American Dream with a much needed boost this year, *Indiana Jones and the Last Crusade* served as a knight in shining armor for the American spirit, as our hero defeats an external enemy with values that are clearly in opposition to the ideals of freedom, Christianity, and benevolent adventure embodied in the film. It was the second biggest film of the year, right behind *Batman,* and contributed to another fantastic year for Paramount.

However, that sense of pride in American values relied largely on a trip to a mythical past instead of being able to connect these realizations to the present moment. The film that was able to combine all these elements and deliver the entire package to the screen was *Field of Dreams*. It created the place in this year's cinema where fantasy coexisted with homespun reality and dreams indeed did come true. The mysterious voice in the Iowa cornfields imploring Roy Kinsella (Kevin Costner) to "Go the Distance!" gave audiences precisely what they needed during this year of national struggle and cinematic crises: here was the encouragement to follow you own dreams.

The reward for Roy in following his dreams is far greater than anything money could buy. In fact, he risks everything he owns for something he cannot explain. Voices send Roy on a cross-country odyssey, picking up cranky writers and legendary baseball players from the past, and he winds up plowing under his entire corn crop to build a baseball diamond where Shoeless Joe Jackson and the 1919 White Sox reappear to play ball. "Is this heaven?" Jackson asks when he sees the field for the first time. "No, it's Iowa," Roy replied, realizing that perhaps this midwestern cornfield was more ethereal than he had first thought. In fact, it is the place where he is finally able to reconnect with his father and have that game of catch they never had time for when he was alive.

The American pastime is mobilized as the perfect backdrop for the drama of recuperation and healing to play out, as the game of baseball is something deeply rooted in our culture as a place where the notions of family and heroism and the ideal of a happy childhood come together in a mythical way. As reclusive novelist Terrence Mann (James Earl Jones) says, "The one constant through all the years has been baseball. America has rolled by like an army of steamrollers, erased like a blackboard, rebuilt, and erased again. Baseball has marked the time. It is a part of our past . . . it reminds us of all that was good and that could be again." And ultimately, it was this incredible nostalgia for the past that created something magical in the present.

Even in the face of the ruthless corporate suits threatening to foreclose on Roy's farm, those who could "see" the magic believed he should keep the field. Terrence Mann insists, "They'll come to Iowa for reasons they can't even fathom . . . innocent as children, longing for the past. They'll pass over the money without even thinking about it: for it is money they have and peace they lack. And they'll watch the game and it'll be as if they dipped themselves in magic waters." And, in the end, they come. They wind down long country roads for miles and miles to see the baseball diamond in the middle of nowhere. The image of car headlights illuminating the screen is reminiscent of President Bush's campaign trope of "a thousand points of light," finally bringing the audience their kinder, gentler America that had been missing from the cinema for most of the year.

NOTES

1. All box office data and financial information were found in *Variety* from January 1989 through January 1990 and in the Motion Picture Association of America's "1989 U.S. Economic Review."

2. For an insightful discussion on the corporate holdings of TimeWarner and their relationship to *Batman,* refer to Meehan 47–65.

3. For more on this concept see Schatz 73–106.

4. For a detailed explanation, see Holt 22–29.

5. In *Spike, Mike, Slackers, and Dykes,* John Pierson notes the irony of these strange bedfellows with a picture of giant posters for *Roger & Me* and *Batman* showcased next to one another on the side of the Warner Bros. Burbank studio.

1980 – 1989

Select Academy Awards

1980

Best Picture: *Ordinary People*, Paramount

Best Actor: Robert De Niro in *Raging Bull*, United Artists

Best Actress: Sissy Spacek in *Coal Miner's Daughter*, Universal

Best Supporting Actor: Timothy Hutton in *Ordinary People*, Paramount

Best Supporting Actress: Mary Steenburgen in *Melvin and Howard*, Universal

Best Director: Robert Redford, *Ordinary People*, Paramount

Best Original Screenplay: Bo Goldman, *Melvin and Howard*, Universal

Best Adapted Screenplay: Alvin Sargent, *Ordinary People*, Paramount

Best Cinematography: Geoffrey Unsworth, Chislain Cloquet, *Tess,* Columbia

Best Film Editing: Thelma Schoonmaker, *Raging Bull,* United Artists

Best Music (Original Score): Michael Gore, *Fame*, MGM

Best Music (Song): Michael Gore and Dean Pitchford, "Fame" from *Fame,* MGM

1981

Best Picture: *Chariots of Fire,* Ladd Co.

Best Actor: Henry Fonda in *On Golden Pond,* Universal

Best Actress: Katharine Hepburn in *On Golden Pond,* Universal

Best Supporting Actor: John Gielgud in *Arthur,* Orion

Best Supporting Actress: Maureen Stapleton in *Reds,* Paramount

Best Director: Warren Beatty, *Reds,* Paramount

Best Original Screenplay: Colin Welland, *Chariots of Fire*, Ladd. Co.

Best Adapted Screenplay: Ernest Thompson, *On Golden Pond*, Universal

Best Cinematography: Vittorio Storaro, *Reds,* Paramount

Best Film Editing: Michael Kahn, *Raiders of the Lost Ark,* Paramount

Best Music (Original Score): Vangelis, *Chariots of Fire*, Ladd Co.

Best Music (Song): Burt Bacharach, Carole Bayer Sager, Christopher Cross and Peter Allen, "Arthur's Theme" from *Arthur*, Orion

1982

Best Picture: *Gandhi,* Columbia

Best Actor: Ben Kingsley in *Gandhi,* Columbia

Best Actress: Meryl Streep in *Sophie's Choice*, Universal

Best Supporting Actor: Louis Gossett Jr. in *An Officer and a Gentleman*, Paramount

Best Supporting Actress: Jessica Lange in *Tootsie*, Columbia

Best Director: Richard Attenborough, *Gandhi*, Columbia

Best Original Screenplay: John Briley, *Gandhi*, Columbia

Best Adapted Screenplay: Costa-Gavras and Donald Stewart, *Missing*, Universal

Best Cinematography: Billy Williams, Ronnie Taylor, *Gandhi*, Columbia

Best Film Editing: John Bloom, *Gandhi*, Columbia

Best Music (Original Score): John Williams, *E.T. the Extra-Terrestrial*, Universal

Best Music (Song): Jack Nitzsche and Buffy Saint-Marie and Will Jennings, "Up Where We Belong" from *An Officer and a Gentleman*, Paramount

■ 1983

Best Picture: *Terms of Endearment*, Paramount

Best Actor: Robert Duvall in *Tender Mercies*, Universal

Best Actress: Shirley MacLaine in *Terms of Endearment*, Paramount

Best Supporting Actor: Jack Nicholson in *Terms of Endearment*, Paramount

Best Supporting Actress: Linda Hunt in *The Year of Living Dangerously*, MGM

Best Director: James L. Brooks, *Terms of Endearment*, Paramount

Best Original Screenplay: Horton Foote, *Tender Mercies*, Universal

Best Adapted Screenplay: James L. Brooks, *Terms of Endearment*, Paramount

Best Cinematography: Sven Nykvist, *Fanny and Alexander*, Embassy

Best Film Editing: Glenn Farr, Lisa Fruchtman, Stephen A. Rotter, Douglas Stewart, Tom Rolf, *The Right Stuff*, Ladd Co.

Best Music (Original Score): Bill Conti, *The Right Stuff*, Ladd Co.

Best Music (Song): Giorgio Moroder and Keith Forsey and Irene Cara, "Flashdance . . . What a Feeling" from *Flashdance*, Paramount

■ 1984

Best Picture: *Amadeus*, Orion

Best Actor: F. Murray Abraham in *Amadeus*, Orion

Best Actress: Sally Field in *Places in the Heart*, TriStar

Best Supporting Actor: Haing S. Ngor in *The Killing Fields*, Warner Bros.

Best Supporting Actress: Peggy Ashcroft in *A Passage to India*, Columbia

Best Director: Milos Forman, *Amadeus*, Orion

Best Original Screenplay: Robert Benton, *Places in the Heart*, TriStar

Best Adapted Screenplay: Peter Shaffer, *Amadeus*, Orion

Best Cinematography: Chris Menges, *The Killing Fields*, Warner Bros.

Best Film Editing: Jim Clark, *The Killing Fields*, Warner Bros.

Best Music (Original Score): Maurice Jarre, *A Passage to India*, Columbia

Best Music (Song): Stevie Wonder, "I Just Called to Say I Love You" from *The Woman in Red*, MGM

1985

Best Picture: *Out of Africa*, Universal

Best Actor: William Hurt in *Kiss of the Spider Woman*, Island Alive

Best Actress: Geraldine Page in *The Trip to Bountiful*, Island Best Pictures

Best Supporting Actor: Don Ameche in *Cocoon*, Twentieth Century Fox

Best Supporting Actress: Anjelica Huston in *Prizzi's Honor*, Twentieth Century Fox

Best Director: Sydney Pollack, *Out of Africa*, Universal

Best Original Screenplay: William Kelley, Pamela Wallace, and Earl W. Wallace, *Witness*, Paramount

Best Adapted Screenplay: Kurt Luedtke, *Out of Africa*, Universal

Best Cinematography: David Watkin, *Out of Africa*, Universal

Best Film Editing: Thom Noble, *Witness*, Paramount

Best Music (Original Score): John Barry, *Out of Africa*, Universal

Best Music (Song): Lionel Richie, "Say You, Say Me" from *White Nights*, Columbia

1986

Best Picture: *Platoon*, Orion

Best Actor: Paul Newman in *The Color of Money*, Buena Vista

Best Actress: Marlee Matlin in *Children of a Lesser God*, Paramount

Best Supporting Actor: Michael Caine in *Hannah and Her Sisters*, Orion

Best Supporting Actress: Dianne Wiest in *Hannah and Her Sisters*, Orion

Best Director: Oliver Stone, *Platoon*, Orion

Best Original Screenplay: Woody Allen, *Hannah and Her Sisters*, Orion

Best Adapted Screenplay: Ruth Prawer Jhabvala, *A Room with a View*, Cinecom International

Best Cinematography: Chris Menges, *The Mission*, Warner Bros.

Best Film Editing: Claire Simpson, *Platoon*, Orion

Best Music (Original Score): Herbie Hancock, *Round Midnight*, Warner Bros.

Best Music (Song): Giorgio Moroder and Tom Whitlock, "Take My Breath Away" from *Top Gun*, Paramount

■ **1987**

Best Picture: *The Last Emperor,* Columbia

Best Actor: Michael Douglas in *Wall Street,* Twentieth Century Fox

Best Actress: Cher in *Moonstruck,* MGM

Best Supporting Actor: Sean Connery in *The Untouchables,* Paramount

Best Supporting Actress: Olympia Dukakis in *Moonstruck,* MGM

Best Director: Bernardo Bertolucci, *The Last Emperor,* Columbia

Best Original Screenplay: John Patrick Shanley, *Moonstruck,* MGM

Best Adapted Screenplay: Mark Peploe and Bernardo Bertolucci, *The Last Emperor,* Columbia

Best Cinematography: Vittorio Storaro, *The Last Emperor,* Columbia

Best Film Editing: Gabriella Christiani, *The Last Emperor,* Columbia

Best Music (Original Score): Ryuichi Sakamoto, David Byrne, and Cong Su, *The Last Emperor,* Columbia

Best Music (Song): Frankie Previte, John DeNicola, and Donald Markowitz, "(I've Had) The Time of My Life" from *Dirty Dancing,* Vestron

■ **1988**

Best Picture: *Rain Man,* MGM

Best Actor: Dustin Hoffman in *Rain Man,* MGM

Best Actress: Jodie Foster in *The Accused,* Paramount

Best Supporting Actor: Kevin Kline in *A Fish Called Wanda,* MGM

Best Supporting Actress: Geena Davis in *The Accidental Tourist,* Warner Bros.

Best Director: Barry Levinson, *Rain Man,* MGM

Best Original Screenplay: Ronald Bass and Barry Morrow, *Rain Man,* MGM

Best Adapted Screenplay: Christopher Hampton, *Dangerous Liaisons,* Warner Bros.

Best Cinematography: Peter Biziou, *Mississippi Burning,* Orion

Best Film Editing: Arthur Schmidt, *Who Framed Roger Rabbit,* Buena Vista

Best Music (Original Score): Dave Grusin, *The Milagro Beanfield War,* Universal

Best Music (Song): "Carly Simon, "Let the River Run" from *Working Girl,* Twentieth Century Fox

■ **1989**

Best Picture: *Driving Miss Daisy,* Warner Bros.

Best Actor: Daniel Day-Lewis in *My Left Foot,* Miramax

Best Actress: Jessica Tandy in *Driving Miss Daisy,* Warner Bros.

Best Supporting Actor: Denzel Washingon in *Glory,* TriStar

Best Supporting Actress: Brenda Fricker in *My Left Foot,* Miramax

Best Director: Oliver Stone, *Born on the Fourth of July,* Universal

Best Original Screenplay: Tom Schulman, *Dead Poets Society,* Buena Vista

Best Adapted Screenplay: Alfred Uhry, *Driving Miss Daisy,* Warner Bros.

Best Cinematography: Freddie Francis, *Glory,* TriStar

Best Film Editing: David Brenner, Joe Hutshing, *Born on the Fourth of July,* Universal

Best Music (Original Score): Alan Menken, *The Little Mermaid,* Buena Vista

Best Music (Song): Alan Menken and Howard Ashman, "Under the Sea" from *The Little Mermaid,* Buena Vista

WORKS CITED

AND CONSULTED

Anderson, Carolyn. "Diminishing Degrees of Separation: Class Mobility in Movies of the Reagan-Bush Era." *Beyond the Stars: Stock Characters in American Popular Film.* Ed. Paul Loukides and Linda K. Fuller. Bowling Green, Oh.: Bowling Green State U Popular P, 1990. 141–63.

Ansen, David. "A Ferocious Vietnam Elegy." *Newsweek* 5 Jan. 1987: 57.

———. "Searing, Nervy, and Very Honest." *Newsweek* 3 July 1989: 65–66.

Atkinson, Michael. *Blue Velvet.* London: BFI Publishing, 1997.

Auty, Chris. "Review: *Poltergeist.*" *Monthly Film Bulletin,* Sept. 1982: 205.

Barol, Bill, Karen Springen, and Jennifer Foote. "The Eighties Are Over." *Newsweek* 4 Jan. 1988: 40–48.

Baumgarten, Ruth. "Review: *The Loveless.*" *Monthly Film Bulletin,* September 1982: 203.

Bell, Elizabeth, Lynda Haas, and Laura Sells, eds. *From Mouse to Mermaid: The Politics of Film, Gender, and Culture.* Bloomington: Indiana UP, 1995.

Berman, Larry. "Looking Back on the Reagan Presidency." *Looking Back on the Reagan Presidency.* Ed. Larry Berman. Baltimore: Johns Hopkins UP, 1990. 3–17.

Blumenthal, Sidney. "Reaganism and the Neokitsch Aesthetic." *The Reagan Legacy.* Ed. Sidney Blumenthal and Thomas Byrne Edsall. New York: Pantheon, 1988. 251–94.

Boozer, Jack. *Career Movies: American Business and the Success Mystique.* Austin: U of Texas P, 2002.

———. "The Lethal Femme Fatale in the Noir Tradition." *Journal of Film and Video* 51.3–4 (Fall-Winter 1999–2000): 28.

———. "*Wall Street*: The Commodification of Perception." *Journal of Popular Film & Television* 17.3 (Fall 1989): 90–99.

Bouzereau, Laurent. "*Blue Velvet:* An Interview with David Lynch." *Cineaste* 15.3 (1987): 39.

Brauerhoch, Annette. "Mixed Emotions: *Mommie Dearest*—Between Melodrama and Horror." *Cinema Journal* 35.1 (1995): 53–64.

Bukatman, Scott. *Blade Runner.* London: BFI, 1997.

Bundtzen, Lynda K. "'Don't Look At Me': Woman's Body, Woman's Voice in *Blue Velvet.*" *Western Humanities Review* 42.3 (1988): 187–203.

Campbell, Duncan. "Raid on Hideout 'Named after Cold War Film.'" *Guardian* 17 Dec. 2003.

Canby, Vincent. "Amid Gloom, Good Comedy Staged an Exhilarating Comeback." *New York Times* 26 Dec. 1982: H17–18.

———. "Breakneck Pace." *New York Times* 12 June 1981.

———. "Coming to Grips with the American Experience." *New York Times* 20 Dec. 1981: 17.

———. "Mommie—A Guilt-Edged Caricature." *New York Times* 8 Nov. 1981: 13.

———. "'Nine to Five,' Office Comedy; Revolt of the Women." *New York Times* 19 Dec. 1980: C20.

———. "Unexpected Dividends at a Festival." *New York Times* 2 May 1982: D19.

Cannon, Lou. *President Reagan: The Role of a Lifetime.* New York: Simon & Schuster, 1991.

Carter, Hodding. *The Reagan Years.* New York: George Braziller, 1988.

Cavell, Stanley. *Pursuits of Happiness: The Hollywood Comedy of Remarriage.* Cambridge, Mass.: Harvard UP, 1981.

Cha-Jua, Sundiata K. "Mississippi Burning: The Burning of Black Self-Activity." *Radical History Review* 45 (1989): 124–36.

Clover, Carol. *Men, Women, and Chainsaws: Gender in the Modern Horror Film.* Princeton: Princeton UP, 1992.

Cook, Brad. "Upgrade to New Adventures with Tron 2.0." *http://www.apple.com/games/articles/2004/04/tron2/.* 14 Sept. 2004.

Corliss, Richard. "Fire This Time." *Time* 9 Jan. 1989: 54–59.

———. "*Platoon*: Vietnam, the Way It Really Was on Film." *Time* 26 Jan. 1987: 54–62.

Corrigan, Timothy. *A Cinema without Walls: Movies and Culture after Vietnam.* New Brunswick: Rutgers UP, 1991.

Crouch, Stanley. "Do the Race Thing." *Village Voice* 20 June 1989: 73.

Crowdus, Gary. "Review: *Blade Runner.*" *Cineaste* 12.2 (1982): 60.

Culhane, John. "Special Effects Are Revolutionizing Film." *New York Times* 4 July 1982: H1, H13–14.

Davies, Gareth. "The Welfare State." *The Reagan Presidency: Pragmatic Conservatism and Its Legacies.* Ed. W. Elliot Brownlee and Hugh Davis Graham. Lawrence: UP of Kansas, 2003. 209–32.

Dunn, Charles W., and J. David Woodard. "Ideological Images for a Television Age: Ronald Reagan as Party Leader." *The Reagan Presidency: An Incomplete Revolution?* Ed. Dilys M. Hill, Raymond A. Moore, and Phil Williams. Houndmills, Eng.: Macmillan, 1990. 115–31.

Ebert, Roger. "*Blue Velvet.*" *Chicago Sun-Times* 19 Sept. 1986. http://rogerebert.suntimes.com/apps/pbcs.dll/article?AID=/19860919/REVIEWS/609190301/1023. 13 Aug. 2006.

———. "Star Trek IV: The Voyage Home." *Chicago Sun-Times* 26 Nov. 1986. *http://rogerebert.suntimes.com/apps/pbcs.dll/article?AID=/19861126/REVIEWS/611260301/1023.* 13 Aug. 2006.

Ehrlich, Matthew C. *Journalism in the Movies.* Urbana: U of Illinois P, 2004.

Erie, Steven, and Martin Rein. "Welfare: The New Poor Laws." *What Reagan Is Doing to Us.* Ed. Alan Gartner, Colin Greer, and Frank Riessman. New York: Harper & Row, 1982.

Faludi, Susan. *Backlash: The Undeclared War against American Women.* New York: Crown, 1991.

Federal Deposit Insurance Corporation. "The S&L Crisis: A Chrono-Bibliography." *http://www.fdic.gov/bank/historical/s&1.*

Francis, Roberta W. "The History behind the Equal Rights Amendment." http://www.equalrightsamendment.org/era.htm.

Francke, Lizzie. *Script Girls.* London: BFI, 1994.

Friedan, Betty. *The Second Stage.* New York: Summit Books, 1981.

Frye, Northrop. *A Natural Perspective.* New York: Harvest Books, 1965.

Gehring, Wes D. *Romantic vs. Screwball Comedy: Charting the Difference.* Lanham, Md.: Scarecrow Press, 2002.

Gold, Richard. "Van Sant's 'Drugstore Cowboy' . . ." *Variety* 11–17 Oct. 1989: 17.

Goldinger, Carolyn, and Margaret C. Thompson, eds. *Historic Documents of 1983.* Washington, D.C.: Congressional Quarterly Inc., 1984.

"Goodbye to the Gipper." *Newsweek* 9 Jan. 1989: 18–23.

Goode, Stephen. "The Reagan Legacy." *Insight on the News* 27 Oct. 1997. 10–13.

Gray, Frances. *Women and Laughter.* Charlottesville: UP of Virginia, 1994.

Greene, Gayle. "The Empire Strikes Back." *Nation* 10 Feb. 1992: 166–70.

Gup, Ted. "Racism in the Raw in Suburban Chicago." *Time* 17 Oct. 1988: 25.

Harmetz, Aljean. "Hollywood's Video Gamble." *New York Times Magazine* 28 March 1982: 40–48.

———. "Summer '82 Is Hollywood's Most Lucrative Ever." *New York Times* 8 Sept. 1982: C22.

———. "What Movies Will Be the Big Winners This Summer?" *New York Times* 17 May 1982: C11.

Hartlaub, Peter. "A mere 20 years ago, 'Red Dawn' depicted a nation invaded, overpowered. Only that nation was us." *San Francisco Chronicle* 30 June 2004.

Harwood, Sarah. *Family Fictions: Representations of the Family in 1980s Hollywood Cinema.* New York: St. Martin's, 1997.

Haskell, Molly. "Lights . . . Camera . . . Daddy." *Nation* 28 May 1983: 673–75.

Hearty, Kitty Bowe. "The Decade's Best." *Premiere* 3.3 (Nov. 1989): 106–07.

Heilbrun, Carolyn. *Writing a Women's Life.* New York: Norton, 1988.

Hershberg, James G. "The War in Afghanistan and the Iran-Contra Affair: Missing Links?" *Cold War History* 3.3 (April 2003): 23–48.

Hoberman, J. "Return to Normalcy." *Village Voice* 23 Sept. 1986: 56.

———. "Review: *The Loveless.*" *Village Voice* 24 Jan. 1984: 56.

Holt, Jennifer. "In Deregulation We Trust: The Synergy of Politics and Industry in Reagan-Era Hollywood." *Film Quarterly* 55.2 (Winter 2001–02): 22–29.

Hunt, Albert R. "The Campaign and the Issues." *The American Elections of 1980.* Ed. Austin Ranney. Washington, D.C.: American Enterprise Institute for Public Policy Research, 1981.

Imig, Douglas. *Poverty and Power: The Political Representation of Poor Americans.* Lincoln: U of Nebraska P, 1996.

International Television and Video Almanac 1989. New York: Quigley, 1990.

Jaehne, Karen. "*Blue Velvet.*" *Cineaste* 15.3 (1987): 38–41.

James, Nick. "Modern Times: UK Critics' Top Ten Since 1978." *Sight and Sound* 12.12 (Dec. 2002): 20–23.

Jameson, Fredric. "Nostalgia for the Present." *Classical Hollywood Narrative: The Paradigm Wars.* Durham, N.C.: Duke UP, 1992. 253–73.

Jeffords, Susan. *Hard Bodies: Hollywood Masculinity in the Reagan Era.* New Brunswick: Rutgers UP, 1994.

Kael, Pauline. *Hooked.* New York: E. P. Dutton, 1989.

———. *Taking It All In.* New York: Holt, Rinehart & Winston, 1984.

Kasson, John F. *Houdini, Tarzan, and the Perfect Man: The White Male Body and the Challenge of Modernity in America.* New York: Hill & Wang, 2001.

Kellner, Douglas. "From 1984 to One-Dimensional Man: Reflections on Orwell and Marcuse." *Current Perspectives in Social Theory* (1990): 223–52.

———. *Media Culture: Cultural Studies, Identity and Politics between the Modern and the Postmodern.* New York: Routledge, 1995.

———. *Media Spectacle and the Crisis of Democracy.* Boulder, Colo.: Paradigm Press, 2005.

———. *Television and the Crisis of Democracy.* Boulder, Colo.: Westview, 1990.

Kengor, Paul. "Comparing Presidents Reagan and Eisenhower." *Presidential Studies Quarterly* 28:2 (Spring 1998). 366–93.

Kent, Steven. *The Ultimate History of Video Games*. 1994. Reprint, Roseville, Calif.: Prima Publishing, 2001.

Kroll, Jack. "How Hot Is Too Hot?" *Newsweek* 3 July 1989: 64–65.

Lane, Christina. "From *The Loveless* to *Point Break*: Bigelow's Trajectory in Action." *Cinema Journal* 37.4 (1998): 59–81.

Langer, Susanne. "The Comic Rhythm." *Feeling and Form*. New York: Charles Scribner's Sons, 1953.

Layton, Lynne. "*Blue Velvet*: A Parable of Male Development." *Screen* 35.4 (Winter 1994): 374–93.

Lehman, Peter. *Running Scared: Masculinity and the Representation of the Male Body*. Philadelphia: Temple UP, 1993.

Leo, John. "A Chilling Wave of Racism." *Time* 25 January 1988: 57.

Malbin, Michael J. "The Convention, Platforms, and Issue Activists." *The American Elections of 1980*. Ed. Austin Ranney. Washington, D.C.: American Enterprise Institute for Public Policy Research, 1981.

Manning, Jason. "The Midwest Farm Crisis of the 1980s." http://eightiesclub.tripod.com/id395.htm.

Martz, Larry, and Robert Parry. "'I am going to tell the truth.'" *Newsweek* 5 March 1990: 16–17.

Maslin, Janet. "Futuristic 'Blade Runner.'" *New York Times* 25 June 1982: C10.

———. "Yanks on the Moors." *New York Times* 21 Aug. 1981: C12.

McBride, Joseph. "Batman Swoops to Conquer." *Variety* 28 June–4 July 1989: 1–2.

McGilligan, Pat, and Mark Rowland. "American Film Critics Poll: The 80's." *American Film* 15.2 (Nov. 1989): 23–29.

McLeland, Susan. "Barbarella Goes Radical: Hanoi Jane and the American Popular Press." *Headline Hollywood: A Century of Film Scandal*. Ed. Adrienne McLean and David Cook. New Brunswick: Rutgers UP, 2001.

Meehan, Eileen. "'Holy Commodity Fetish, Batman!': The Political Economy of a Commercial Intertext." *The Many Lives of the Batman*. Ed. Roberta Pearson and William Uricchio. New York: Routledge, 1991. 47–65.

Michener, James A. "You Can Call the 1980s 'The Ugly Decade.'" *New York Times* 1 January 1987: 27.

"Milken, Michael Robert." *Columbia Encyclopedia*, 6th ed., 2001. http://www.bartleby.com/65/mi/Milken-M.html.

Mills, Nicolaus. "Culture in an Age of Money." *50 Years of Dissent*. Ed. Nicolaus Mills and Michael Walzer. New Haven: Yale UP, 2004. 173–83.

Milne, Tom. "Review: *Blade Runner*." *Monthly Film Bulletin* Sept. 1982: 194.

Moore, Susanna. "The Metal Age." *New Stateman and Society*. 18 Aug. 1989: 36–37.

Motion Picture Association of America. "1989 U.S. Economic Review." Encino, Calif.: MPAA, 1990.

———. "1996 U.S. Economic Review." Encino, Calif.: MPAA, 1997.

———. "2003 MPA Market Statistics." http://www.mpaa.org/researchStatistics.asp.

Mulvey, Laura. "Netherworlds and the Unconscious: Oedipus and *Blue Velvet*." *Fetishism and Curiosity*. London: BFI, 1996. 137–54.

Nadel, Alan. *Flatlining on the Field of Dreams: Cultural Narratives in the Films of President Reagan's America*. New Brunswick: Rutgers UP, 1997.

Naficy, Hamid. *An Accented Cinema: Exilic and Diasporic Filmmaking*. Princeton: Princeton UP, 2001.

Negra, Diane. "*An American Werewolf in London*: Horror, Satire and the European Misadventure." *America First: Naming the Nation in US Film*. Ed. Mandy Merck. London: Routledge, 2007.

"1987 in Film." *Wikipedia. http://en.wikipedia.org/wiki/1987_in_film*. August 2004.

Niskanen, William A. "Reaganomics." *Concise Encyclopedia of Economics. http://www.econlib.org/library/Enc/Reaganomics.html*. 1999.

Orlofsky, Stephen, ed. *Facts on File* 43.2208 (March 1983).

Orwell, George. *1984*. 1948. New York: Signet, 1961.

Palmer, William J. *The Films of the Eighties: A Social History*. Carbondale: Southern Illinois UP, 1993.

Pfeil, Fred. *White Guys: Studies in Postmodern Domination & Difference*. London: Verso, 1995.

Pierson, John. *Spike, Mike, Slackers, and Dykes*. New York: Hyperion, 1997.

Pizzo, Stephen, Mary Fricker, and Paul Muolo. *Inside Job: The Looting of America's Savings & Loans*. New York: Harper Perennial, 1991.

Pollitt, Katha. *Reasonable Creatures: Essays on Women and Feminism*. New York: Knopf, 1994.

Powell, Bill. "The Pacific Century." *Newsweek* 22 Feb. 1988: 42–51.

Powers, John. "Bleak Chic." *American Film* 12.5 (March 1987): 46–51.

Prince, Stephen. *A New Pot of Gold: Hollywood under the Electronic Rainbow, 1980–1989*. Berkeley: U of California P, 2000.

Public Opinion. "Closing the Book on the Reagan Presidency." Jan.-Feb. 1989: 40.

"The Reagan Legacy." *Nation* 28 June 2004: 3–4.

Roberts, Stanley V. "Poll Finds Less Optimism in U.S. on Future, a First under Reagan." *New York Times* 21 Feb. 1988: 1.

Robinson, Michael J. "The Media in 1980: Was the Message the Message?" *The American Elections of 1980*. Ed. Austin Ranney. Washington, D.C.: American Enterprise Institute for Public Policy Research, 1981.

Rodley, Chris. *Lynch on Lynch*. London: Faber & Faber, 1997.

Rodnitzky, Jerry L. *Feminist Phoenix: The Rise and Fall of a Feminist Counterculture*. Westport, Conn.: Praeger, 1999.

Rogin, Michael. *Ronald Reagan, The Movie: and Other Episodes in Political Demonology*. Berkeley: U of California P, 1987.

Rosenblatt, Roger. "Women Are Getting Out of Hand." *Time* 18 July 1983: 72.

Russo, Vito. *The Celluloid Closet: Homosexuality in the Movies*. New York: Harper & Row, 1987.

Ryan, Michael, and Douglas Kellner. *Camera Politica: The Politics and Ideology of Contemporary Hollywood Film*. Bloomington: Indiana UP, 1988.

Sammon, Paul M. *Future Noir: The Making of Blade Runner*. New York: Harper Prism, 1996.

Schatz, Thomas. "The Return of the Hollywood Studio System." *Conglomerates and the Media*. Ed. Erik Barnouw et al. New York: New Press, 1997. 73–106.

Schlossstein, Steven. *The End of the American Century*. New York: Congdon & Weed, 1989.

Schneider, William. "The November 4 Vote for the President: What Did It Mean?" *The American Elections of 1980*. Ed. Austin Ranney. Washington, D.C.: American Enterprise Institute for Public Policy Research, 1981.

———. "The Political Legacy of the Reagan Years." *The Reagan Legacy*. Ed. Sidney Blumenthal and Thomas Byrne Edsall. New York: Pantheon, 1988. 51–98.

Shattuc, Jane. "Postmodern Misogyny in *Blue Velvet*." *Genders* 13 (Spring 1992): 73–89.

Sherman, Janann, ed. *Interviews with Betty Friedan*. Jackson: U of Mississippi P, 2002.

Staples, Brent. "Cinematic Segregation in a Story about Civil Rights." *New York Times* 8 Jan. 1989: H1+.

Stern, Lesley. "The Oblivious Transfer: Analyzing *Blue Velvet*." *Camera Obscura* 30 (May 1992): 76–90.

Stewart, James B. *Den of Thieves*. New York: Simon & Schuster, 1991.

Sunstein, Cass. "The Right-Wing Assault." *American Prospect* 14 (March 2003). http://www.prospect.org/print/V14/3/sunstein-c.html. 18 October 2006.

Thompson, Kristin. *Storytelling in the New Hollywood*. Cambridge, Mass.: Harvard UP, 1999.

Time. "Behind the Numbers." 12 Sept. 1988: 22.

———. "Leap Year." 17 Jan. 1983: 67.

Tincknall, Estella. *Mediating the Family: Gender, Culture, and Representation*. London: Hodder Arnold, 2005.

Tolchin, Martin, and Susan Tolchin. *Buying into America: How Foreign Money Is Changing the Face of Our Nation*. New York: Times Books, 1988.

Toplin, Robert Brent. *History by Hollywood: The Use and Abuse of the American Past*. Urbana: U of Illinois P, 1986; London: Verso Press, 1995.

Troy, Gil. *Morning in America: How Ronald Reagan Invented the 1980s*. Princeton: Princeton UP, 2005.

Wasko, Janet. *Hollywood in the Information Age*. Cambridge: Polity Press, 1994.

Weiler, Michael, and W. Barnett Pearce. "Ceremonial Discourse: The Rhetorical Ecology of the Reagan Administration." *Reagan and Public Discourse in America*. Ed. Michael Weiler and W. Barnett Pearce. Tuscaloosa: U of Alabama P, 1992. 11–42.

Will, George. "How Reagan Changed America." *Newsweek* 9 Jan. 1989: 13–17.

Wills, Garry. *Reagan's America: Innocents at Home*. New York: Doubleday, 1987.

———. *Under God: Religion and American Politics*. New York: Simon & Schuster, 1990.

Wood, Robin. *Hollywood from Vietnam to Reagan*. New York: Columbia UP, 1986.

Yacowar, Maurice. "The White Man's Mythic Invincibility: *Die Hard*." *Jump Cut* 34 (1989): 2–4.

"The Year in Review." *Film Almanac*. New York: World Almanac, 1988. 24A–27A.

CONTRIBUTORS

CHRISTINA BANKS and MICHAEL BLISS are the co-authors of *What Goes Around Comes Around: The Films of Jonathan Demme* (1996). They are currently working on a study of the films of Dario Argento.

JACK BOOZER is a professor of film in the Department of Communication at Georgia State University. He is the author of *Career Movies: American Business and the Success Mystique* (2002). He has edited the forthcoming anthology *The Process of Film Adaptation: Voices from Page to Screen,* and has a chapter, "Murder in Televirtuality," in the forthcoming collection *Killing Women: The Visual Culture of Gender and Violence.*

WARREN BUCKLAND is author of five books: *Directed by Steven Spielberg* (2006), *Film Studies* (second edition, 2003), *Studying Contemporary American Film* (with Thomas Elsaesser, 2002), *The Cognitive Semiotics of Film* (2000), and *The Film Spectator* (1995). He also edits the journal the *New Review of Film and Television Studies.* He lives in New York.

LEGER GRINDON is a professor of film studies and the director of the Film and Media Culture Program at Middlebury College in Vermont. He is the author of *Shadows on the Past: Studies in the Historical Fiction Film* (1994) and the forthcoming *Knockout: The Boxer and Boxing in American Cinema.*

RHONDA HAMMER is a research scholar at the UCLA Center for the Study of Women and a lecturer in Women's Studies, Communications, and Education at UCLA. She has produced educational videos and is the author of articles, chapters, and books in the areas of cultural studies, feminism, communications, and media literacy, including *Antifeminism and Family Terrorism: A Critical Feminist Perspective* (2002) and a book co-authored with Peter McLaren, David Sholle, and Susan Reilly, *Rethinking Media Literacy: A Critical Pedagogy of Representation* (1995).

JENNIFER HOLT is an assistant professor of Film and Media Studies at the University of California–Santa Barbara. Her articles on film and television history have appeared in various journals, including *Film Quarterly,* and in the anthologies *Quality Popular Television* (2003) and *Media Ownership: Research and Regulation* (2006).

DOUGLAS KELLNER is George Kneller Chair in the Philosophy of Education at UCLA and the author of many books on social theory, politics, history, and culture, including *Camera Politica: The Politics and Ideology of Contemporary Hollywood Film,* co-authored with Michael Ryan (1988); *Critical Theory, Marxism, and Modernity* (1989); *Jean Baudrillard: From Marxism to Postmodernism and Beyond* (1990); works in cultural studies such as *Media Culture* (1995) and *Media Spectacle* (2003); a trilogy of books on postmodern theory, with Steve Best; a trilogy of books on the Bush administration, including *Grand Theft 2000* (2001); and his latest book, *Media Spectacle and the Crisis of Democracy* (2005).

ALAN NADEL, the William T. Bryan Professor of American Literature and Culture at the University of Kentucky, is the author of numerous books and articles on American literature, film, and culture. His most recent books are *Flatlining on the Field of Dreams: Cultural Narratives in the Films of President Reagan's America* (1997) and *Television in Black-and-White America: Race and National Identity* (2005).

DIANE NEGRA is a Reader in the School of Film and Television Studies at the University of East Anglia. She is the author of *Off-White Hollywood: American Culture and Ethnic Female Stardom* (2001), editor of *The Irish in Us: Irishness, Performativity, and Popular Culture* (2006), and co-editor of *A Feminist Reader in Early Cinema* (2002) and *Interrogating Postfeminism: Gender and the Politics of Popular Culture* (2007).

DERON OVERPECK is a doctoral candidate in Critical Studies in Film, Television, and Digital Media at UCLA. His dissertation focuses on American exhibitor trade organizations and their responses to changes in the film industry in the 1970s and 1980s.

STEPHEN PRINCE is a professor of communication at Virginia Tech. He is the author of numerous books on film history and criticism, including *Classical Film Violence: Designing and Regulating Brutality in Hollywood Cinema, 1930–1968* (2003) and *Movies and Meaning: An Introduction to Film* (4th ed., 2007).

JOANNA E. RAPF is a professor of English and film and video studies at the University of Oklahoma and a regular visiting professor in the Department of Film and Television Studies at Dartmouth College. Her books include *Buster Keaton: A Bio-Bibliography* (1995), *On the Waterfront: A Handbook* (2003), and *Interviews with Sidney Lumet* (2005). She has contributed to a number of anthologies, including *American Cinema of the 1940s* (2006), and her essays have appeared in such journals as *Film Quarterly, The Cinema Journal,* and *Literature/Film Quarterly.*

INDEX